LISTIFIED!

Britannica's 300 lists that will blow your mind

Andrew Pettie

Illustrated by
Andrés Lozano

BRITANNICA
BOOKS

List of Contents

A List to Get Us Started

Five great things about reading this book

1. You will find out about everything from amphibious bicycles to erupting volcanoes. This book will take you on an adventure where you will meet giant millipedes, microscopic robots, prehistoric monsters, and exploding stars. It will open your mind to an amazing world of knowledge as vast, fascinating, and bizarre as the universe itself. So if you need to use the bathroom, now is the time to go.

2. You will explode with laughter. As I wrote *Listified!*, there were so many funny and interesting things to tell you that sometimes I couldn't squeeze them all into a list. So, to fill the book with even more jokes, facts, and stories, I've added notes at the bottom of the page.* Look out, too, for the little arrows like this» that will zoom you straight to a related topic in another part of the book.

3. All the facts have been verified by Britannica researchers. So where does all the information in *Listified!* come from? If you turn to page 407, you will find a selection of the books and articles I used to create each chapter. A brilliant team of researchers who eat encyclopedias for breakfast** then used even bigger books and websites to check that every fact is correct.

4. You can read it in any order. Get lost in *Listified!* for however long you've got. From 30 seconds to several hours—or even days!—at a time.

5. You can test your family and friends and pretend that you already knew all the mind-blowing information in this book. Which, very shortly, you will!

Enjoy the book!

Andrew Pettie

Andrew Pettie

---

*Like this one!

» To find out about some things that really do zoom, see page 316.

**This is not strictly true. The favorite breakfast of Britannica's managing editor for this book is a toasted baguette and a big pot of tea.

Chapter 1

Space

A list of things you'll encounter in this chapter:

Egg-shaped galaxies

A sandwich

A supermassive black hole

Dark matter*

A stretched-out satellite

Leftover space boots

Astronaut bathroom habits

A white dwarf

Halley's Comet

A large peach

The King of the Kuiper belt

A lost pair of scissors

Gemstone rain

A guinea pig

*Admittedly, it might be difficult to spot.

Right: An artist's interpretation of what the Big Bang might have looked like. Despite it being called the Big Bang, scientists don't think the start of the universe created a loud explosive noise. They think it probably gave off a humming sound that would have been too low-pitched for humans to hear.

*A light-year is a unit of measurement equivalent to the distance light travels in a year. One light-year is approximately 6 trillion miles (9 trillion km).

**The observable universe is all the objects that are close enough to Earth for their light to have reached us in the time since the universe began. We can see these objects with the naked eye, telescopes, or probes. Although we don't yet know by how much, the universe is probably larger than we can observe. And it is still expanding.

What's the Matter?

The stuff that scientists think the universe is made of

Observable matter—less than 5 percent

Amazingly, all the matter and energy that we can observe in the universe, including the Earth, the Sun, and other stars and galaxies, add up to less than 5 percent of the universe's total mass.

Dark matter—27 percent

As the name suggests, dark matter is made of some invisible and currently unknown stuff that does not absorb, reflect, or give off light, so we cannot observe it directly.* However, we do know dark matter exists because it creates a force of gravity, which affects other objects in space such as stars and galaxies.

Dark energy—68 percent

From the Big Bang onward, the universe has been expanding. According to the laws of gravity, the rate at which it's expanding should be slowing down. However, when scientists measured the universe's rate of expansion, they were shocked to discover that the opposite was true: the expansion was speeding up! No one has any idea how or why this is happening but scientists have called the mysterious force causing it "dark energy."

*Scientists are trying to find out more about dark matter in special underground laboratories. These laboratories are located as deep as 7,900 feet (2,400 m) below the Earth's surface so that the delicate measuring instruments scientists use to search for dark matter won't be disturbed by any background noise.

Intergalactic

The five main types of galaxy*

1. Spiral galaxies
These are the most common type of galaxy. Spiral galaxies feature clusters of gas and dust, called arms, spreading out from a central disc in a spiral pattern.

2. Barred spiral galaxies
These are similar to spiral galaxies but have a straight bar of stars in the center. Our own galaxy, the Milky Way, is a barred spiral.

3. Lenticular galaxies
Sometimes called "armless spiral galaxies," lenticular galaxies are the shape of a flattened disc or lens.

4. Elliptical galaxies
These are egg-shaped galaxies. They are usually red in color, with their light coming from red giant stars.**

5. Irregular galaxies
Often relatively small, these galaxies lack a distinct shape or form.

Spiral galaxy

Barred spiral galaxy

Lenticular galaxy

Elliptical galaxy

Irregular galaxy

---

*The word "galaxy" comes from the Greek word *galaxias*, which means "milky." It is a reference to the way our own galaxy, the Milky Way, looks in the sky.

**Curiously, both the very biggest and the very smallest galaxies tend to be elliptical.

Galaxy Quest

The Milky Way in numbers

100 billion–400 billion The number of stars in the Milky Way.* The precise figure is currently impossible to count.

100 billion The minimum number of planets that scientists estimate are found in the Milky Way.

13.6 billion The estimated number of years ago that the galaxy was born, which is 200 million years after the Big Bang and the start of the universe.

4.5 billion The number of years until the Milky Way will merge with our neighboring galaxy, Andromeda, forming what scientists have nicknamed "Milkomeda."

225 million The number of years it takes for the Milky Way to rotate once.

14 million The diameter in miles (22 million km) of the supermassive black hole sitting at the center of the galaxy. It's called Sagittarius A* (the * is part of its name!).

1.4 million The speed in miles per hour (2.2 million km/h) at which the Milky Way is moving through space.

100,000 The diameter of the Milky Way in light-years.

20 The number of times the arm of the Milky Way containing our solar system has orbited the center of the galaxy. Each orbit takes around 225 million years.

4 The number of spiral arms emerging from the Milky Way's central bar.

Our galaxy, the Milky Way, as it would look if seen from the outside.

*The Milky Way is only a medium-sized galaxy. The largest known galaxy is called IC 1101 and has more than 100 trillion stars.

The Hole Truth

Seven things that would (probably) happen if a satellite fell into a black hole

A black hole is a very dense point in space where the force of gravity is so strong that not even light can escape its pull. Black holes are formed from dying stars and come in different sizes.* There are thought to be billions of them throughout the universe.

1. As the satellite approaches the black hole, it will detect a completely black sphere in the middle, from which no light will be visible.

2. The satellite will travel through swirling circular patterns of light. These patterns are created by the black hole's extraordinarily strong gravitational pull bending rays of light given off by the surrounding stars.

3. Time will do funny things. Where the satellite is entering the black hole, time will tick forward as usual. But from the perspective of those outside the black hole looking in, the satellite will appear to be moving very, very slowly. This is because the force of gravity from a black hole is strong enough to distort time as well as light.

4. The gravity from the black hole will drag the satellite at the speed of light toward its center, a single point known as a singularity.

5. The difference between the two gravitational forces—the pull on the side of the satellite closest to the black hole and the force pulling on the side farthest away from the black hole—will stretch the satellite out like an enormous string of spaghetti.

6. As the satellite is pulled even closer to the singularity, the light from all the stars in the visible universe will compress into a tiny dot of light behind it.

7. After this point, the satellite will be in total darkness. It is now inside a black hole.**

---

*The black hole with the smallest known mass is approximately four times heavier than the Sun. Some black holes are tens of billions of times heavier.

**No one knows what would happen next because we have no information about what may or may not exist on the other side. Some scientists think that traveling through a black hole could lead to a different part of the universe through a "wormhole"—or even to an entirely different universe.

Heavens Above

Nine space objects that you can see without a telescope

The entries in the list are in descending order of how easy they are to see.

1. The Sun*

2. The Moon

3. Venus

4. The International Space Station

5. Jupiter

6. Mars

7. Comets

8. Meteors

9. Supernovae**

Bird's-Eye View

Five human-made structures you can see from space

1. **Pyramids of Giza**, Egypt"

2. **Xihoumen Bridge**, China

3. **Kennecott Copper Mine**, United States

4. **Greenhouses of Almería**, Spain

5. **Palm Islands**, United Arab Emirates

Space Dust

The five main types of nebulae

"Nebula" means "cloud" and it's the word used to describe enormous—and often stunningly beautiful—clouds of dust and gas found in outer space.

1. Emission nebulae
Clouds of very hot gas. This is where new stars are often formed. These nebulae are usually red.

2. Reflection nebulae
Clouds of dust that reflect light from a nearby star, or stars. New stars are also formed here. These nebulae are usually blue.

3. Dark nebulae
Clouds of dust that are so dense they block out the light from whatever is behind them.

4. Planetary nebulae*
Giant shells of gas given off by some stars at the ends of their lifetimes.

5. Supernova remnants
A supernova is an explosion caused by a massive star at the end of its life. When the supernova is over, a large portion of the star's matter is blown into space as a supernova remnant.

Right: This emission nebula is Messier 8, the Lagoon Nebula.

---

*Obviously. Although you should never look directly at the Sun because it could damage your eyes.

**The last supernova from a star in the Milky Way that could be seen with the naked eye was recorded in 1604. Kepler's Supernova, named after the German astronomer Johannes Kepler, who described it, became, at its peak, the brightest star in the night sky.

" To find out the height of the tallest of these incredible pyramids, see page 262.

*Planetary nebulae have nothing to do with planets. They were given the name because they can look like little planets when seen through a telescope.

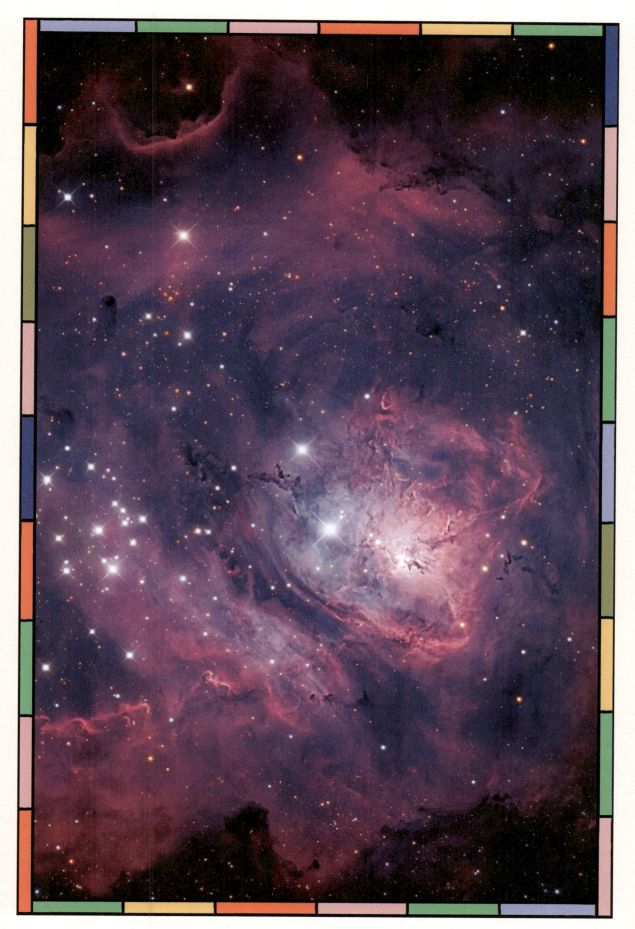

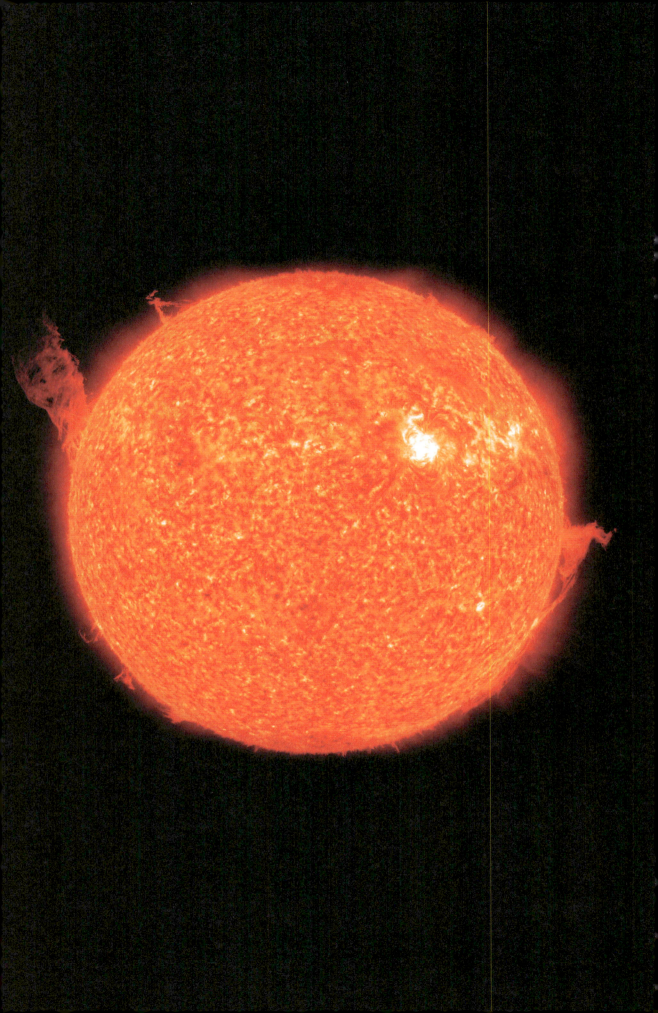

Sunny Delight

The Sun in numbers

Our world quite literally revolves around the Sun.* Here are some of its most impressive stats:

6.5 billion The estimated number of years before the Sun uses up all its fuel and shrinks down to become a white dwarf.

4.5 billion The Sun's age in years.

93 million The distance between the Sun and Earth in miles (150 million km).**

27 million The temperature of the Sun's core in degrees Fahrenheit (15 million°C).

1.3 million The number of planet Earths you could fit inside the Sun.

864,000 The width of the Sun in miles (1,400,000 km).

170,000 The number of years it takes for energy to travel from the Sun's inner core to its surface.

10,000 The approximate temperature of the surface of the Sun in degrees Fahrenheit (5,500°C).

280 The speed, in miles per second (450 km/sec) at which solar wind*** travels through the solar system.

99.8 The percentage of the solar system's total mass that is made up by the Sun.

92.1 The percentage of the Sun that is made up of hydrogen.

25 The approximate number of Earth days it takes for a point on the Sun's equator to spin around once. Because the surface of the Sun isn't solid like the Earth's crust, different parts of it spin around at different speeds.

6 The difference in miles (10 km) between the diameter of the Sun measured at its equator, and its diameter when measured between its north and south poles. This means that the Sun is the closest thing to a perfect sphere observed in nature.

Left: The Sun is a ball of superheated gas. Its surface is constantly moving—there are sudden bursts of energy called solar flares, jets of hot gas called spicules, and enormous gas eruptions called loop prominences.

---

*The solar system consists of the Sun and all the objects in space that travel around it, including the Earth, planets, moons, asteroids, and comets.

**This distance is also a unit of measurement known as an Astronomical Unit (AU).

***Solar wind is created by particles from the Sun's corona (or outer atmosphere) that are accelerated to such high speeds that they can escape the Sun's gravitational field.

You're a Star

The five life stages of a star like the Sun

Stars are created from giant clouds of dust and gas that are pulled together by gravity over thousands of years. Once they have formed, stars produce energy by converting hydrogen into helium at their cores. They then develop in a series of stages, each of which has its own name and characteristics.

1. Average-sized star A small or average-sized star, such as the Sun, will stay the same shape and size for around 10 billion years.

2. Red giant As the star approaches the end of its life, it slowly gets bigger and cooler, becoming a red giant. (This will happen to the Sun in around 5 billion years.)

3. Planetary nebula As a red giant starts to run out of hydrogen, it releases glowing outer layers of gas.

4. White dwarf When a red giant has used up all its hydrogen and other fuel, the star's leftover core is called a white dwarf.

5. Black dwarf A white dwarf slowly cools until, eventually, it stops giving off light and heat, becoming a black dwarf.*

Average-sized star

Red giant

Planetary nebula

White dwarf

Black dwarf

*However, because it takes a white dwarf at least hundreds of billions of years to cool down, the universe isn't old enough for any black dwarfs to have formed yet.

You're a Mega Star

The four life stages of a star bigger than the Sun

All stars are created in the same way. However, large stars that have a mass more than one and a half times greater than the Sun's go through different stages during their life.

1. Massive star Big stars use up their hydrogen more quickly, which means they don't live as long as average-sized stars. The biggest stars will burn themselves out in just a few million years.

2. Red supergiant When a large star approaches the end of its life, it becomes a red supergiant, which can be more than 1,000 times bigger than the Sun and is the largest type of star in the universe.

3. Supernova At the end of its life, a red supergiant throws out its outer layers in a massive explosion.

4. Neutron star, or black hole What happens next depends on the mass of the original star. If the star's mass was between one and a half and three times greater than the Sun's, it becomes a neutron star, which is a tiny dense star no more than 12 miles (19 km) wide.* If the star's mass was more than three times greater than the Sun's, it becomes a black hole instead.

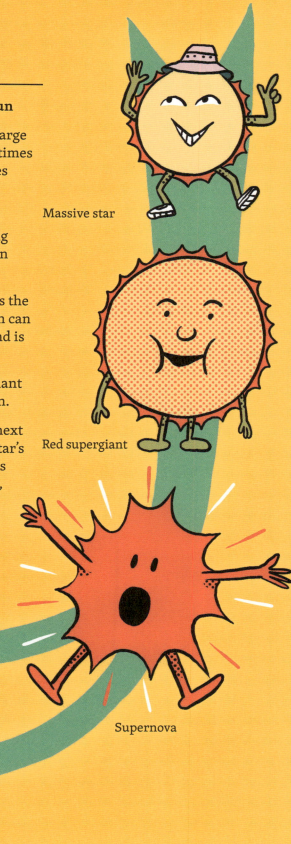

Massive star

Red supergiant

Supernova

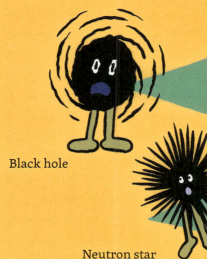

Black hole

Neutron star

*Neutron stars are amazingly dense. A single teaspoon of a neutron star would weigh 4 billion tons (3.6 billion tonnes), which is roughly 700 times heavier than the Great Pyramid of Giza in Egypt. They are also the fastest spinning objects in the universe and can rotate 700 times in one second.

Great Balls of Fire

How five of the biggest stars in the universe measure up to the Sun

The Sun is mind-blowingly big, but in cosmic terms it's actually an average-sized star. The largest stars we've found so far are hundreds of times bigger than the Sun, while others are less than a tenth of its size.

1,700 times bigger than the Sun*— UY Scuti, Milky Way

1,540 times bigger than the Sun— WOH G64, Large Magellanic Cloud**

1,530 times bigger than the Sun— Westerlund 1-26, Milky Way

1,420 times bigger than the Sun— VY Canis Majoris, Milky Way

890 times bigger than the Sun— Betelgeuse,» Milky Way

Starlight Express

How long it takes light from ten famous stars to reach Earth

It can take years for light from the stars to reach Earth. So when you're looking up at the night sky, you're really looking back in time, seeing light that stars gave off hundreds, thousands, millions, and, in some cases, billions of years ago.

1. **The Sun**—8 minutes and 20 seconds
2. **Alpha Centauri**—4 years*
3. **Sirius**—9 years
4. **Vega**—25 years
5. **Aldebaran**—65 years
6. **Canopus**—310 years
7. **Betelgeuse**—642 years
8. **Rigel**—863 years
9. **Deneb**—1,500 years
10. **Icarus**—9,400,000,000 years**

---

*If the Earth was the size of a volleyball, UY Scuti would be a ball with a 125,000-mile (200,000-km) diameter. Try playing with that on the beach.

**The Large Magellanic Cloud is a satellite galaxy that orbits around the Milky Way.

» To find out what could happen to Betelgeuse any . . . moment . . . now, see page 54.

*The estimated times from Alpha Centuri onward have been rounded to the nearest year.

**Icarus, whose official name is MACS J1149+2223 Lensed Star 1, is the farthest individual star ever seen. The light we're seeing from Icarus today was emitted by the star billions of years before the formation of the Earth.

Planetarium

The planets of the solar system by size

Jupiter*—diameter: 86,881 mi (139,822 km)
If Earth was the size of a cherry: Jupiter would be the size of a pumpkin.

Saturn—diameter: 72,367 mi (116,464 km)
If Earth was the size of a cherry: Saturn would be the size of an iceberg lettuce.

Uranus—diameter: 31,518 mi (50,724 km)
If Earth was the size of a cherry: Uranus would be the size of a large peach.

Neptune—diameter: 30,598 mi (49,244 km)
If Earth was the size of a cherry: Neptune would be the size of an apple.

Earth**—diameter: 7,917 mi (12,742 km)
If Earth was the size of a cherry: Earth would be the same size as, um, a cherry.

Venus—diameter: 7,521 mi (12,104 km)
If Earth was the size of a cherry: Venus would be the size of a small cherry.

Mars—diameter: 4,212 mi (6,779 km)
If Earth was the size of a cherry: Mars would be the size of a blueberry.

Mercury—diameter: 3,032 mi (4,879 km)
If Earth was the size of a cherry: Mercury would be the size of a peppercorn.

*Jupiter is two and half times bigger in mass than all the rest of the planets in the solar system combined.

**Earth is the only planet in the solar system that isn't named after a god or goddess from ancient Roman or Greek mythology. The word "Earth" comes from Old English and German words meaning "ground," although no one knows who first named our planet "the Earth."

Light Speed

The planets of the solar system in order of how long it takes light from the Sun to reach them

Mercury—3.2 minutes

Venus—6 minutes

Earth—8.5 minutes

Mars—11.5 minutes

Jupiter—43 minutes

Saturn—1 hour, 23 minutes

Uranus—2 hours, 45 minutes

Neptune—4 hours, 9 minutes

Spin Cycle

The planets of the solar system by day length

The length of a day is measured by how long it takes a planet to spin on its axis—an imaginary line that runs through a planet's core.

Venus—5,832 hours*

Mercury—1,408 hours

Mars—25 hours

Earth—24 hours

Uranus—17 hours

Neptune—16 hours

Saturn—11 hours

Jupiter—10 hours

Taking the Temperature

The planets of the solar system by average surface temperature

Venus—864°F (462°C)

Mercury—332°F (167°C)

Earth—59°F (15°C)*

Mars—minus 80°F (62°C)

Jupiter—minus 234°F (–145°C)

Saturn—minus 288°F (–178°C)

Uranus—minus 320°F (–195°C)

Neptune—minus 331°F (–201°C)

---

*It takes less time for Venus to orbit the Sun (5,400 hours) than it does for the planet to spin once on its axis. This means that a day on Venus lasts longer than its year.

*Earth's position in the solar system and the composition of its atmosphere are two reasons that our planet can support life as we know it. Other stars are orbited by planets where life could potentially exist. However, we have yet to find life on them.

A World of Your Own

The three ingredients you need
to make a planet

1. Dust

2. Gas

3. Gravity*

*Planets form from the dust and gas that is left
over in space after the creation of a star. As these
clouds of dust and gas orbit the star, gravity
gradually pulls them together to form clumps
of matter. Over time, some of these clumps grow
big enough to become planets.

The ten biggest moons in the solar system

There are more than 200 moons orbiting the planets of our solar system. Earth has only one moon, but some planets have many!* Here are the largest moons in the solar system, measured by their width:

1. **Ganymede**, orbits Jupiter—3,270 mi (5,262 km)

2. **Titan**, orbits Saturn—3,200 mi (5,150 km)

3. **Callisto**, orbits Jupiter—2,996 mi (4,821 km)

4. **Io**,** orbits Jupiter—2,264 mi (3,643 km)

5. **The Moon**, orbits Earth—2,159 mi (3,475 km)

6. **Europa**, orbits Jupiter—1,940 mi (3,122 km)

7. **Triton**, orbits Neptune—1,682 mi (2,707 km)

8. **Titania**, orbits Uranus—981 mi (1,578 km)

9. **Rhea**, orbits Saturn—950 mi (1,529 km)

10. **Oberon**, orbits Uranus—946 mi (1,523 km)

Below: Europa is the smallest of the four moons of Jupiter that were discovered by the famous astronomer Galileo.

*For example, Saturn has at least 82 moons, and Jupiter has at least 79. Mercury and Venus have none.

**Io is the most volcanically active moon or planet in the solar system. It has hundreds of volcanoes on its surface, some spewing out fountains of molten lava that are dozens of miles high.

Moonstruck

The eight phases of our Moon

Half of the Moon's surface is always lit up by the Sun (except during a lunar eclipse). However, as the Moon orbits Earth, we see different parts of the sunlit side. This makes it appear as though the Moon is changing shape. Over the course of a lunar cycle, which takes just under 30 days, the Moon goes through eight recognizable changes of appearance called phases.

1. New Moon When the illuminated side of the Moon is not visible from Earth because the Moon is positioned between the Earth and the Sun.*

2. The waxing crescent During this phase, the croissant-shaped sunlit part of the Moon gets bigger and brighter.

3. The first quarter Despite the name, this is when half the Moon is illuminated. This happens around one week after a New Moon.

4. The waxing gibbous*** When more than half of the Moon's sunlit side can be seen.

5. The full Moon The Moon is now on the opposite side of the Earth than the Sun and is fully illuminated.

6. The waning gibbous Having reached its point of maximum brightness, the sunlit part of the Moon now starts to get smaller.

7. The last quarter The second phase during which exactly half the Moon is illuminated by the Sun.

8. The waning crescent The final phase in the lunar cycle when only a thin crescent of the Moon is visible.

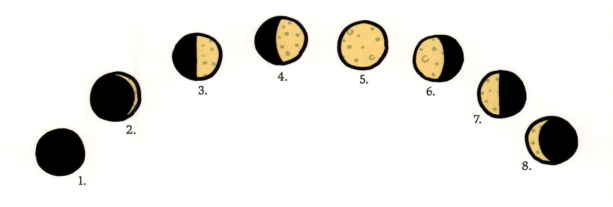

*A total solar eclipse, when the precise positioning of the Moon blocks out the light from the Sun, is only possible during the New Moon phase of the lunar cycle.

**"Waxing" and "waning" are old-fashioned words used to describe things that are getting bigger (waxing) or smaller (waning).

***The word "gibbous" comes from the Latin *gibbus*, meaning "hump," which nicely describes the shape of the Moon in this phase.

We Will Rock You

How to tell the difference between asteroids, meteors, and other flying space rocks

Asteroids are rocky objects that orbit the Sun and that are smaller than planets.

Meteoroids are small pieces of rock or metal that orbit the Sun.

Meteors are streaks of light that can be seen in the sky when a meteoroid comes close enough to Earth to enter its atmosphere, burn up, and vaporize.*

Meteorites are meteors that don't vaporize as they enter the Earth's atmosphere, but instead survive the trip and land on Earth's surface.

Comets consist of clusters of ice and dust that orbit the Sun. As the comet's orbit takes it closer to the Sun, the solar wind vaporizes some of the ice and dust, creating the comet's "tail."**

Dwarf planets are objects that orbit the Sun and are bigger than comets or asteroids, but don't quite qualify as planets. The largest known dwarf planet in the solar system is Pluto.

I used to be a planet

Pluto

*Meteors are sometimes called "shooting stars" even though they are chunks of vaporizing rock and not stars at all. When lots of meteoroids enter Earth's atmosphere at the same time, it is called a "meteor shower."

**This means that a comet's tail always points away from the Sun, in the same direction as the solar wind.

Cold as Ice

The Kuiper belt in numbers

The Kuiper belt is a distant region of the solar system. It is thought to contain millions of comets, asteroids, and other rocky or icy objects.

1 trillion+ The estimated number of comets in the Kuiper belt.

2.7 billion The distance in miles (4.4 billion km) from the Sun to the nearest edge of the Kuiper belt.

1.86 billion The width of the Kuiper belt in miles (3 billion km).

2006 The year Pluto was downgraded from being a planet to a dwarf planet.*

1992 The year American astronomers David Jewitt and Jane Luu discovered the first Kuiper belt object.** They wanted to name their find "Smiley" but it has since been catalogued as "1992 QB1." Boring!

1,476 The width of the dwarf planet Pluto in miles (2,376 km). Pluto is sometimes called the "King of the Kuiper belt" because it is the largest known object in it.

200 The number of years it takes comets from the Kuiper belt to orbit the Sun.

9 The number of stars astronomers have found with structures that are similar to the Kuiper belt around them.

4 The number of hours in a day on the dwarf planet Haumea, which is one of the fastest spinning large objects in the solar system.

*A small planet that shares its orbit with other objects is called a dwarf planet. Most known dwarf planets are in the Kuiper belt.

**Pluto was actually the first Kuiper belt object to be found, in 1930. However, at that time, scientists didn't know it was in the Kuiper belt (they thought it was a planet). It wasn't until David Jewitt and Jane Luu's discovery that scientists found that the Kuiper belt was a region in the solar system filled with many rocky or icy objects.

Alien Worlds

Nine extraordinary exoplanets*

1. Gj 436 b

Distance from Earth: 30 light-years.

Amazing feature: Ultraviolet rays from a nearby star are causing Gj 436 b's atmosphere to evaporate, leaving behind a cloudlike trail that is millions of miles long.

2. Gj 1214 b

Distance from Earth: 40 light-years.

Amazing feature: It could have no land whatsoever, and the planet's surface may be covered by one enormous, hot, watery ocean.

3. 55 Cancri e

Distance from Earth: 40 light-years.

Amazing feature: The side of the planet that faces its star could be covered with molten lava.

4. HD 189733 b

Distance from Earth: 63 light-years.

Amazing feature: It possibly rains glass on this exoplanet.

5. 2MASS J2126-8140

Distance from Earth: 104 light-years.

Amazing feature: It has the longest orbit of any planet yet discovered, as it revolves around a red dwarf star that is 600 billion miles away. That's 7,000 times farther than the distance between the Earth and the Sun.

6. TrES-2b

Distance from Earth: 750 light-years.

Amazing feature: This exoplanet reflects less than 1 percent of the light that hits it. Known as the "Dark Planet," TrES-2b is blacker than a lump of coal.

7. HAT-P-7b

Distance from Earth: 1,000 light-years.

Amazing feature: The rain here could be made up of colorful gemstones, including rubies and sapphires.

8. TrES-4b

Distance from Earth: 1,400 light-years.

Amazing feature: It is one of the largest known exoplanets but has a very low density—roughly the same as cork.**

9. PSR B1620-26 b

Distance from Earth: 5,600 light-years.

Amazing feature: At an estimated 13 billion years old, it's more than twice as old as Earth and almost as old as the universe itself, which was born 13.8 billion years ago.***

---

*An exoplanet is a planet that orbits a star other than our Sun. The first exoplanets were discovered in the early 1990s. Since then, more than 4,000 have been discovered. However, there are trillions more out there to find!

**This means that despite TrES-4b being more than one and a half times bigger than Jupiter, it would still float in a bathtub (if there was a bathtub large enough to hold it!).

***PSR B1620-26 b has been given the nickname "Methuselah" after a figure from the Bible who was said to have lived to the age of 969.

Ten of the most powerful space rockets ever launched

1. N1

Maximum thrust: 10,200,000 pound-force (lbf) (45,400 kilonewtons [kN]), which is roughly the same thrust force* as 165 jumbo jet engines.

Missions: Built as the Soviet equivalent to the Saturn V (see below), the N1 had four test launches between 1969 and 1972 but never made it all the way into outer space.

2. Saturn V

Maximum thrust: 7,900,000 lbf (35,100 kN), or 127 jumbo jet engines.**

Missions: Saturn V carried the lunar modules for the Apollo missions, including Apollo 11, which put the first humans on the Moon. Its final mission was in 1973.

3. Space Shuttles

Maximum thrust: 7,900,000 lbf (35,000 kN), or 127 jumbo jet engines.

Missions: The six reusable space shuttles flew a combined total of 135 missions between 1981 and 2011.

4. Falcon Heavy

Maximum thrust: 3,400,000 lbf (15,200 kN), or 55 jumbo jet engines.

Missions: The Falcon Heavy is capable of delivering large payloads (passengers or cargo) to orbit and supporting future missions to the Moon or Mars. To promote Falcon Heavy's first launch in 2018, the privately owned rocket carried an electric sports car as its cargo, which was then released into outer space.

5. Ares I-X

Maximum thrust: 3,400,000 lbf (15,000 kN), or 55 jumbo jet engines.

Missions: Ares I-X was launched once in 2009 as a prototype to test and develop technology for later NASA rockets.

6. Ariane 4

Maximum thrust: 2,700,000 lbf (12,120 kN), or 44 jumbo jet engines.

Missions: Built for the European Space Agency, Ariane 4 carried satellites into space on more than 100 missions between 1988 and 2003.

---

*Thrust is the name of the force from a rocket's engine that moves it through the air. So the rocket's thrust force is a measure of how powerful it is.

**Like jumbo jet engines, space rockets are very loud. When Saturn V launched, it generated 204 decibels of noise, which is almost as loud as a nuclear explosion. Rocket launch pads now have special sound-dampening systems that use water to reduce the noise.

7. Atlas V

Maximum thrust:
2,400,000 lbf (10,600 kN),
or 38 jumbo jet engines.

Missions: First launched in 2002, the Atlas V carried satellites and equipment for the International Space Station and is still in use today.

8. Angara-A5

Maximum thrust: 1,700,000 lbf (7,680 kN), or 27 jumbo jet engines.

Missions: This Russian prototype rocket was launched on a single test flight in 2014.

9. Delta IV Heavy

Maximum thrust: 1,400,000 lbf (6,280 kN), or 22 jumbo jet engines.

Missions: Over 11 missions between 2004 and 2019, the Delta IV Heavy carried military observation satellites and an uncrewed test flight of NASA's Orion spacecraft.

10. Delta IV Medium

Maximum thrust: 800,000 lbf (3,560 kN), or 12 jumbo jet engines.

Missions: A total of 29 launches between 2002 and 2019, some of which carried satellites into Earth orbit.

Below: Space Shuttle *Endeavour* launches on one of many missions to build the International Space Station.

Star Trek

How long it would take to drive around the galaxy

If you were driving a car at 60 miles per hour (100 km/h), this is approximately how long it would take to travel from the Earth to various exciting space destinations.*

Into space—1 hour

To the Moon—6 months

To Venus—45 years

To Mars—62 years

To Mercury—91 years

To the Sun—175 years

To Jupiter—720 years

To Saturn—1,655 years

To Uranus—3,310 years

To Neptune—5,135 years

To Pluto—6,850 years

To the outer edge of the Kuiper belt—8,365 years

To the edge of the solar system**—17,000 years

To the nearest star outside the solar system***—45 million years

Across the Milky Way—1.12 trillion years

*However, driving through space in a car is impossible for a number of practical reasons, including the lack of oxygen, gravity, or road signs.

**One way to define the outer edge of the solar system is to use the heliosphere, which is the area of space affected by the Sun's magnetic field and solar wind. The edge of the heliosphere is known as the heliopause.

***After the Sun, the nearest star to Earth is Proxima Centauri, which is around 25 trillion miles (40 trillion km) away. So take some snacks for the journey.

High Jump

How high a human being could jump on nine different planets and moons

On Earth, the average human being can do a standing jump roughly 1.6 ft (0.5 m) straight up in the air and stay off the ground for roughly half a second.* But how high and for how long could the same human jump on another planet or moon, where the force of gravity is different?

1. Enceladus (a moon of Saturn)—140 ft (42.6 m)

About as high as: The statue of Christ the Redeemer, Rio de Janeiro, Brazil.

Off the ground for: 1 minute.

2. Ceres (a dwarf planet)—57 ft (17.5 m)

About as high as: A four-story building.

Off the ground for: 22 seconds.

3. Pluto (a dwarf planet)—25 ft (7.6 m)

About as high as: A giraffe.

Off the ground for: 10 seconds.

4. The Moon—10 ft (3 m)

About as high as: The ceiling of the average room.

Off the ground for: 4 seconds.

5. Mars—4.3 ft (1.3 m)

About as high as: A cow.

Off the ground for: 2 seconds.

6. Mercury—4.3 ft (1.3 m)

About as high as: Ahem, another cow.

Off the ground for: 2 seconds.

7. Venus—1.8 ft (0.55 m)

About as high as: Three steps on a flight of stairs.

Off the ground for: 0.7 seconds.

8. Saturn—1.5 ft (0.47 m)**

About as high as: A golden retriever.

Off the ground for: Half a second.

9. Jupiter—0.6 ft (0.19 m)

About as high as: A banana.

Off the ground for: A quarter of a second.

Christ the Redeemer

*The highest recorded standing jump on Earth is 5 feet 5 inches (1.65 m), by Brett Williams from the United States.

**Because Saturn and Jupiter are made mostly of gas, you would need to be standing on something solid, such as the outside of a spaceship, to jump within their atmospheres. The height of your jump would still be related to the strength of each planet's gravitational pull.

Space Creatures

Twenty types of animal that have been to space

1. Fruit flies*
2. Monkeys and apes
3. Mice
4. Dogs
5. Rats
6. Rabbits
7. Cats
8. Tortoises
9. Spiders
10. Worms
11. Ants
12. Bees
13. Turtles
14. Newts
15. Geckos
16. Fish
17. Jellyfish
18. Frogs
19. Guinea pigs
20. Tardigrades**

*The flies reached an altitude of 68 miles (108 km) before safely parachuting back down to Earth in a special capsule.

**Tardigrades are microscopic invertebrates that can survive almost anywhere. In 2007, they became the first animals to survive after being fully exposed to outer space without the protection of a spaceship or space suit. To find out more about these remarkable creatures, see page 156.

Friends in High Places

Five jobs that satellites do

There are currently more than 2,000 working satellites* orbiting the Earth. These are the key functions they perform:

1. Observe the universe Scientific satellites such as the Hubble Space Telescope observe other planets, stars, and distant parts of the universe, sending amazing photographs back to Earth.

2. Help us to navigate Satellite-based navigation systems such as GPS (which stands for Global Positioning System) use a network of satellites in Earth orbit. By bouncing a signal off several satellites, the GPS locator in your phone or other digital devices can calculate exactly where you are to within a few feet.

3. Send communications Some satellites have dishes like giant mirrors that bounce signals from one place on Earth to another. This enables us to use the Internet, make phone calls to people all around the world, and watch TV shows in our homes.

4. Spy on other countries Military satellites monitor activities in other countries, such as the movement of troops.

5. Monitor weather and climate By watching Earth's cloud and other weather patterns from above, satellites can help us to predict when and where it is going to rain. They also play a part in figuring out how much the planet is warming due to climate change.

The Hubble Space Telescope

---

*There are also more than 3,000 satellites that are no longer working. These dead satellites are examples of "space junk." Scientists estimate there are more than 34,000 pieces of space junk currently orbiting the Earth.

Celestial Bodies

Nine things that can happen to astronauts' bodies in space

Going into space is amazing—a human experience that is truly out of this world. But space travel also has some strange and interesting effects on the human body, which astronauts prepare and train hard to face before setting off on their great adventures.

1. Space sickness

When astronauts first reach space, some of them suffer from space sickness, also called "Space Adaptation Syndrome." Symptoms can include headaches and feeling tired or nauseous. Thankfully, space sickness typically only lasts for a few days.

2. Puffy head

Without gravity to pull bodily fluids such as water and blood downwards, more of them flow to the upper half of the body. This causes an astronaut's head to become swollen and puffy.*

3. Blurry vision

The swelling of astronauts' heads also slightly changes the shape of their eyeballs and optic nerves, which can affect their eyesight. The change isn't usually permanent, but it can take years for some astronauts' eyesight to return to normal.

4. Growth spurt

An astronaut's body grows around 2 inches (5 cm) taller while it's in space. This is because Earth's gravity is no longer pulling the bones in the spine closer together. Once astronauts return to Earth, they shrink back down to their normal size.

5. Weaker muscles

Because of the lack of gravity in space, your muscles no longer have to work as hard to move your body or, in the case of your heart, pump blood around your blood vessels. Over time, this makes all the muscles weaker, which is one of the reasons astronauts exercise for around two hours each day. Even so, they can lose up to 30 percent of their total muscle mass during a long space mission.

6. Lost fingernails

The pressurized air inside a space suit makes the rubber inner linings of the gloves hard and stiff, like bicycle tires. If an astronaut in a space suit has to work with their hands for several hours at a time, the constant friction and pressure on the fingertips can cause the fingernails to fall off in a painful condition called "delamination."

*To reduce the flow of blood and other bodily fluids from their legs up to the top half of their bodies, astronauts now wear tight restrictive bands called "compression cuffs" around their thighs.

7. Less sleep

Astronauts typically sleep for a shorter amount of time while they're in space. Their sleep is also shallower and more easily disturbed. Scientists think this may be connected to the lack of gravity or the fact that, in space, astronauts don't experience the usual cycle of night and day.** But there is one positive effect . . .

8. No more snoring!

The lack of gravity in space helps air to pass more easily through the mouth, nose, and throat. This means that people very rarely snore in space.

9. More pee

An increase of fluid gathering in certain areas of the body fools it into thinking that it is carrying too much water. The body then produces more urine (pee). So, as with long car journeys, astronauts should go to the bathroom shortly before liftoff.

RESTROOM

**On Earth, human sleep patterns are partly controlled by the 24-hour cycle of night and day. In space, the Sun no longer rises and sets once a day, so getting a good "night's" sleep becomes much more difficult. To find out what important things happen to the body during sleep, see page 215.

Life in Space

Six things future astronauts should know before staying on the International Space Station

As they orbit Earth, astronauts in the International Space Station live in what's known as "microgravity," which is the floating state in which people appear to be weightless and even heavy objects are easy to move. This is because the pull of Earth's gravity is much weaker in space than it is on the planet's surface.

1. There are no refrigerators in space, so all food must be heat-treated or freeze-dried to keep it from going bad.*

2. Salt and pepper are only available in liquid form.**

3. Astronauts are given a special no-rinse shampoo to wash their hair, which was originally developed for hospital patients who were unable to take a shower.

4. Using the toilet in microgravity could be a messy business. To avoid creating a major space incident, astronauts should first clamp themselves on the toilet seat using the special leg straps provided. The toilet then works like a vacuum cleaner, sucking all the air, poop, and pee away and into a waste tank.***

5. Because there is no "up" or "down" in microgravity, astronauts can sleep in any position they like. Most astronauts use sleeping bags located in the small crew cabins.

6. Like most people with full-time jobs, astronauts get days off. Popular pastimes for astronauts include watching movies, listening to music, playing computer games, talking to their families on Earth, and, perhaps most memorable of all, looking out the window.

Right: The International Space Station orbits Earth around 16 times a day. Here, it can be seen over the Sahara.

*Ordering takeout is also frowned upon, as the cost would be . . . astronomical.

**If astronauts tried to sprinkle salt and pepper on their food as we do on Earth, the grains would float away. There is even a danger they could clog the space station's air vents or damage vital equipment.

***A toilet on the International Space Station can cost as much as $23 million to build and install.

Fly Me to the Moon

The seven crewed missions to the Moon (so far . . .)

1. Apollo 11 (July 20, 1969)

Landing site: Sea of Tranquility.*

Moonwalkers: Neil Armstrong and Buzz Aldrin.

Time spent on the Moon: 21 hours and 36 minutes.

Memorable moment: Armstrong places his left foot onto the surface of the Moon, saying the words: "That's one small step for man, one giant leap for mankind."**»

2. Apollo 12 (November 19, 1969)

Landing site: Ocean of Storms.

Moonwalkers: Charles Conrad and Alan Bean.

Time spent on the Moon: 31 hours and 31 minutes.

Memorable moment: Part of the rocket taking Conrad and Bean back to the Apollo 12 command module is deliberately dropped down to crash onto the surface of the Moon. Scientists measure the impact and find that the vibrations from the resulting "Moonquake" last for more than half an hour.

3. Apollo 13 (April 11, 1970)

Landing site: The astronauts failed to reach the Moon.

Astronauts on the mission: James Lovell, John Swigert, Fred Haise.

Time spent on the Moon: None.

Memorable moment: An oxygen tank explodes during the flight, affecting the Apollo 13 command module's supply of electricity, light, and water—leading John Swigert to say to the mission control team back on Earth: "Houston, we've had a problem here." (Swigert is often misquoted as saying: "Houston, we have a problem.") The planned Moon landing is canceled but, miraculously, the three-man crew manages to navigate the damaged command module 200,000 miles (322,000 km) back to Earth, where it lands safely in the Pacific Ocean on April 17.

4. Apollo 14 (February 5, 1971)

Landing site: Fra Mauro formation.

Moonwalkers: Alan Shepard and Edgar Mitchell.

Time spent on the Moon: 33 hours and 31 minutes.

Memorable moment: Alan Shepard hits two golf balls across the surface of the Moon using a makeshift golf club adapted from a piece of space equipment.

---

*The "seas" on the Moon are actually large plains of rock caused by ancient volcanic eruptions. They were named "seas" by early astronomers who mistakenly thought they were full of water.

**Neil Armstrong meant to say: "That's one small step for a man," which makes more sense and is grammatically correct. However, this couldn't be heard clearly in the transmission.

» Buzz Aldrin became the second person to walk on the Moon during this mission. To find out about other people who came a close second, see page 358.

5. Apollo 15 (July 30, 1971)

Landing site: Hadley-Apennine.

Moonwalkers: David Scott and James Irwin.

Time spent on the Moon: 66 hours and 55 minutes.

Memorable moment: A lunar roving vehicle or "Moon buggy" is used for the first time, allowing astronauts to drive 17.5 miles (28 km) across the surface of the Moon.

6. Apollo 16 (April 20, 1972)

Landing site: Descartes Highlands.

Moonwalkers: John Young and Charles Duke.

Time spent on the Moon: 71 hours and 2 minutes.

Memorable moment: On the return journey to Earth, command module pilot Ken Mattingly did a spacewalk in deep space.

7. Apollo 17 (December 11, 1972)

Landing site: Taurus-Littrow.

Moonwalkers: Eugene Cernan and Harrison Schmitt.

Time spent on the Moon: 75 hours.

Memorable moment: Astronaut Ronald Evans loses his pair of scissors on the way to the Moon, which are vital for opening food packets. Cernan and Schmitt give him one of their pairs and later find Evans's scissors as they are packing equipment before returning to Earth. They keep this a secret from Evans and present the lost scissors to him a month later at a party to celebrate the successful mission.

Moon landings

Leftovers

Eighteen things that humans have left on the surface of the Moon

1. Footprints, including the first one, made by astronaut Neil Armstrong's "giant leap for mankind" in 1969.*

2. A TV camera that Neil Armstrong and Buzz Aldrin used to film the first Moon landing.

3. Part of the Eagle lunar module that Armstrong and Aldrin used to travel from the Apollo 11 space rocket to the surface of the Moon and back.

4. A gold replica of an olive branch, which is a traditional symbol of peace.

5. Several United States flags.**

6. A small silicon disc, which is inscribed with miniaturized statements from the leaders of 74 countries. The disc has the words "From Planet Earth, July 1969" in the center.

7. A copy of the Bible.

8. Seismometers, which measure vibrations in the ground, and other scientific equipment used by astronauts to conduct lunar experiments.

9. Mirrors used to reflect laser beams sent to the Moon from large telescopes on Earth. The laser beams helped scientists to calculate the exact distance between the Earth and the Moon, and to track its orbit.

10. Twelve pairs of space boots that were left on the Moon at the end of the Apollo 11 mission because the crew needed to lighten their load for the return journey to Earth.

11. Two medals and a 3.5-inch- (9-cm-) tall aluminum sculpture called "Fallen Astronaut" were among objects left behind to commemorate American astronauts and Soviet cosmonauts who had died during earlier space missions and training exercises.

12. Ashes of the American geologist Gene Shoemaker, who discovered many comets and planets.

13. A hammer and a feather that were part of an experiment demonstrating how gravity works on the Moon.

14. A signed photograph of astronaut Charles Duke's family.

15. Two golf balls, which astronaut Alan Shepard hit across the surface of the Moon.

16. Three lunar rovers, which astronauts used to explore the Moon's surface.

17. Ninety-six bags of astronauts' pee and poop.

18. A commemorative plaque that reads: "Here men from the planet Earth first set foot upon the Moon. July 1969, A.D. We came in peace for all mankind."

---

*Because there is no wind, rain, or other weather on the Moon, the astronauts' footprints are still there today.

**The flags contained special extendable metal poles so that they could be seen when they were unfurled, even though there is no wind on the Moon to blow them.

Appliance of Science

Ten everyday inventions that were originally created for space travel

1. Dustbusters The small handheld vacuum cleaner known as a "Dustbuster" is based on a lightweight machine used to collect samples of rock and dust from the surface of the Moon.

2. Camera phones These use technology that NASA developed when they were creating cameras for use on space missions. They needed to be small enough to fit on spacecraft yet capable of taking pictures of scientific quality.

3. Athletic shoes A shock-absorbent rubber molding originally designed for astronauts' helmets inspired the cushioned soles of most modern sports shoes and sneakers.

4. Foil blankets These thin metallic sheets, which are now used on Earth to protect people from extreme temperatures, evolved from a lightweight insulator for spacecraft.

5. Water purification systems In the 1960s, NASA created a machine to purify astronauts' drinking water. The same technology is now widely used in filtering systems that kill the bacteria in swimming pools.

6. Invisible braces NASA invented a special see-through material to protect radar equipment without blocking the radar's signal. It has since been used to develop "invisible" braces for your teeth.

7. Freeze-dried food NASA did a lot of research into how to create the most lightweight food for space flights, where every ounce of weight on board matters. One technique they developed was freeze-drying, which retains 98 percent of the food's nutrients with just 20 percent of its original weight. Freeze-dried food is now used on Earth for expeditions when people have to carry their own food, such as climbing and camping trips.

8. Baby formula Most modern baby formula contains a special ingredient to make it more nutritious. Its origins can be traced back to an algae-based substance used to provide extra nutrition for long-term space travel.

9. Artificial limbs Modern prosthetic (artificial) arms, legs, and joints rely on innovations originally designed for space vehicles, including shock-absorbing materials, artificial muscle systems, and robotic moving parts and sensors.

10. Portable computer The first ever portable computer, known as the Grid Compass, was used on space shuttle missions in the 1980s. Nicknamed SPOC,* it could communicate with other devices on board and was used to launch satellites from the space shuttle.

*The nickname SPOC stands for Shuttle Portable On-Board Computer but many people think it is also a fun reference to Spock, a half-human, half-alien character from the science-fiction TV and film series *Star Trek*.

Space Oddities

Ten surprising things that have been sent into space

1. Fossilized bones and eggshells from a duck-billed dinosaur called *Maiasaura peeblesorum* were sent to space in Spacelab 2, which was on board the Space Shuttle *Challenger* in 1985.

2. Salami pizza was delivered via space rocket to cosmonaut Yuri Usachov on board the International Space Station.

3. Pieces of wood and fabric from the Wright brothers'" Flyer 1 were placed inside Apollo 11's lunar module. "Flyer 1" was the name given to the first airplane to make a powered flight.

4. Luke Skywalker's lightsaber—the one from *Return of the Jedi*—was sent to the International Space Station to mark 30 years of the Star Wars movies.

5. Amelia Earhart's watch was brought to the International Space Station 82 years to the day after Earhart's pioneering transatlantic flight. The American pilot was the first woman to fly solo across the Atlantic.

6. An electric sports car! To mark the first launch of SpaceX's Falcon Heavy rocket, a car was released in outer space and is traveling on a solar orbit carrying it toward Mars.*

7. Gene Roddenberry's ashes were sent into outer space in a rocket. Roddenberry created the famous science-fiction TV and film series *Star Trek*.

8. LEGO figures were sent to Jupiter on NASA's Juno space probe. Three figures were chosen: the mythological god Jupiter, his wife Juno, and the Italian astronomer Galileo.

9. Two golden records were carried on the Voyager 1 and Voyager 2 space probes.**

10. A sandwich was smuggled onto NASA's Gemini 3 space mission by astronaut John Young.*** It was a corned beef sandwich.

" To find out more about the Wright Brothers and some other sets of famous siblings, see pages 348–349.

*The car's radio was apparently playing the David Bowie song "Life on Mars?" as it was launched from the rocket.

**The golden records were intended to introduce the story of Earth to any alien life that discovered the probes. The sounds on the discs, which could be played like an old-fashioned vinyl record, included natural sounds from Earth, such as wind, thunder, and the sounds of birds, whales, and other animals; a selection of music from different cultures and periods of history; and spoken greetings from human beings in 55 different languages.

***NASA doesn't usually approve of astronauts eating sandwiches in space because breadcrumbs could damage the spacecraft's delicate equipment.

Eye in the Sky

The James Webb Space Telescope in numbers

The best-known space telescope is NASA's Hubble Space Telescope, which was launched in 1990. But soon there will be a new telescope on the block. The James Webb* Space Telescope (JWST) is the first of a new generation of space telescopes that will probe even farther into the far reaches of the universe.

13.5 billion The number of years the telescope will look back in time. Its creators hope to detect the heat given off by the first galaxies born after the Big Bang.

10 billion The estimated total cost of the project in dollars.

1 million The sun protection factor, or SPF, given by the JWST's sun shield, which protects the telescope's sensitive instruments. The sunscreen people put on their skin typically has an SPF of between 8 and 50.

14,000 The telescope's weight in pounds (6,350 kg), which is about the same as a school bus.

100 The number of times more powerful the JWST will be than the Hubble Space Telescope.

69 The length of the sun shield in feet (21 m). It is 46 feet (14 m) wide and has the surface area of a tennis court.

22 The number of different countries collaborating on the project.

21 The width in feet (6.5 m) of JWST's primary mirror.

18 The number of gold-coated hexagonal segments on its mirror.

10 The planned length in years from design to launch of the JWST.

–370 The approximate temperature in degrees Fahrenheit (–223°C) that the telescope has to be kept at for its instruments to work properly.

Left: A NASA engineer looks at segments of the telescope's primary mirrors before they are sent for cryogenic testing. This will subject the mirrors to extremely cold temperatures, similar to those in space.

*James Webb was in charge of NASA between 1961 and 1968. He played an important role in the Apollo space missions, which put the first person on the Moon in July 1969, just a few months after Webb had retired from his job.

Strangers in the Night

Seven reasons that might explain why we haven't yet encountered alien life

Our galaxy, the Milky Way, is very big and very old. It contains hundreds of billions of stars and planets. Mathematical probability suggests that at least one of those planets should contain intelligent alien life. So why haven't we seen or heard any firm evidence that aliens exist?

1. There aren't any aliens out there to find. Perhaps human beings are the only intelligent life-forms in the whole universe. (This is mathematically unlikely but still possible.)

2. There is alien life on other planets but it's not intelligent. For example, tiny microscopic creatures could be living on other planets but because they're not broadcasting any signals or able to travel into space themselves, it's very hard or even impossible for us to find them.

3. The universe can be a dangerous place, so perhaps other alien civilizations did once exist on other planets but were then wiped out by an exploding supernova or a giant asteroid strike, a bit like the one that we think killed the dinosaurs.»

4. Space is so very big—the Milky Way alone is 100,000 light-years across—that it is possible aliens have been sending signals into space but they just haven't reached us yet.

5. We haven't been looking for long enough. Radio telescopes, which can be used to listen for signals sent from outer space, were only invented 80 years ago. And we've only been actively searching for signs of alien life for around 60 years.* In galactic terms, that's hardly any time at all.

6. Alien technology might be too advanced. Intelligent aliens could already be trying to contact us here on Earth using a form of communication or technology that we don't yet recognize or understand.**

7. It is possible that very advanced alien civilizations have found out about intelligent life on Earth (i.e., humans) but are deliberately ignoring us. Not because some of us have bad table manners but perhaps because they have wisely decided not to disturb us or our way of life.

»To find out more about the asteroid that scientists think could have wiped out the dinosaurs, see page 149.

*The first radio message deliberately broadcast to communicate with aliens was sent by the American astronomer Frank Drake on November 16, 1974. Drake sent 168 seconds of sound that included a map of where our solar system is located.

**This would be a bit like trying to have a conversation with a cave person on a cell phone.

Endgame

Three theories about what will happen at the end of the universe

Most scientists think that the universe will die, albeit a very, very long time in the future. But they disagree on exactly how and when this will happen. Here are the three main theories:

1. The Big Crunch The expansion of the universe will slow down, the universe will reach its maximum size, and then it will start to shrink. This contraction of the universe will eventually lead to a "Big Crunch." At this point, a new Big Bang will happen and the universe will start all over again!

2. The Big Freeze The universe will continue to expand and expand. So, eventually, all the energy in the universe will be so spread out that no new stars can form.*

3. The Big Rip The expansion of the universe will accelerate so fast that everything will start to tear apart—starting with galaxies and going on to destroy stars, planets, and even atoms so that nothing is left.**

---

*Most scientists think that the Big Freeze, which is also known as "heat death," is the most likely.

**Don't let this worry you. These events will happen so far in the future that Earth—and the rest of the universe—will be completely different from the place it is now.

For Future Reference

A timeline of future space events

Any moment The star Betelgeuse, which is currently a red supergiant star, will explode in a spectacular supernova.*

2024 The Parker Solar Probe will make its first close approach of the Sun.**

2030s The decade when NASA plans to send its first crewed missions to Mars.***

2061 Halley's Comet, arguably the most famous comet, will pass relatively close to Earth.

2123 An especially long lunar eclipse will occur, lasting 1 hour and 46 minutes.

2134 Halley's Comet is back again!

2177 Pluto completes its first full orbit since its discovery in 1930.

3000 Due to the motion of the Earth in space, Gamma Cephei will eventually align with our North Pole and replace Polaris as the north star.

4385 Comet Hale-Bopp, which was one of the brightest and most widely seen comets of the 20th century, returns to the inner solar system.

After 100,000 years VY Canis Majoris will explode in a supernova that will be visible from Earth.

After 296,000 years The Voyager 2 space probe will pass within 4.3 light-years of Sirius, the brightest star in the night sky.

After 4.5 billion years The Milky Way will merge with the Andromeda Galaxy.

After 5 billion years The Sun will cool and grow bigger as it becomes a red giant.

---

*In fact, this could have already happened, as it will take the light from the Betelgeuse supernova 650 years to reach us here on Earth.

**The Parker Solar Probe holds the record for being the fastest-moving human-made object. On its closest approach to the Sun, the probe will travel at around 430,000 miles per hour (700,000 km/h), which is fast enough to take you from Philadelphia to Washington, DC, in one second.

***Many of the astronauts who will be involved in these missions to Mars are still children today. So it could be you!

Chapter 2

Nature

A list of things you'll encounter in this chapter:

A cosmic calendar

Red diamonds

A mountain taller than Everest

The world's stinkiest fruit

A rock that looks like a camel

Skeletal snowflakes

Moonbows

Spider lightning

Frozen iguanas*

The world's speediest glacier

A humongous fungus

The belly button of the world

A plant that eats reptiles

*You'll need to look up!

A Cosmic Year

The entire history of the universe and Earth condensed to a single year

The Earth has been around for 4.5 billion years. And the universe has been around even longer—for 13.8 billion years! Imagine that the entire history of the universe is scaled down to fit into a single year, so that the Big Bang happens just after midnight on January 1 and right now, the moment you're reading this sentence, is just before midnight on December 31.* Here's how everything fits together . . .

January 1—The Big Bang.”

January 14—There is a flash of gamma rays, which are thought to be associated with the formation of black holes.

January 22—The first galaxies form.

March 16—The Milky Way forms.

September 2—Our solar system forms.

September 6—Earth forms.

September 7—The Moon forms, probably after the Earth collides with another planet.

September 14—The first single-celled life appears on Earth.

December 5—The first multicellular life (organisms that have more than one cell) appears on Earth. They breathe oxygen to survive.

December 14—The first arthropods emerge, the ancestors of insects (such as beetles) and crustaceans (such as crabs).

December 17—The first fish and early amphibians emerge.

December 20—The first land plants emerge.

December 21—The first insects and seeds emerge.

December 23—The first reptiles emerge.

December 25—Dinosaurs start to roam the Earth. (Just in time for Christmas dinner!)

December 26—The first mammals emerge.

December 27—The first birds emerge.

December 28—The first flowers emerge.

December 30—A giant asteroid hits Earth, causing many different species of animal (such as dinosaurs) to become extinct.

December 31, early afternoon—The first great apes emerge, from which humans will evolve.

December 31, late evening—Early humans emerge.

December 31, one second before midnight—The end of the last ice age. Humans begin farming their food rather than hunting or finding it.

December 31, midnight about to strike—You are reading this book!

---

*This way of scaling down the entire history of the universe to fit into a 365-day year is sometimes known as the "cosmic calendar." Using this scale, each day represents 37.8 million years, each hour represents 1.5 million years, and each second represents 437.5 years. The average human lifespan of 70 to 80 years takes just 0.16 seconds of time on the cosmic calendar.

» To find out more about the Big Bang, see page 10.

Journey to the Center of the Earth

Earth's four layers, from crust to core

1. Crust—up to 43.5 mi (70 km) below the surface*
Temperature: 392–2,120°F (200–1,160°C)
Made of: Mostly silica, aluminum, and oxygen

2. Mantle—up to 1,800 mi (2,900 km) below the surface
Temperature: 1,832–6,692°F (1,000–3,700°C)
Made of: Semi-solid iron, magnesium, and silicon

3. Outer core—up to 3,220 mi (5,180 km) below the surface
Temperature: 8,312–9,392°F (4,500–5,200°C)**
Made of: Liquid iron and nickel

4. Inner core—up to 4,000 mi (6,400 km) below the surface
Temperature: 9,392°F (5,200°C)
Made of: Solid iron and nickel

*The crust makes up only 1 percent of the planet's total volume. Its thickness varies a lot. Under the ocean, it can be as little as 3.1 miles (5 km) thick. Beneath the continents, it can be up to 14 times thicker.

**The hottest part of the inside of the Earth is a region called the Bullen discontinuity, which lies at the boundary between the outer and inner cores.

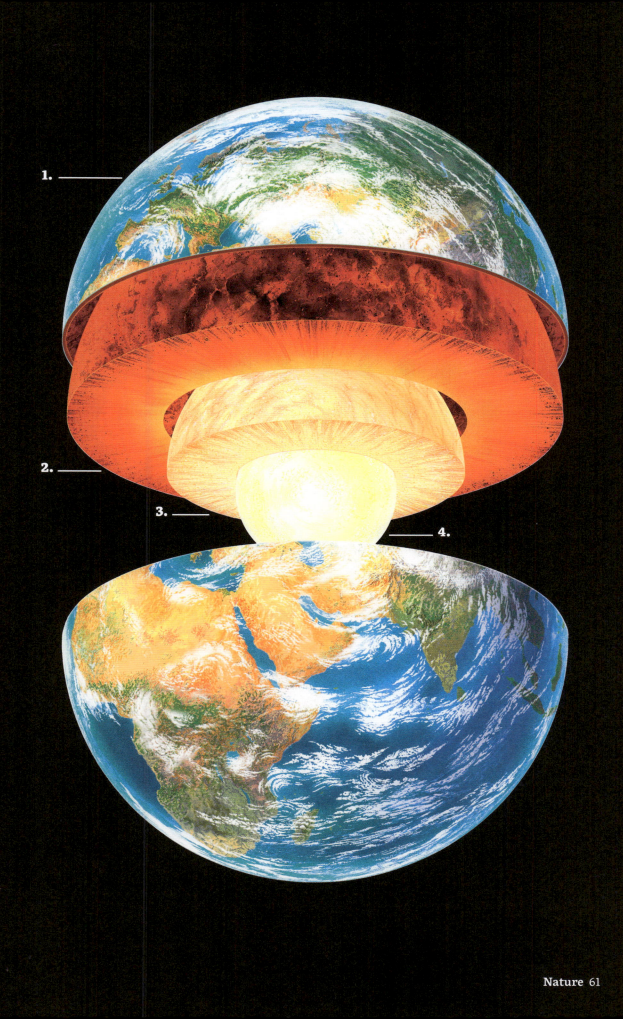

1. _____

2. _____

3. _____

4.

The World on a Plate

The Earth's seven major tectonic plates

The Earth's crust is divided into seven major and 15 minor tectonic plates. The minor plates slot into the spaces between the major plates like jigsaw pieces.*

1. Pacific Plate**
2. North American Plate
3. South American Plate
4. Eurasian Plate
5. African Plate
6. Indo-Australian Plate
7. Antarctic Plate

*The movement of tectonic plates causes most earthquakes and volcanoes. The major plates typically move between 1.2 and 2 inches (3 and 5 cm) each year, which is roughly the speed at which your fingernails grow.

**Approximately 90 percent of earthquakes and more than 75 percent of volcanoes occur around the edge of the Pacific Plate, along what is called the Ring of Fire.

Ground Force

The ten biggest recorded earthquakes

The strength of earthquakes is measured on the moment magnitude scale. The higher the number, the bigger the earthquake.*

1. **Valdivia, Chile,** in 1960—9.5 magnitude**

2. **Prince William Sound, Alaska, United States,** in 1964—9.2 magnitude

3. **Indian Ocean, near Indonesia,** in 2004—9.1 magnitude

4. **Pacific Ocean, near Japan,** in 2011—9.1 magnitude

5. **Kamchatka, Russia,** in 1952—9 magnitude

6. **Offshore of Ecuador,** in 1906—8.8 magnitude

7. **Offshore of Maule, Chile,** in 2010—8.8 magnitude

8. **Rat Islands, Alaska, United States,** in 1965—8.7 magnitude

9. **Assam, India,** in 1950—8.6 magnitude

10. **Sumatra, Indonesia,** in 2005—8.6 magnitude

*An earthquake that can barely be felt by humans measures 1 on the scale, while an earthquake measuring 8 or more is likely to make permanent changes to the landscape and cause huge destruction.

**The largest earthquake ever recorded caused a giant ocean wave, known as a tsunami, to roll from the coast of Chile in South America for thousands of miles across the Pacific Ocean before reaching islands as far away as Hawaii and the Philippines.

Blowing Their Tops

Eight of the biggest volcanic eruptions in recorded history

A volcano is formed by molten rock called magma that rises toward the Earth's surface. Bubbles of gas form inside the magma as it rises. In some volcanoes, the bubbles can't escape, so the pressure builds up until—kaboom!—the volcano erupts, sending hot gases, ash, lava, and rock spewing out into the air. The power of volcanic eruptions is measured using the Volcanic Explosivity Index (VEI). The index goes from 1 to 8, with each level being ten times more powerful than the one before.

1. Mount Thera, Greece, around 1610 BCE—VEI 7

Scientists think this volcano on the Greek island of Santorini exploded with a force 100 times more powerful than the eruption of Mount Vesuvius that destroyed Pompeii. (See entry 8.)

2. Changbaishan, China, around 1000 CE—VEI 7

This massive eruption in eastern China spewed volcanic dust and ash over an area three times the size of Alaska.

3. Mount Tambora, Indonesia, in 1815—VEI 7

In the largest volcanic explosion ever recorded, the sounds of the eruption were heard on the island of Sumatra, more than 1,200 miles (1,930 km) away. The enormous cloud of volcanic ash it fired into the air left a covering of dust across an area more than twice the size of California.*

4. Ambrym, Vanuatu, in 50 CE—VEI 6

Since its biggest eruption, in 50 CE, this volcanic island has been one of the world's most active volcanoes. It has erupted almost 50 times since 1774.

5. Krakatoa, Indonesia, in 1883—VEI 6

When this huge volcanic island erupted, the sound could be heard as far away as Perth, Australia, which is more than 1,800 miles (3,000 km) away.** Large quantities of ash from the eruption covered a total area that was roughly the size of Texas.

6. Novarupta, United States, in 1912—VEI 6

In the biggest volcanic blast of the 20th century, Novarupta sent about 6.7 cubic miles (28 km³) of volcanic material into the air. The ash fell over a huge area, including covering an area roughly the size of Puerto Rico in more than a foot (30 centimeters) of ash.

7. Mount Pinatubo, Philippines, in 1991—VEI 6

The eruption created a towering column of ash that rose up 22 miles (35 km) into the atmosphere. This giant ash cloud covered an area the size of the state of Mississippi, blocking out the sun for 36 hours.

8. Mount Vesuvius, Italy, in 79 CE—VEI 5

This famous eruption spewed a column of volcanic material up into the sky at a rate of 1.5 million tons (1.4 million tonnes) per second. The nearby Roman cities of Pompeii and Herculaneum were buried in up to 60 feet (18 m) of molten rock and ash.

---

*The eruption of Mount Tambora threw vast clouds of volcanic gas and ash into the atmosphere, which had a major impact on Earth's climate, lowering temperatures around the world by between 0.7 and 1.3°F (0.4 and 0.7°C).

**It also created a giant wave or tsunami the height of a ten-story building, threw 600 tons (544 tonnes) of coral onto the shore, and carried a steamship a mile (1.5 km) inland. The dust and ash thrown up into the atmosphere caused red sunsets around the world for up to three years after.

This image shows the powerful eruption of Anak Krakatau in 2009. This volcano was created by lava that had been ejected from nearby Krakatoa. Its name means "Child of Krakatoa."

On Top of the World

The ten tallest mountains in the world measured from base to peak

1. **Mauna Kea, Hawaii**—33,500 ft (10,210 m)*

2. **Mount Everest, China/Nepal**—29,032 ft (8,849 m)

3. **K2, China/Pakistan**—28,251 ft (8,611 m)

4. **Kangchenjunga, India/Nepal**—28,169 ft (8,586 m)

5. **Lhotse, China/Nepal**—27,940 ft (8,516 m)

6. **Makalu, China/Nepal**—27,766 ft (8,463 m)

7. **Cho Oyu, China/Nepal**—26,906 ft (8,201 m)

8. **Dhaulagiri, Nepal**—26,795 ft (8,167 m)

9. **Manaslu, Nepal**—26,781 ft (8,163 m)

10. **Nanga Parbat, Pakistan**—26,660 ft (8,126 m)

Solid as a Rock

The three types of rock

1. Igneous rock—made from molten lava
Examples: obsidian and pumice

2. Sedimentary rock—made from layers of sand, mud, and small stones
Examples: chalk and limestone

3. Metamorphic rock—made from rocks that have been put under great pressure and heat inside the Earth
Examples: slate and marble

Tough Stuff

Mohs scale of hardness

Mohs scale was created in 1812 by the German geologist Friedrich Mohs to compare the hardness of different minerals. The higher the number on the scale, the harder the mineral. To find out where a substance should rank on the scale, you use it to scratch each of the minerals listed. For example, you would be able to scratch gypsum with your fingernail, but not calcite, so your fingernail has a hardness of 2.5—softer than calcite but harder than gypsum.

10. Diamond

9. Corundum

8. Topaz*

7. Quartz

6. Orthoclase

5. Apatite**

4. Fluorite

3. Calcite***

2. Gypsum

1. Talc

Right: A hiker inside The Wave, a giant sandstone rock formation in the Vermilion Cliffs National Monument, Arizona.

---

*Mount Everest is the highest mountain in the world above sea level. But when Mauna Kea is measured all the way from its underwater base to its peak, it is significantly taller than Mount Everest.

*A drill designed for making holes in bricks would score 8.5.

**A kitchen knife would score 5.5.

***A copper coin would score 3.5.

Planet Rock

Five amazing rock formations that look like other things

1. Richat Structure—looks like an eye

Where: Mauritania

What: A huge dome-shaped structure in the Sahara Desert that is about 30 miles (48 km) wide and formed from rocks that are more than 90 million years old.*

2. Moeraki Boulders—looks like giant black marbles

Where: New Zealand

What: A group of more than 50 spherical black stones that began forming more than 60 million years ago.

3. Wave Rock—looks like an ocean wave

Where: Australia

What: A smooth, curved wall of rock that's 49 feet (15 m) high and 361 feet (110 m) long. Formed by water erosion, it's part of Hyden Rock, a granite outcrop that is more than 2.7 billion years old.

4. Giant's Causeway—looks like stairs

Where: Northern Ireland

What: These large columns of rock rise up from the ground like steps and fit together neatly thanks to their hexagonal shape. They're thought to have been created by volcanic activity around 50 million years ago, and there are more than 40,000 of them along the coast.

5. Camel Rock—looks like, well, you guessed it . . .

Where: Turkey

What: The rock was originally formed millions of years ago from compressed volcanic ash. By a strange coincidence, this particular rock has eroded to create the outline of a certain humped animal.

---

*Also known as the "Eye of the Sahara," the Richat Structure was once thought to have been created by a meteorite landing on Earth. Water erosion is now considered the more likely explanation.

Richat Structure

Moeraki Boulders

Wave Rock

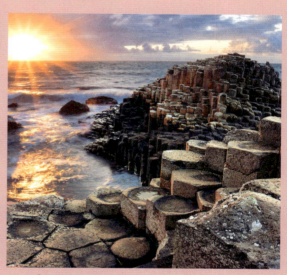

Giant's Causeway

Camel Rock

Rich Pickings

Twelve of the most expensive natural substances in the world

1. Red diamond—$5 million per gram

Red diamonds are so rare that only around 30 high-quality examples are thought to exist.*

2. Painite—$300,000 per gram

This red-brown gem is named after the British mineralogist Arthur Pain, who first unearthed it in Myanmar in the 1950s. Pain thought he'd found a ruby until it was later identified as a new type of gemstone.

3. Grandidierite—$129,500 per gram

Grandidierite is a beautiful green-blue gemstone that was first discovered in Madagascar in 1902, by the French explorer Alfred Grandidier.

4. Taaffeite—$12,500 per gram

This pink or purple gemstone is more than a million times rarer than diamond. It was first discovered in a jeweler's shop in Dublin, Ireland, in 1945 and is the only gemstone to have been first identified after it had been crafted into a piece of jewelry.

5. Da Hong Pao tea—$1,400 per gram

This tea from southern China is so expensive because the bushes from which the tea leaves are picked are extremely rare.

6. Rhodium—$317 per gram

The most precious metal in the world is most commonly used in car exhausts, where it helps to filter out nitrous gas, which can damage the environment.

7. Palladium—$80 per gram

This silvery-white precious metal is sometimes used to make jewelry, and often used in car engines.

8. Iridium—$59 per gram

One of the rarest elements to be found naturally on Earth, iridium is also one of the toughest metals. You can find it in the tips of pens and in crucibles—containers that are designed to withstand very high temperatures.

9. Gold—$50 per gram

Despite its rarity, gold has been found on every continent on Earth.» Pure gold is so soft you can mold it with your hands and just 1 ounce (28 g) can be stretched into thin wire 50 miles (80 km) long.

10. Platinum—$32 per gram

This precious metal is so rare that all the platinum that has ever been mined would fit into an average-sized living room. It has many uses, from jewelry and medicine to dentists' tools and electronics.

11. Italian white truffles—$9 per gram

Truffles are a type of fungus that grow underground and that many people eat. Pigs and dogs are great truffle-hunters because of their excellent sense of smell. Humans have used these animals to root out truffles for thousands of years.

12. Saffron—$4 per gram

Made from the flower of the autumn crocus plant, saffron is the world's most expensive spice. It is used for flavoring food and as a natural medicine.**

---

*The world's largest red diamond, which weighs 0.04 ounce (1.022 g, about the same weight as a paper clip), is called the Moussaieff Red Diamond. It is thought to be worth $8 million.

» To discover a surprising place where gold can be found (hint: it's closer than you think), see page 206.

**Saffron is so expensive because the autumn crocus plant is hard to grow, the flowers have to be handpicked, and you need 400 of them to produce just 0.04 ounce (1 g) of saffron.

Following a Pattern

The Fibonacci sequence in nature

The Fibonacci sequence is one of the most famous number sequences in mathematics. It begins: 0, 1, 1, 2, 3, 5, 8, 13, 21, 34, 55, 89 . . . You find the next number by adding the previous two numbers together. One of the extraordinary things about this sequence is that these Fibonacci numbers are found in many places in nature. Here are five places that you can spot them:

1. In seed heads

If you look at the center of a sunflower, you can see spirals of seeds curving clockwise and counterclockwise. If you count all of the spirals that curve counterclockwise and then all that curve clockwise you will come up with two numbers that are next to each other in the Fibonacci sequence.* The sunflower on the opposite page has 21 counterclockwise spirals (marked in yellow) and 34 clockwise spirals (marked in blue).

2. On pine cones

As with seed heads, you can see spirals in pine cones that curve counterclockwise and clockwise. The number of spirals going in each direction will likewise be two numbers that are next to each other in the Fibonacci sequence. The pine cone on the opposite page has eight counterclockwise spirals (marked in yellow) and 13 clockwise spirals (marked in blue).

3. On Romanesco broccoli

You can see spirals that curve counterclockwise and clockwise in the florets of a Romanesco broccoli. As with sunflower seed heads and pinecones, the number of spirals going in each direction will be two numbers that are next to each other in the Fibonacci sequence. The Romanesco broccoli floret on the opposite page has 13 counterclockwise spirals (marked in yellow) and 21 clockwise spirals (marked in blue).

4. Flower petals

If you count the number of petals on a flower, you will often find that the total number adds up to a number from the Fibonacci sequence. For example, lilies have three petals, buttercups have five, and most marigolds have 13. The flower shown in the image opposite is a tiger-flower, which is a type of lily that has three petals.

5. Fruit

The seeds of some fruit are arranged in sections that are Fibonacci numbers. For example, if you look at the cross section of a banana you will see three segments, and an apple cross section shows five segments, such as the one shown on the opposite page.

---

*This seed pattern is the most efficient way to pack as many seeds as possible into a circular space.

Sunflower

Pine cone

Romanesco broccoli

Tiger-flower

Apple

Big Stink

Eight of the smelliest things on the planet

1. Stinking corpse lily This giant red flower smells like a combination of rotting meat, old fish, and sweaty socks. It releases this terrible stench to attract flies that help to spread its pollen to other flowers.

2. Lesser anteater Although this furry creature looks cute, don't get too close. It is more than five times smellier than a skunk and uses its dreadful stench to keep predators away.

3. Eastern skunk cabbage This red wetland plant smells like a dead skunk. It uses its unique scent to attract insects.

4. Durian fruit Known as the world's stinkiest fruit, the durian has a smell like rotten onions. The odor is so disgusting that you are not allowed to carry one on public buses and trains in Japan.*

5. Stink bug Do not bother a stink bug. When threatened or injured, these powerful little insects release an intense, spicy smell that can take hours to go away.

6. Vieux Boulogne cheese Scientists used a special smelling machine—which they called an "electronic nose"—to prove that Vieux Boulogne is officially the smelliest cheese on Earth.

7. Dog stinkhorn This slime-capped mushroom smells so terrible that you can sometimes detect its presence in a forest before you spot it on the ground.

8. Hoatzin bird This blue-faced bird from South America is known as the "skunk bird" or "stinkbird" for good reason: it smells like cow poop.

*Although if you're brave enough to eat a durian fruit, the yellow flesh inside tastes nice and sweet, like custard.

Mount Everest

Grand Canyon

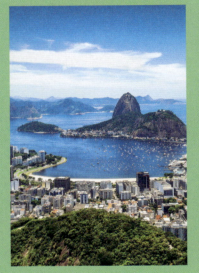
Harbor of Rio de Janeiro

Great Barrier Reef

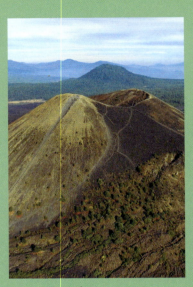
Paricutín Volcano

Victoria Falls

Aurora borealis

Wonderlands

The seven natural wonders of the world

These seven amazing phenomena were chosen by Seven Natural Wonders, an organization dedicated to protecting and promoting the environment.

1. Mount Everest, China/Nepal
The highest mountain in the world (above sea level) is more than 60 million years old and still growing: It gets approximately 0.25 inches (6 mm) taller each year.*

2. Grand Canyon, United States
At 277 miles (446 km) long and 1 mile (2 km) deep,** this huge gorge is known for its dramatic landscapes of red, orange, and brown rocks. It was formed by plate tectonics and the movement of the Colorado River over millions of years.

3. Harbor of Rio de Janeiro, Brazil
This spectacular natural harbor is overlooked by a ring of granite mountains, including the famous Sugarloaf Mountain. It is the largest bay in the world by volume of water.

4. Great Barrier Reef, Australia***
The world's largest coral reef system is made up of some 3,000 individual reefs. It covers a surface area of 134,000 square miles (348,000 km²), making it roughly the same size as Germany.

5. Paricutín Volcano, Mexico
This 9,210-foot- (2,808-m-) tall volcano was chosen as a natural wonder because it is one of the youngest volcanoes on Earth. When Paricutín first erupted in 1943, it grew 164 feet (50 m) in a day and 500 feet (150 m) in a week, firing ash and flames thousands of feet into the air. The volcano stayed active until 1952.

6. Victoria Falls, Zambia/Zimbabwe
At more than 5,577 feet (1,700 m) wide and 328 feet (100 m) tall, Victoria Falls is the largest single curtain of flowing water on the planet. At peak times of the year, an estimated 132,000,000 gallons (500 million l) of water flow over it each minute. That's enough water to fill 200 Olympic-sized swimming pools.

7. Aurora borealis, the night sky
Also known as the Northern Lights, the aurora borealis are multicolored patterns of light created when solar winds, which are given off by the Sun, come into contact with Earth's magnetic field. One of the best places to see them is from the International Space Station, which sometimes passes right through the lights as it orbits Earth.

---

*Mount Everest is constantly being pushed upward by the force of two tectonic plates that collided underneath it.

**The village at the bottom of the canyon, Supai, is so hard to get to that it is the only place in the United States where the mail is still delivered by mules.

***The Great Barrier Reef is home to more than 1,600 species of fish—approximately 4.7 percent of the world's estimated total.

Journey to the Top of the Clouds

Ten common types of cloud and how to spot them

Clouds are formed when water vapor, which is invisible, turns into tiny water droplets or ice crystals. These float in the air as clouds until the droplets or crystals grow large enough to fall to the ground as rain or snow.

1. Stratus Covering most or all of the sky, these clouds are flat, featureless, and gray. If you're feeling gloomy, this is the cloud for you.

2. Cumulus Bright white on the top and a darker grayish-white underneath, Cumulus clouds are the most familiar type of puffy clouds.

3. Stratocumulus These are similar in shape to Cumulus clouds, but are flatter, thicker, and darker. Stratocumulus clouds are usually grouped close together with very little blue sky visible between them.

4. Cumulonimbus If you spot these large towers of threatening-looking dark clouds, it is a sign to reach for the umbrella: A storm is approaching.

5. Nimbostratus *Nimbus* is the Latin word for "rain cloud." Nimbostratus clouds form a dark layer, sort of like a big, wet blanket, which reaches across the sky and is thick enough to hide the Sun from view. When these clouds are around, it will rain a lot.

6. Altocumulus These rounded white or gray clouds are often tightly grouped together and look like tufts of wool arranged in a pattern.

7. Altostratus These clouds form a white or gray blanket across the sky. Although patches of blue sky can't usually be seen when Altostratus clouds appear, the Sun is often visible as a dim yellow disc shining through them.

8. Cirrocumulus These clouds are found at high altitudes and take the form of tiny clumps that look a little like confetti in the sky. They are the rarest of the ten main cloud types as they don't hang around for long and often change into Cirrus or Cirrostratus clouds.

9. Cirrostratus These subtle clouds cover most or all of the sky like a thin, milky veil.

10. Cirrus You can see plenty of blue sky around Cirrus clouds, which are thin, wispy clouds that look a little like brushstrokes and are found high in the atmosphere. They are the fastest moving of the ten cloud types and are made of ice crystals. You will usually see them during fair weather.

Sunlight zone

Twilight zone

Midnight zone

The abyss

The trenches

Journey to the Bottom of the Sea

The ocean's five zones

1. Sunlight zone—up to 656 ft (200 m) below the surface

Scientific name: Epipelagic zone

What it is like: With plenty of sunlight, warmer waters, and little water pressure, this is where most marine creatures live. You'll find everything from dolphins and fish, such as tuna and mackerel, to turtles and whales—maybe even a human having a swim."

2. Twilight zone—up to 3,281 ft (1,000 m) below the surface

Scientific name: Mesopelagic zone

What it is like: Faint sunlight is visible, along with the lights of bioluminescent organisms that give off their own glow. Some very peculiar-looking creatures live here, including squidworms, gulper eels, and lanternfish, as well as krill, cuttlefish, jellyfish, and whale sharks.

3. Midnight zone—up to 13,100 ft (4,000 m) below the surface

Scientific name: Bathypelagic zone

What it is like: No sunlight can reach the midnight zone at all, and yet a surprisingly large number of marine species live here, including octopuses, eels, Greenland sharks, and sperm whales.

4. The abyss—up to 19,686 ft (6,000 m) below the surface

Scientific name: Abyssopelagic zone

What it is like: A few creatures have adapted to the cold and dark of the abyss, including fish such as anglerfish and black swallowers* and invertebrates such as basket stars and tiny squid.

5. The trenches—up to 36,100 ft (11,000 m) below the surface

Scientific name: Hadal zone

What it is like: It's not only the total lack of sunlight and water temperatures just above freezing that make this the toughest underwater environment on Earth. The pressure from all the water above is equivalent to the weight of a pickup truck per square inch (2.5 cm²). Amazingly, some life still thrives here, including liparid fish, sea cucumbers, and tube worms.

»To find out what happens to the human body if you dive deep underwater, see page 242.

*Thanks to its hugely extendable stomach, the 9.8-inch (25-cm) black swallower is able to eat prey twice its length and ten times its weight. Gulp.

Surface Features

What the Earth is covered with

Water—71 percent
Land—29 percent*

Water World

Where all the water on Earth is found

There are approximately
326 million trillion gallons
(1.23 billion trillion liters) of water
on Earth, making it the most common
substance on the planet's surface.** Here
are all the different places you can find it:

Oceans and seas—97.4 percent

Groundwater—0.75 percent

**Ice caps, glaciers, and
snow**—1.7 percent

Frozen ground—0.02 percent

Lakes—0.006 percent

In the soil—0.001 percent

In the atmosphere—0.0009 percent***

Swamps—0.00078 percent

Rivers—0.00015 percent

**Living organisms, including
humans**—0.000078 percent

Making a Splash

The ten tallest waterfalls in the world

1. **Angel Falls,** * **Venezuela**—
   3,212 ft (979 m)

2. **Tugela Falls, South Africa**—
   3,110 ft (948 m)

3. **Mattenbachfälle, Switzerland**—
   3,050 ft (930 m)

4. **Tres Hermanas Falls, Peru**—
   2,999 ft (914 m)

5. **Oloʻupena Falls, Hawaii**—
   2,953 ft (900 m)

6. **Yumbilla Falls, Peru**—2,938 ft (896 m)

7. **Vinnufallet, Norway**—2,837 ft (865 m)

8. **Skorga, Norway**—2,835 ft (864 m)

9. **James Bruce Falls, Canada**—
   2,756 ft (840 m)

10. **Puʻukaʻoku Falls, Hawaii**—
    2,756 ft (840 m)

Right: Angel Falls

---

*Around one fifth of the land on Earth
is permanently covered in snow.

**There is the same amount of water on Earth
now as there was when the Earth formed
4.5 billion years ago. In fact, the next cup of
water you drink could contain molecules
of water that were drunk by a dinosaur.
Let's hope it brushed its teeth.

***Over a 100-year period, an average water
molecule spends just over 98 years in the ocean,
20 months as ice, about two weeks in rivers and
lakes, and less than a week in the atmosphere.

*Angel Falls is more than three times taller than
the Eiffel Tower in Paris, France. In fact, it is so
tall that in warmer, drier weather, all the water
cascading over the top evaporates into a fine mist
before it hits the bottom.

Crystal-Gazing

Thirty-five different types of snowflake

Although no two individual snowflakes are exactly the same,* scientists have given names to groups of snowflakes that have similar shapes.

1. Simple prisms
2. Hexagonal plates
3. Stellar plates
4. Sectored plates
5. Simple stars
6. Stellar dendrites
7. Fernlike stellar dendrites**
8. Solid columns
9. Hollow columns
10. Bullet rosettes
11. Isolated bullets
12. Simple needles
13. Needle clusters
14. Crossed needles
15. Sheaths
16. Cups
17. Capped columns
18. Multiply capped columns
19. Capped bullets
20. Double plates
21. Hollow plates
22. Scrolls on plates
23. Columns on plates
24. Split plates and stars
25. Skeletal forms
26. Twin columns
27. Arrowhead twins
28. Crossed plates
29. Triangular forms
30. Twelve-branched stars
31. Radiating plates
32. Radiating dendrites
33. Irregulars
34. Rimed
35. Graupel

---

*It is possible for two simple snowflakes (such as simple needles) to look similar in shape, even when viewed through a microscope. However, larger complex snowflakes (such as stellar dendrites) are a different story. It is mathematically so unlikely that two complex snowflakes are the same shape, that scientists can say with confidence that it has not happened once in all the snow that's fallen during Earth's 4.5-billion-year history. But don't let that stop you from checking.

**Fernlike stellar dendrites are very thin and light. They can form the kind of powdery snow that's great for making snowballs.

Over the Rainbow

Nine different types of rainbow

Rainbows are caused by rays of light shining through water droplets in the atmosphere. When sunlight passes through the droplets, it bends and spreads out, forming a band of colors.*

1. Primary rainbow The classic. The color sequence of a primary rainbow is: red, orange, yellow, green, blue, indigo, violet.

2. Double rainbows This is when a faint, secondary rainbow appears above the first one. They're caused by light reflecting twice inside the raindrop. This second reflection** causes the color sequence of the rainbow to be reversed: red is now on the inner section of the arch, while violet is on the outer.

3. Twinned rainbows These are the rarest type of rainbows, when two rainbows start from the same base but then split to form a primary and secondary arc across the sky. They are usually caused by a rain cloud that contains different sizes and shapes of raindrops.

4. Reflection rainbows Sometimes sunlight reflects off a flat body of water first and then bounces up to create a rainbow in the air above the water. This is called a reflection rainbow.

5. Reflected rainbows This is the name for any rainbow you see reflected on the surface of a flat body of water, such as a lake.

6. Monochrome rainbows These rainbows only display one color, which is usually red. They happen at sunrise or sunset, when sunlight has to travel farther through Earth's atmosphere because the Sun is low in the sky. This "scatters" the light with shorter wavelengths (yellow, green, blue, indigo, and violet) so only the longer-wavelength red and orange are visible.

7. Supernumerary rainbows These are smaller rainbows in lighter, pastel colors that appear as an extra colored band running inside the first rainbow. They form when sunlight bounces off small water droplets of 0.04 inches (1 mm) or less.

8. Fogbows Because the water droplets in fog are much smaller than raindrops, fogbows have much fainter colors than rainbows. They mostly appear white with a reddish tinge on the outer edge and a bluish tinge on the inner edge.

9. Moonbows These are also called lunar rainbows. Moonbows are created in the same way as rainbows but with moonlight—which is actually just sunlight reflected by the Moon. They form the same spectrum of colors but are usually fainter.

---

*Rainbows often look like arches, but they are actually full circles. Rainbows only look like arches when seen from the ground because the bottom part is often blocked by the horizon.

**A rainbow's order is defined by the number of times that light reflects inside the water droplets. Primary rainbows are first-order rainbows and double rainbows are second-order. It is possible to see third- and fourth-order rainbows too, but they become increasingly faint as the number increases. Scientists in a laboratory have detected a 200th-order rainbow!

Right: A double rainbow over the Raja Ampat Islands in Indonesia

Flashdance

Eleven types of lightning and how to recognize them

Lightning is a bright burst of electricity produced by a thunderstorm. It works in the same way as the spark you sometimes see (and the small shock you feel) when you rub your feet across carpet and then touch something metal. Except on a much, much bigger scale!*

1. Cloud-to-ground This is the least common but most dangerous of the three main categories of lightning (which are the first three listed here) because the lightning flash jumps from the cloud and terminates on or "strikes" the Earth.**

2. Ground-to-cloud Here the lightning strike starts on the ground, often from a skyscraper or other tall, human-made object. Then any forks of lightning branch upward toward the sky.

3. Intracloud The most common form of lightning takes place inside a cloud, which means the lightning flash may not be fully visible to someone on the ground. This is sometimes called sheet lightning because it illuminates the sky with a bright "sheet" of light.

4. Spider lightning This is made when a horizontal forked lightning flash happens inside a cloud but is slow enough to be visible from the ground. The name comes from the spiderlike way the lightning "crawls" sideways across the sky.

5. Cloud-to-air lightning This particularly dramatic form of lightning jumps out of the side of a thundercloud and ends in the clear air outside the storm.

6. Bead lightning It is unknown exactly why this occurs, but one theory suggests that parts of the lightning channel are slanted away from the observer. This makes some parts seem brighter than others. It looks like a string of beads and is also known as pearl lightning.

7. Bolt from the blue lightning This type of lightning travels horizontally some distance away from the thunderstorm before dropping down vertically to strike the Earth.***

8. Ribbon lightning A ribboned lightning effect happens in thunderstorms with strong horizontal winds that blow each stroke of the lightning flash slightly to one side.

9. Sprites These are bursts of electricity that happen high above the thunderstorm. They appear as faint, vertical red columns of light but are hard to see from the ground.

10. Heat lightning This is a lightning flash that appears not to be followed by a thunderclap. The lightning happens so far away that the thunder's sound waves break up before they reach the person watching the lightning.

11. Staccato lightning This type of lightning creates a single bright cloud-to-ground flash, often with lots of downward-pointing branches.

---

*A bolt of lightning is 0.8–1.2 inches (2–3 cm) wide, so roughly the width of your thumb, and is approximately 50,000°F (27,760°C), which is five times hotter than the surface of the Sun.

**Lightning strikes most frequently over Lake Maracaibo, Venezuela. In just one night, the sky above the lake can be illuminated with 40,000 bolts of lightning.

***Because its final strike point can be up to 10 miles (16 km) away from the storm, a bolt from the blue can be seen even when there are clear skies overhead, which is how it gets its name.

Spider lightning
in Tucson, Arizona

Skyfall

Nine surprising things that have fallen out of the sky

1. Red rain

The microscopic freshwater algae called *Haematococcus pluvialis* produces a red pigment or color when it is under stress. If the red algae mixes with rainwater, it can cause a phenomenon called "blood rain," which has been witnessed in India, Spain, and the United States, among other places.*

2. Frozen iguanas

The iguanas that live in Florida like to make their homes in the branches of tall trees. However, when it gets too cold, their cold-blooded bodies stop functioning properly, and they can no longer hold on to the branches. Freezing iguanas then start falling from above and will stay lying motionless on the ground until the temperature warms up, when they spring back to life.**

3. Mud

In 1902, a huge dust storm formed dust clouds over Illinois. The clouds were blown eastward across the United States until they met a large group of rain clouds over New York and New Jersey. The dusty and rainy clouds combined to form a refreshing shower of mud.

4. Fish

There are several theories as to why it sometimes rains fish, which it has done in lots of parts of the world, including India, Australia, and Canada. One explanation is that it's caused by a whirling column of air and mist called a waterspout. When a waterspout forms above water, it can suck fish and other marine creatures up from lakes or the sea before carrying them inland and dropping them on confused people holding umbrellas.***

*Dust from the Sahara Desert can also cause red rain; dust from the Gobi Desert can cause yellow rain; while volcanic dust and ash cause black rain.

**To cope with the problem, the National Weather Service in Miami now sends out "iguana rain" warnings if cold weather is approaching.

***Fish fall from the sky so often in Mexico that there is a name for it—*lluvia de peces*—which means "rain of fish."

5. Frogs

The same thing happens to frogs. In 1873, the magazine *Scientific American* reported a "shower of frogs which darkened the air and covered the ground for a long distance" after a rainstorm in Kansas City.

6. Satellites

There are more than 2,000 working and 3,000 broken satellites currently orbiting Earth. When they stop working, they become space junk. Over the last 50 years, more than 5,900 tons (5,400 tonnes) of space junk have survived reentry to the atmosphere to land back on Earth.

7. Meat

In 1876, people in Kentucky in the United States witnessed a flurry of meaty flakes fall from a cloudless sky. Two men who tasted the meat thought it probably came from a sheep or a deer. Scientists who tested the flakes thought the most likely explanation was that some passing vultures had disgorged, or thrown up, the meat while flying overhead.

8. Golf balls

Residents of Punta Gorda, Florida, were left scratching their heads on September 1, 1969, when dozens of golf balls dropped out of the sky. The most convincing theory to explain them is that a passing storm had scooped up water from a lake on a golf course, along with lots of lost balls, before dropping it all on the nearby town.

9. Spiders

The spooky phenomenon known as "spider rain" is caused by millions of tiny spiders engaging in a behavior called ballooning. First, the spiders go to an exposed high place. They then release silk threads from their abdomens, which are picked up and carried away by the wind, with the flying spiders coming along for the ride. Ballooning spiders can travel anything from a few feet to hundreds of miles. It's a technique mostly used by baby spiders, which are called spiderlings, to find new territory.

Breaking the Ice

Glaciers in numbers

Glaciers are vast, slow-moving rivers of ice. They are formed by layers of snow that become compressed over hundreds of years. They are found flowing down the slopes of high mountains and in the Arctic and Antarctic.

198,000 The estimated number of glaciers in the world.

15,500 The depth in feet (4,700 m) of the thickest glaciers in Antarctica.*

270 The length in miles (435 km) of the world's largest glacier, the Lambert Glacier in Antarctica. It is 60 miles (97 km) wide.

230 The height in feet (70 m) that global sea levels would rise if all the glaciers in the world melted at once.

150 The number of feet (46 m) per day that the world's speediest glacier, the Jakobshavn Glacier in Greenland, can move.

91 The percentage of the world's glaciers found in Antarctica.

69 The percentage of the world's fresh water found in glaciers.»

36.3 The average depth of ice in inches (92.2 cm) that has melted off the top of all the world's glaciers each year since 2010.**

30 The percentage of the Earth's surface covered by glaciers during the last ice age.

10 The percentage of the Earth's surface covered by glaciers today.

0.04 The minimum size in square miles (0.1 km²) that a sheet of ice needs to be, in order to be considered a glacier.

---

*Glaciers often appear blue because, unlike red and yellow waves of light, blue light can move through snow and ice. The longer the light has traveled through the ice, the deeper blue it appears.

» Glaciers are a vital source of clean water for hundreds of millions of people around the world. To find out how humans could use this water, see page 256.

**Glaciers are melting four times more quickly today than they were in the 1980s.

Going with the Flow

The ten longest rivers in the world*

1. **Nile River, Africa**—4,132 mi (6,650 km)

2. **Amazon River, South America**—4,000 mi (6,400 km)**

3. **Yangtze River, Asia**—3,915 mi (6,300 km)

4. **Yellow River, Asia**—3,395 mi (5,464 km)

5. **Paraná River, South America**—3,032 mi (4,880 km)

6. **Congo, Africa*****—2,900 mi (4,700 km)

7. **Mississippi River, North America**—2,340 mi (3,766 km)

8. **Ob, Russia**—2,268 mi (3,650 km)

9. **Yenisey, Russia**—2,167 mi (3,487 km)

10. **Amur River, Asia**—1,755 mi (2,824 km)

*The shortest river in the world is the Roe River in Montana. It is 201 feet (61 m) long.

**However, the Amazon River is notoriously difficult to measure because there is much debate about where it starts and ends. This is the minimum length that scientists believe it could be.

***The Congo is the only major river to cross the equator twice.

Land Ahoy!

Ten extremely remote islands

1. Pitcairn Island, South Pacific Ocean

Location: 3,300 mi (5,300 km) from New Zealand

Most of the 50 or so people who live on the island today are descendants of the crew of the British ship HMS *Bounty* and the Polynesian people who already lived there. In 1790, the *Bounty*'s crew had to hide on the island after seizing control of the ship from its unpopular captain, William Bligh.

2. Easter Island, South Pacific Ocean

Location: 2,340 mi (3,767 km) from South America

One of the local Rapa Nui people's names for this isolated volcanic island is *Te Pito o Te Henua*, which means the "belly button of the world."*

3. Amsterdam Island, Indian Ocean

Location: 2,140 mi (3,450 km) from Australia

Due to the extreme isolation of this volcanic island, many of the plants and creatures that live there are not found anywhere else in the world.

4. Kerguelen Islands, Indian Ocean

Location: 2,050 mi (3,299 km) from Madagascar

These mountainous, glacier-filled islands are home to animals that thrive in cold weather, such as seals, terns, and penguins—plus between 50 and 100 scientific researchers.

5. Tristan da Cunha, South Atlantic Ocean

Location: 1,750 mi (2,816 km) from South Africa

Tristan da Cunha has a population of around 260 people but with no airport or airstrip, it can only be reached by boat.

*Easter Island is famous for its statues of humans with giant heads that are thought to have been made by the Rapa Nui people around 1000 CE. The statues are known as *moai* and there are nearly 1,000 of them. The largest is more than 32 feet (10 m) tall and weighs 82 tons (75 tonnes), which is heavier than ten African elephants. One theory of how the Rapa Nui moved these colossal statues the 11 miles (18 km) from the quarry to where they now stand is that they slowly "walked" each stone across the island. Two teams of people might have used ropes to rock a *moai* forward, while a third team followed behind, using another rope to keep it stable.

6. Crozet Islands, Indian Ocean

Location: 1,500 mi (2,400 km) from Antarctica

In 1887, a group of boys on a beach in Australia found a dead albatross with a rusty tin band attached to its neck with a note reading: "13 shipwrecked refugees are on the Crozet islands, 4 August, 1887." The bird had flown 3,480 miles (5,600 km) in 45 days to deliver its message. A rescue mission was launched, but no trace of the shipwrecked men was found on any of the islands. They were presumed to have drowned attempting to seek food on a self-built boat. Today, the islands are a nature reserve inhabited by around 25 scientific researchers.

7. Niue, South Pacific Ocean

Location: 1,340 mi (2,160 km) from New Zealand

Niue is an independent country with its own flag, government, and a population of around 1,500 people." The roads are so quiet that there are no traffic lights.

8. Diego Garcia, Indian Ocean

Location: 1,196 mi (1,925 km) from Sri Lanka

When seen from above, this coral island, or atoll, forms the shape of a "V." It is currently home to a United States military base, which includes a hamburger restaurant and tenpin bowling alley.

9. Saint Helena, South Atlantic Ocean

Location: 1,150 mi (1,850 km) from Angola

This volcanic island was uninhabited when it was discovered by the Spanish in 1502, but today it has a population of around 4,500 people. Saint Helena is most famous for being the place where the French general and leader Napoleon Bonaparte was exiled and imprisoned between 1815 and 1821, when he died.

10. Laurie Island, South Atlantic Ocean

Location: 795 mi (1,280 km) from the Falkland Islands

The island is home to around 30 research scientists as well as the oldest Antarctic research station, which has been in continuous operation since 1903.

Easter Island (*moai* not to scale)

» Niue is a very small country. To find out which country is the smallest in the world, see pages 258–259.

Trees of Life

Rain forests in numbers

Rain forests are one of the Earth's most amazing and important natural habitats. There are two kinds. Tropical rain forests are found close to the equator and are warm and moist. Temperate rain forests are found in parts of the world with milder temperatures.

390 billion The estimated number of individual trees in the tropical Amazon rain forest.*

100 million The number of years ago that tropical rain forests started to grow.

50 million The number of people who live in rain forests around the world.

1,300 The number of species of butterfly that have been recorded by scientists in a single region of the Peruvian Amazon rain forest.**

80 The percentage of flowers in the Australian rain forests that are not found anywhere else in the world.

75 The minimum amount of rain in inches (190 cm) that must fall in a forest in a year for it to be considered a rain forest.

50 The percentage of the Earth's land animals that live in tropical rain forests.

2.5 The percentage of the Earth's total surface covered by rain forest today.

Amazon rain forest

*The Amazon rain forest is thought to be home to one in ten known species on Earth, including 2.5 million insect species, 40,000 plant species, and 3,000 species of freshwater fish.

**In comparison, the United States is home to around 750 species of butterfly.

Dry Patches

The ten biggest deserts in the world

A desert is defined as an area of land that receives very little precipitation, such as rain, sleet, or snow. This means that frozen, icy places, such as Antarctica, also count as deserts.*

1. **Antarctica**—5,500,000 sq mi (14,200,000 km²)

2. **Arctic**—5,400,000 sq mi (13,985,000 km²)

3. **Sahara,** ** **Africa**—3,300,000 sq mi (9,000,000 km²)

4. **Arabian Desert, Asia**—890,000 sq mi (2,300,000 km²)

5. **Gobi Desert, Asia**—502,000 sq mi (1,300,000 km²)

6. **Kalahari Desert, Africa**—360,000 sq mi (930,000 km²)

7. **Patagonian Desert, South America**—260,000 sq mi (673,000 km²)

8. **Rubʻ al-Khali, Saudi Arabia**—250,000 sq mi (650,000 km²)

9. **Great Victoria Desert,** *** **Australia**—250,000 sq mi (647,000 km²)

10. **Great Basin, North America**—190,000 sq mi (492,000 km²)

Sahara

*Approximately one third of all the land on Earth is desert.

**The Sahara is roughly the same size as China. It is also getting bigger: scientists estimate the Sahara has grown more than 10 percent in the last 100 years due to the world's climate becoming hotter.

***The Great Victoria Desert is one of ten named deserts in Australia, which together cover 18 percent of the country. However, an even larger area of land receives so little rain that it counts as desert. This means that, when you add all the driest parts of the country together, around 1,029,000 square miles (2,665,800 km²)—or 35 percent of Australia—is actually desert.

The Only Way Is Up

Six of the fastest-growing plants

1. Bamboo The current world-record holder. The speediest species of bamboo can grow up to 36 inches (91 cm) in a day.*

2. Duckweed This small, flowering marine plant goes through its entire lifecycle in 30 hours and can double its total mass every couple of days.**

3. Kudzu Also known as Japanese arrowroot, this climbing vine grows so quickly on top of other trees and plants that it soon kills them by blocking out the sunlight. Kudzu can grow up to 1 foot (30 cm) a day.

4. Acacia This pretty, flowering shrub is mostly found in tropical parts of the world. It can grow as much as 30 feet (10 m) a year.

5. Giant sequoia Mainly known for their size and long lifespans, giant sequoia trees are also fast growers, especially in the early years of their life, when they can grow up to 6 feet (2 m) a year.

6. Cress Often added to soups, salads, and sandwiches, cress is the fastest growing herb. It starts growing just 24 hours after the seed is planted and can shoot up 2 inches (5 cm) in its first week.

Right: Giant pandas live in China and love to eat bamboo. They can eat as much as 84 pounds (38 kg) of bamboo leaves, shoots, and stems per day, which weighs more than the average eight-year-old!

*So if you're patient enough to spend a few hours staring at sticks of bamboo, you will see them growing before your eyes. (Though do check first that you're not looking at a fence.)

**This means that if duckweed had enough light, food, and space to reproduce continuously at maximum efficiency for four months, all the duckweed grown would have a combined mass four times bigger than the Earth's. Because duckweed grows so fast, scientists are investigating whether it could be used as an environmentally friendly source of energy known as a biofuel.

Mushroom Magic

Fungi in numbers

50 billion The approximate amount of money in dollars spent each year on mushrooms you can eat.

103,900,000 million The size in square feet (9.65 million m²) of the honey mushroom found in the Malheur National Forest, Oregon. It covers an area of more than 1,500 soccer fields and is thought to be the single largest living organism on Earth.*

3.8 million The estimated number of species of fungi in the world, including mushrooms, yeasts, lichens, rust, and mold.

2,000+ The number of new species of fungi discovered each year.

80 The number of mushroom species that glow in the dark, thanks to a light-emitting chemical that attracts insects.**

8 The length in miles (13 km) of fungi filaments, or thin strands, that researchers have found in a single teaspoon of soil.

*This honey mushroom is found 3 feet (1 m) underground, and is estimated to have been alive for more than 2,400 years. It is also known as the "humongous fungus."

**Humans can also use the glowing mushrooms to find their way home through the woods at night.

When Plants Attack

Seven species of plant that eat meat

1. Tropical pitcher plant This plant's prey is attracted by its sweet-smelling nectar. If the prey gets too close, it falls into the "pitcher," a long tube-shaped cup that is coated on the inside with a sticky wax, making it hard to escape. The pitcher is big enough to trap not just insects but also small reptiles, amphibians, and mammals, which the plant then slowly digests over a couple of months.*

2. Sundew Sometimes called "living flypaper," the sundew has long, tentacle-like leaves covered in sticky hairs. Its nectar attracts all kinds of bugs, including flies, mosquitoes, and spiders, and once one gets stuck on a leaf, the plant will curl inward to start digesting its victim.

3. Cobra lily Insects are drawn to the cobra lily by the nectar on its tongue-shaped outer leaves. But once an insect has fallen to the bottom of its pitcher, it's almost impossible to escape, partly because the plant then curls up to hide the tiny exit hole. The cobra lily also confuses and exhausts its prey by having multiple see-through sections in the side of its pitcher that look like exits but offer no way out.**

4. *Brocchinia reducta* Most meat-eating plants use sweet-smelling nectar to lure in insects. But the long, slim sides of this plant's prey-catching pitcher have an added appeal: they reflect ultraviolet light, which human eyes can't see but is attractive to insects.

5. Venus flytrap*** The two sticky, eyelid-shaped leaves of this plant are designed to snap shut in an instant, trapping prey inside. To stop the flytrap being set off by false alarms, such as a falling leaf, it will only shut if an insect has touched two different hairs inside its trap within 20 seconds. The leaves then snap together in around a tenth of a second.

6. Butterwort The sticky, pearl-colored goo on the leaves of this plant looks a bit like butter. Mistaking these shiny droplets for water, insects land on the butterwort's leaves, then find themselves glued to the sticky gunk. The plant then slowly digests the insect.

7. Bladderwort Found mostly in lakes and rivers, the bladderwort has a stem that floats on the surface, from which small sacklike traps grow. When an insect touches the hairs inside a sac, a hidden door opens, sucking in a stream of water that drags the insect inside too! When a sac is full of water, the door closes, allowing the bladderwort to start digesting its catch of the day.

Right: An unfortunate bug has been trapped by the leaf of a sundew plant.

---

*Monkeys, which are too big to fall prey to the plant, have been seen drinking rainwater out of its pitchers, giving the plant the nickname "monkey cups."

**The cobra lily gets its name from its unusually shaped leaves, which look like the curved head and forked tongue of a cobra snake about to strike.

***Despite its name, only around 5 percent of a Venus flytrap's diet is flies. It also likes to gobble up spiders and grasshoppers.

Weight of the World

How much all the living organisms on Earth weigh

If you gathered together all the living organisms on Earth in one huge pile, it would weigh an estimated 601 billion tons (545 billion tonnes). Here's what proportion of the total weight different types of organism would contribute:

Plants—82.5 percent

Bacteria—12.8 percent

Fungi—2.2 percent

Archaea*—1.3 percent

Protists—0.7 percent

All animals, including humans**—0.4 percent

Viruses—0.04 percent

That's Life

The percentage of species that we know about—and those we haven't discovered yet

Scientists think there are at least 8.7 million species of organisms alive on Earth. That's amazing. But even more mind-boggling is the fact that the vast majority of these species have yet to be discovered.

14 percent
The living species we know about.

86 percent
The living species we've yet to find.

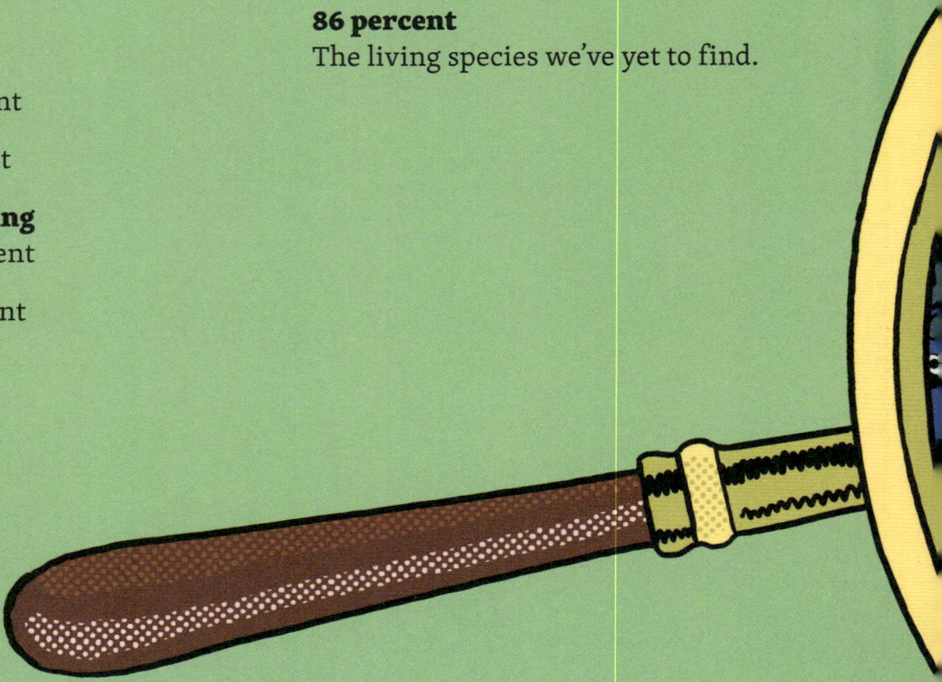

---

*Archaea and protists are both types of tiny single-celled organisms similar to bacteria.

**All the human beings in the world weigh approximately 66 million tons (60 million tonnes), which accounts for just 0.01 percent of the weight of all the living things on Earth.

86 percent: species
we've yet to find

14 percent: species
we know about

Chapter 3

Dinosaur Times

A list of things you'll encounter in this chapter:

High-jumping raptors

Prehistoric alligators

A tiny bug slayer

Dinosaur feathers

An innocent "egg thief"

T-rex clones

An *Argentinosaurus* egg

A coprolite* collection

Dramatic bite marks

Apollonia, Prince, and Twinky

Lying stones

A theory about dinosaur gas

Woody the *Aachenosaurus*

A chicken

*This is fossilized poop!

Lost Worlds

The three time periods* when
dinosaurs ruled the Earth

1. Triassic Period:

252–201 million years ago

Dimorphodon

2. Jurassic Period:

201–145 million years ago

Allosaurus

3. Cretaceous Period:

145–66 million years ago

Spinosaurus

*Dinosaurs emerged during the Mesozoic Era,
which spans the period of time between 252
and 66 million years ago. The Mesozoic is
subdivided into three shorter time periods:
the Triassic, Jurassic, and Cretaceous.

These images show a selection of the dinosaurs and other creatures that would have lived during these time periods.

Sharovipteryx

Icarosaurus

Eoraptor

Eozostrodon

Daiopterix

Brachiosaurus

Morganucodon

Guanlong

Ornithocheirus

Deinosuchus

Sphecomyrma

Triceratops

Before the Dinosaurs

Five prehistoric creatures that look like dinosaurs but were actually alive before them

1. *Eryops*

Lived: 299–273 million years ago.

Fossils found: In what is now Germany and the Southwest of America.

What: A large carnivore that lived both on land and in water.

Size: 6.6 feet (2 m), which is as long as a seal.

Profile: *Eryops* was a fierce predator that had sharp teeth. These teeth would have made it impossible for *Eryops* to chew, so it trapped fish in its strong jaws then threw back its head to swallow them in a big gulp. This is similar to the way that modern crocodiles and alligators eat.

2. *Dimetrodon*

Lived: 286–270 million years ago.

Fossils found: In what is now Europe and North America.

What: A carnivorous four-legged reptile with a sail-like fin on its back.

Size: 15 feet (4.5 m), which is twice as long as a horse.

Profile: Paleontologists are unsure what *Dimetrodon*'s fin was used for. Two theories are that it served a purpose in heating and cooling the *Dimetrodon*, or it was a means of signaling to other animals—maybe even showing off to other *Dimetrodons*!

3. *Cotylorhynchus*

Lived: Around 275 million years ago.

Fossils found: In what is now North America.

What: A giant four-legged reptile that ate plants and had strong, paddle-like hands.

Size: More than 3.3 feet (1 m) tall and 20 feet (6 m) long, which is as long as the biggest crocodiles.

Profile: *Cotylorhynchus* looked a bit like a lizard that's been inflated with a bicycle pump. However, despite its huge body, *Cotylorhynchus* had a relatively small head—not much bigger than a human's.

4. *Estemmenosuchus*

Lived: Around 267 million years ago.

Fossils found: In what is now Russia.

What: A powerful, four-legged herbivorous reptile with a large skull and several sets of antler-like horns.

Size: 13 feet (4 m), which is as long as a hippo.

Profile: The name *Estemmenosuchus* means "crowned crocodile," although in reality it probably wasn't that scary and looked more like a large cow.

5. *Inostrancevia*

Lived: Around 265–250 million years ago.

Fossils found: In what is now Russia.

What: A carnivorous four-legged reptile with two long, saber-like teeth.

Size: 11.5 feet (3.5 m) long, which is roughly the size of a modern alligator, although *Inostrancevia* was almost twice as heavy.

Profile: *Inostrancevia* was a fearsome predator. Its sharp canine teeth, which it used to bite and tear into prey, could grow up to 6 inches (15 cm) long.

Eryops

Dimetrodon

Cotylorhynchus

Estemmenosuchus

Inostrancevia

They're Alive!

Twenty types of creature that lived alongside the dinosaurs and are still with us today

1. **Sea sponges**—650 million years old
2. **Horseshoe crabs**—540 million years old
3. **Lampreys**—520 million years old
4. **Jellyfish**—500+ million years old
5. **Nautiluses**—500 million years old
6. **Scorpions**—437 million years old
7. **Sharks**—420 million years old
8. **Coelacanths***—400 million years old
9. **Cockroaches**—320 million years old
10. **Turtles**—260 million years old
11. **Shrimp**—250 million years old
12. **Lobsters**—242 million years old
13. **Crocodiles**—230 million years old
14. **Sturgeons**—200 million years old
15. **Salamanders**—170 million years old
16. **Snakes**—167 million years old
17. **Bees**—130 million years old
18. **Frogs**—130 million years old
19. **Ants**—120 million years old
20. **Solenodons****—73 million years old

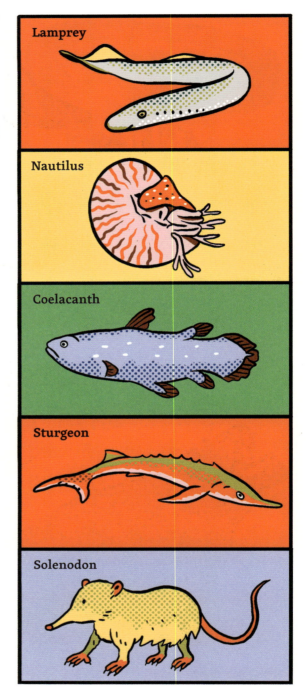

Lamprey

Nautilus

Coelacanth

Sturgeon

Solenodon

*Coelacanths are a type of fish that were thought to have become extinct along with the dinosaurs 65 million years ago until a live coelacanth was discovered in 1938.

**Solenodons are a rare type of shrew-like mammal that are only found today on the islands of Cuba and Hispaniola.

Gardeners' World

Ten prehistoric plants and fungi that are still alive today

1. Mushrooms—Appeared about 800 million years ago

Mushrooms were one of the very first complex organisms to appear on Earth. Some giant prehistoric mushrooms grew around 400 million years ago. Their trunks could be 23 feet (7 m) high and 3 feet (1 m) wide. That's taller than a giraffe!

2. Ferns—Appeared about 359 million years ago

Ferns predate dinosaurs, flowers, and even seeds. Surviving examples include the hard fern, soft tree fern, and staghorn fern.

3. Horsetails—Appeared about 350–360 million years ago

There were once lots of varieties of these primitive plants but only about 20 species remain today. Horsetails have thin, hollow green stems with horizontal bands, similar to bamboo.

4. Mosses—Appeared about 300 million years ago

Moss was one of the very first plants on Earth. There are around 12,000 species still growing all around the world.

5. Cycads—Appeared about 280 million years ago

Cycads, which look like palms and ferns, first grew on Earth in the Permian Period at the same time as *Dimetrodon*—the reptile with the sail-like fin on its back. Modern examples include the sago palm and Eastern Cape giant cycad.

6. Magnolia—Appeared about 140 million years ago

Magnolia plants and their close relatives date back to a time before bees even existed, so prehistoric beetles pollinated them instead.

7. Black pepper—Appeared about 110 million years ago

The black pepper plant, which is a flowering vine, evolved at roughly the same time as the first pollinating insects, such as bees and wasps. Its dried fruit, called peppercorns, is what makes the pepper you sprinkle on your food.

8. *Welwitschia*—Appeared about 100 million years ago

The *Welwitschia*, which is now found in the Namib Desert in Africa, can live to be hundreds, and even thousands, of years old. It's the only living plant that always has just two leaves.

9. Dawn redwoods—Appeared about 90 million years go

T. rex would probably have walked beneath these giant redwood trees, which can grow to be 197 feet (60 m) tall. Dawn redwoods were thought to be extinct before a forest of them was discovered in China in the 1940s.

10. Proteales—Appeared about 80 million years ago

The first ancestors of these beautiful flowering plants were alive at the time of the dinosaurs. Today they are most commonly found in Australia and South Africa.

Over time the *Welwitschia*'s two leaves become tattered and torn, creating the appearance of many leaves.

Meat vs. Veggies

How many dinosaur species ate meat and
how many preferred plants and fruit

65 percent—herbivores

35 percent—carnivores (and omnivores*)

*Omnivores are animals that eat both meat and
plants. Some species of dinosaur were omnivorous
but it is hard for paleontologists to prove exactly
how many.

Leaf Lovers

Nine body parts and characteristics that many herbivorous dinosaurs had in common

1. On all fours Most herbivores walked on four legs either all or some of the time.

2. Grinding teeth They mostly had flat, wide teeth like a cow's, ideal for chewing and mashing up tough plants.

3. Herd instinct Many herbivores stayed in herds for safety. Traveling and working together meant animals could spot predators more easily as well as protect baby dinosaurs and other more vulnerable members of the group.

4. Camouflage Scientists can't tell exactly what color dinosaurs were from fossils alone. But it's likely that some herbivores such as hadrosaurs and ceratopsians used different colors and patterns as camouflage to hide from predators, just as modern reptiles such as snakes do today.

5. Body armor Many herbivores had thick, leathery skin and a tough shield of body armor to protect them from predators. Some had horns, spikes, and shield-like neck frills. *Euoplocephalus* even had armor plating on its eyelids.

6. Tail weapons Some herbivores used their powerful tails to defend themselves. *Kentrosaurus*' tail was covered in sharp spikes. *Ankylosaurus* had large lumps of fused bone at the end of its tail, which it could swing back and forth like a club.

7. Super-sized bodies Many terrifying predators were large compared to modern-day animals. But the true giants of the prehistoric world—such as *Apatosaurus*, *Argentinosaurus*, and *Supersaurus*—were all herbivores. These massive creatures grew so big that only the very largest carnivores, or a group of carnivores, would dare attack them.

8. Big stomachs Herbivores' stomachs were usually bigger and longer than carnivores' because their digestive tracts needed more time to break down and extract nutrients from the plants they ate.*

9. Thick bones Their bones were solid and dense, making them strong but also slower-moving. The plants they wanted to eat were unlikely to be running away from them, so this wasn't a problem!

Ankylosaurus

*Some herbivores may have deliberately swallowed stones, called "gastroliths." These sat in a special muscular stomach called a "gizzard" and helped to mash up plant matter after it had been swallowed. Modern birds and some lizards also have gizzards.

Meat Lovers

Nine body parts and characteristics that many carnivorous dinosaurs had in common

1. Walking tall All carnivores walked on two legs.

2. Sharp teeth Carnivores' teeth were often jagged like steak knives, perfect for attacking prey and tearing flesh. Carnivores also had lots of them: *Spinosaurus*, for example, had as many as 64 pointy teeth that measured between 3 inches (8 cm) and 10 inches (25 cm) long.

3. Pack hunters Some paleontologists think that carnivorous dinosaurs such as tyrannosaurs may have hunted in packs.*

4. Sharp senses More advanced predators such as *Troodon* evolved large eyes and binocular vision,** which made it easier for them to see their prey, especially at night. Scientists think carnivores were also very good at sniffing out prey and rotten flesh to eat.

5. Mighty jaws Larger carnivores such as *Tyrannosaurus rex* had huge, powerful jaws to bite and clamp down on prey.»

6. Killer claws Many carnivores had deadly curved claws on their forelimbs, which they used to grapple with and slash their prey.

7. Slimmer bodies Some smaller, slimmer carnivores, such as the *Velociraptor*, were fast sprinters. Their agility and speed over short distances would have helped them to chase down and catch lizards, frogs, and other creatures.

8. Big hearts, lungs, and livers Carnivores needed big lungs and hearts to breathe in more oxygen, which provided their muscles with more energy and helped them chase down prey. They also had large livers to process the extra protein and fats contained in their meaty diets.

9. Hollow bones Paleontologists think that air spaces in carnivores' bones may have made them lighter and also increased the airflow to the lungs, both of which would have increased the carnivores' speed and helped them chase their prey.

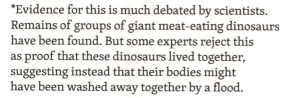

Tyrannosaurus rex

*Evidence for this is much debated by scientists. Remains of groups of giant meat-eating dinosaurs have been found. But some experts reject this as proof that these dinosaurs lived together, suggesting instead that their bodies might have been washed away together by a flood.

**Binocular vision is when an animal can look at a single object using both eyes at the same time, as humans can. This helps them figure out how far away the object is.

» If you want to find out exactly how strong a *T. rex* bite was, turn to page 127.

Top Predators

Seven of the deadliest dinosaurs and their killer features

1. *Spinosaurus*

Killer feature: Its enormous size. *Spinosaurus* was as big as a five-story building.

2. *Tyrannosaurus rex*

Killer feature: The strongest jaws of any dinosaur. Its bite was around 49 times more powerful than a human being's.

3. *Utahraptor*

Killer feature: Its agility. It could jump 15 feet (5 m) into the air.

4. *Carcharodontosaurus*

Killer feature: Its jaw, which was big enough to swallow a human being in a single bite.

5. *Velociraptor*

Killer feature: Its large curved claw on each foot, which it used to wound its prey.

6. *Mapusaurus*

Killer feature: Not only was *Mapusaurus* one of the largest carnivores, it also had sharper teeth than a *T. rex*. Its teeth were curved with a jagged edge, ideal for slicing through flesh.

7. *Coelophysis*

Killer feature: Its speed. *Coelophysis* was a fast, agile hunter that could run at speeds of up to 30 miles per hour (48 km/h). There is also evidence to suggest that it hunted in packs to bring down larger prey.

Utahraptor

In at the Deep End

The biggest prehistoric sea creatures

Shastasaurus—69 ft (21 m)

Shastasaurus was an ichthyosaur that looked like an enormous dolphin. Its large eyes and lack of teeth suggests it hunted squid in the dark ocean depths. It is the largest marine reptile that ever lived.

Megalodon—66 ft (20 m)

Scientists have estimated that a fully-grown megalodon shark could have weighed 65 tons (60 tonnes), which is more than 30 times heavier than a modern great white shark. Megalodon had more than 250 teeth, some of which were 7 inches (17 cm) long.

Mosasaurus—55 ft (17 m)

Mosasaurs were giant swimming lizards and *Mosasaurus* was one of the largest. Marks left by its cone-shaped teeth have been found on turtle shells and ammonites. It became extinct at the same time as the dinosaurs.

Elasmosaurus—46 ft (14 m)

The *Elasmosaurus* was a plesiosaur, one of the giant carnivorous reptiles that ruled the seas while dinosaurs ruled the land. It had a neck that was 23 feet (7 m) long and contained 76 vertebrae, or spine bones—the most of any known animal.

Pliosaurus funkei—42 ft (13 m)

Originally known as "Predator X" before it was given its official name, *Pliosaurus funkei* weighed an estimated 50 tons (45 tonnes), which is nearly as heavy as six elephants.

Temnodontosaurus—39 ft (12 m)

This dolphin-like ichthyosaur had sharp cone-shaped teeth. Its eyes were 8 inches (20 cm) across—almost as big as dinner plates!

Deinosuchus—33 ft (10 m)

This enormous prehistoric alligator was about twice as long as modern alligators. It's thought to have attacked dinosaurs of a similar size: fossils of some tyrannosaurs have bite marks from a *Deinosuchus*.

Dunkleosteus—30 ft (9 m)

Sometimes known as the "*Tyrannosaurus* of the seas," this armored fish was the size of a killer whale. Its bite was powerful enough to crack concrete.

Leedsichthys—30 ft (9 m)

Leedsichthys is thought to be the largest bony fish that has ever lived. Despite its size, *Leedsichthys* only ate small marine animals such as shrimp.

Ophthalmosaurus—16 ft (5 m)

In proportion to the size of its body, this ichthyosaur had the largest eyes of any prehistoric animal. They were as big as grapefruits and took up most of the space in its skull.

Nothosaurus—13 ft (4 m)

Scientists think that nothosaurs walked on land but swam in the seas to hunt fish, like modern seals and sea lions. *Nothosaurus* had long, needlelike teeth, which it could close together like a cage, trapping its prey inside.

Making a Splash

A complete list of all the dinosaurs
that could swim

1. *Spinosaurus—That's it.

*It is thought that *Spinosaurus* lived both on land
and in water, and because it had webbed feet,
scientists believe it was able to swim. There were
lots of large marine creatures living in prehistoric
oceans but they were mostly swimming reptiles,
not dinosaurs.

Off the Scale

Ten of the largest
dinosaurs to walk
the Earth

1. *Argentinosaurus**

Weight: 100 tons
(90 tonnes)
Length: 131 ft (40 m)
As heavy as . . . 20,000 cats

2. *Mamenchisaurus*

Weight: 88 tons
(80 tonnes)
Length: 110 ft (33 m)
As heavy as . . . 17,777 cats

3. *Brachiosaurus*

Weight: 88 tons
(80 tonnes)
Length: 80 ft (25 m)
As heavy as . . . 17,777 cats

4. *Paralititan*

Weight: 83 tons (75 tonnes)
Length: 100 ft (30 m)
As heavy as . . . 16,666 cats

5. *Patagotitan*

Weight: 77 tons (70 tonnes)
Length: 121 ft (37 m)
As heavy as . . . 15,555 cats

6. *Sauroposeidon***

Weight: 66 tons
(60 tonnes)
Length: 112 ft (34 m)
As heavy as . . . 13,333 cats

7. *Dreadnoughtus*

Weight: 65 tons (59 tonnes)
Length: 85 ft (26 m)
As heavy as . . . 13,111 cats

8. *Turiasaurus*

Weight: 53 tons (48 tonnes)
Length: 98 ft (30 m)
As heavy as . . . 10,666 cats

9. *Apatosaurus*

Weight: 45 tons (41 tonnes)
Length: 75 ft (23 m)
As heavy as . . . 9,111 cats

10. *Supersaurus*

Weight: 35 tons (32 tonnes)
Length: 112 ft (34 m)
As heavy as . . . 7,111 cats

Brachiosaurus

Argentinosaurus may have been the heaviest land
animal but the heaviest creature ever to live on
Earth is still the blue whale, which can weigh as
much as 200 tons (180 tonnes), or 40,000 cats.

**Sauroposeidon* is thought to be the tallest ever
dinosaur. Thanks to its extraordinarily long neck,
it could have reached as high as 59 feet (18 m) off
the ground, which is taller than four elephants
stacked on top of each other.

Mini-Monsters

Five prehistoric creatures that were famously small

1. *Kongonaphon*

Lived: 237 million years ago.

Size: The recently discovered species *Kongonaphon kely* (meaning "tiny bug slayer") was just 4 inches (10 cm) tall. This is roughly the size of a modern sparrow and could have easily sat in the palm of your hand.

Claim to fame: *Kongonaphon* is thought to be a common ancestor of much larger dinosaurs and pterosaurs that evolved millions of years later.

2. *Nemicolopterus*

Lived: 113 million years ago.

Size: This small flying reptile had a wingspan of just 10 inches (25 cm), which is about the same as a nightingale.

Claim to fame: The smallest known pterosaur.

3. *Parvicursor*

Lived: 72 million years ago.

Size: *Parvicursor*, whose name means "small runner," measured around 15 inches (39 cm) from the end of its snout to its tail. It weighed about 15.6 ounces (160 g), which is only slightly heavier than a hamster.

Claim to fame: It is one of the smallest non-avian dinosaurs.*

4. *Microraptor*

Lived: 113 million years ago.

Size: This small, birdlike dinosaur was 2 feet (50 cm) long, weighed less than 2 pounds (1 kg), and probably fed on a diet of small lizards and fish. Despite its modest size, *Microraptor* was a relative of the fearsome *Velociraptor* and other much larger carnivores.

Claim to fame: Thought to be the smallest raptor.

5. *Magyarosaurus*

Lived: 72 million years ago.

Size: At 20 feet (6 m) long and weighing 1,654 pounds (750 kg), *Magyarosaurus* was roughly the size of a cow. This was a reasonable size for a dinosaur but very small for a sauropod, most of which were gigantic herbivores such as *Diplodocus* and *Apatosaurus*. *Magyarosaurus* was one of a group of "island dwarf" species that evolved away from other dinosaurs on an island separated from the mainland in what is now Romania.

Claim to fame: One of the smallest sauropods.

*Non-avian dinosaurs are all the dinosaurs except birds.

Out of This World

Eight weird-and-wonderful-looking prehistoric creatures

1. Helicoprion

Lived: 290 million years ago.

As this sharklike marine creature's teeth grew, its older teeth were pushed farther forward. This meant its jaw looked like a circular saw; it continually grew outward as it filled up with more and more teeth.

2. Longisquama

Lived: 235 million years ago.

With six to eight long feather-like spikes sticking out of its back, this omnivore was roughly the size of a guinea pig.

3. Sharovipteryx

Lived: 225 million years ago.

This strange lizard-like flying reptile had wings spread across its back legs instead of across its forelimbs, as most flying creatures do. Scientists have no idea how it was able to walk.

4. Pegomastax

Lived: 200 million years ago.

Pegomastax was a small herbivore that had a sharp beak and was covered in quills, making it look like a cross between a parrot and a hedgehog.

5. Incisivosaurus

Lived: 126 million years ago.

This 3-foot- (1-m-) long omnivore looked like a cross between several animals: It had the head of a raptor, the large front teeth of a rat, the body of an ostrich, and the feet of a chicken.

6. Concavenator

Lived: 125 million years ago.

This 16-foot- (5-m-) long carnivore had two unusual features: pointy feathers" sprouting out of its forearms and a large triangular hump in the middle of its back.

7. Suzhousaurus

Lived: Around 115 million years ago.

With its long arms, sharp claws, and a 20-foot- (6-m-) long body covered in feathers, *Suzhousaurus* looked like a cross between a giant turkey and modern-day sloth, to which it could have been distantly related.

8. Nigersaurus

Lived: 105 million years ago.

This curious-looking herbivore had all its 500 teeth in two parallel rows right at the front of its jaw, which made its head look like an attachment for a vacuum cleaner.

» To find out more about dinosaur feathers, see page 135.

Helicoprion

Longisquama

Sharovipteryx

Pegomastax

Incisivosaurus

Concavenator

Suzhousaurus

Nigersaurus

I Don't Believe It!

Eight dinosaur theories that turned out to be completely wrong

1. All dinosaurs were covered in scales

Scientists now think that lots of meat-eating dinosaurs, including *Tyrannosaurus rex*, probably had a partial covering of feathers.

2. *Tyrannosaurus rex* was a fast runner

Nineteenth-century scientists thought that *T. rex* was a good sprinter. However, in the 20th century, they changed their minds and decided that it would have been lumbering and slow because of its large size. Today, the top speed of a *T. rex* is estimated as being somewhere in the middle, at around 18 miles per hour (29 km/h). This means that a sprinting human being could just about outrun a *T. rex*.

3. Dinosaurs were cold-blooded

Recent research suggests that dinosaurs weren't cold-blooded like lizards and snakes (as was first thought) or warm-blooded like mammals. They are now thought to have been mesotherms, which means that the way dinosaurs regulated their blood temperature was somewhere in between the two,* but this is still being debated.

4. *Diplodocus* lived in a swamp

Some scientists used to think that the largest herbivores—such as *Diplodocus*—must have lived in swamps and lakes because their enormous bodies and long tails would have made it too difficult for them to move around on land. In fact, we now know *Diplodocus* definitely lived on land.

5. *Stegosaurus* had a brain in its bottom

When the first *Stegosaurus* bones were discovered in 1877, scientists were surprised that such a large animal had such a relatively small brain. This is why a paleontologist named Othniel C. Marsh suggested that *Stegosaurus* had a second brain in its pelvis to help control the back section of its body. It was an interesting theory but also completely wrong.

6. Pterosaurs were dinosaurs

Even though they soared in the prehistoric skies above famous dinosaurs such as *Tyrannosaurus rex* and are more closely related to dinosaurs than to any other group of creatures, pterosaurs were actually a separate group of flying reptiles.

7. *Oviraptor* stole other dinosaurs' eggs

The name *Oviraptor* means "egg thief." This omnivorous dinosaur got its name because the first *Oviraptor* fossils were found close to eggs that scientists believed were from a *Protoceratops*. Years later, they realized they'd made a mistake: the eggs were, in fact, *Oviraptor* eggs. Instead of stealing them from another dinosaur, the mother *Oviraptor* was probably protecting her own eggs.

8. Dinosaurs lived for 100 years

Because dinosaurs were thought to be cold-blooded,** scientists once thought that the largest dinosaurs must have been alive for more than 100 years to have time to do all that growing. Today, scientists believe that dinosaurs actually grew fairly quickly, with only a few living to be more than 50 years old.

---

*Cold-blooded means that a creature relies on its surroundings to heat its body. Warm-blooded means that a creature can make its own body heat and stay at a constant temperature. Mesotherms produce body heat that keeps them warmer than their surroundings, but they can't control their exact temperature.

**Cold-blooded animals such as reptiles tend to grow more slowly than warm-blooded animals. Mesotherms tend to grow at a medium rate.

Early images of *Oviraptor* show it eating what were were believed to be *Protoceratops* eggs.

Later, scientists realized that the eggs were actually *Oviraptor* eggs. The *Oviraptor* was protecting the eggs, not stealing them.

Long in the Tooth

The jaw-droppingly big teeth* of nine prehistoric creatures

1. **_Tyrannosaurus rex_**—12 in (30 cm)

2. **_Mapusaurus_**—9 in (22 cm)

3. **_Carcharodontosaurus_**—8 in (20 cm)

4. **_Camarasaurus_**—7.5 in (19 cm)

5. **_Lythronax_**—7.5 in (19 cm)

6. **_Megalodon_**—7.5 in (19 cm)

7. **_Pliosaurus funkei_**—6.5 in (17 cm)

8. **_Spinosaurus_**—5 in (13 cm)

9. **_Brachiosaurus_**—3 in (8 cm)

This enormous tooth belonged to a _Spinosaurus_ and is shown at actual size.

*Carnivorous dinosaurs grew and replaced their teeth throughout their lives. Some grew a new set of teeth every couple of months. (This was handy because it would take millions of years for the first dentists to evolve.)

The estimated biting power of twenty
prehistoric and modern animals

1. **Megalodon**—180,000 newtons

2. *Pliosaurus funkei*—150,000 newtons

3. *Deinosuchus*—100,000 newtons

4. *Tyrannosaurus rex*—57,000 newtons

5. **Great white shark**—17,500 newtons

6. **Saltwater crocodile**—16,000 newtons

7. **American alligator**—13,000 newtons

8. *Carcharodontosaurus*—12,000 newtons

9. **Hippopotamus**—8,000 newtons

10. **Jaguar**—6,000 newtons

11. **Polar bear**—5,300 newtons

12. *Dunkleosteus*—5,000 newtons

13. **Hyena**—4,500 newtons

14. **Lion**—4,500 newtons

15. **Tiger**—4,500 newtons

16. **Gorilla**—4,000 newtons

17. *Velociraptor*—3,000 newtons

18. *Allosaurus*—2,200 newtons

19. **Mastiff (dog)**—2,000 newtons

20. **Piranha**—320 newtons

Megalodon

King of the Tyrant Lizards*

Tyrannosaurus rex in numbers

70 million The number of years since *T. rex* is thought to have appeared on Earth.

15,000 The weight of a large adult *T. rex* in pounds (7,000 kg), which is heavier than two adult hippopotamuses.

1900 The year the first *T. rex* fossils were found, in Hell Creek rock formation, Montana.

500 The number of pounds (225 kg) of meat it could eat in a single bite, which is like swallowing 15,000 hamburgers in one gulp.

400 The estimated weight in pounds (180 kg) that a *T. rex* could lift with its forelimbs. It was probably strong enough to pick up a human being in each hand.

380 The number of bones in a complete *T. rex* skeleton.

66 How many pounds (30 kg) a *T. rex* would weigh at two years old.

60 The approximate number of teeth that *T. rex* had.

50 The approximate number of *T. rex* fossil skeletons that have been found so far.

43 The length of a large *T. rex* in feet (13 m), which is roughly the same as a truck.

33 The length in inches (83 cm) of the longest *T. rex* footprint ever found.

30 *T. rex*'s estimated lifespan in years.

18 The top speed of a *T. rex* in miles per hour (29 km/h).

17 The estimated length of a *T. rex* poop in inches (44 cm).

13 A *T. rex*'s height in feet (4 m), which is about the same as an African elephant.

5 The length of the largest known *T. rex* skull in feet (1.5 m).

0 The number of *T. rex* eggs or nests that have been discovered.**

Tyrannosaurus rex means "king of the tyrant lizards" in Latin.

**By making comparisons with similar species of dinosaur and other animals, scientists think that a freshly hatched baby *T. rex* would have been roughly the size of a turkey and covered with downy feathers to help it keep warm.

T. rex and Friends

Ten dinosaurs that *Tyrannosaurus rex* could have met

Tyrannosaurus rex lived on Earth in the Cretaceous Period between 70 and 66 million years ago. Here are some of the dinosaurs that it might have been friends* with:

1. Pachycephalosaurus
2. Edmontosaurus
3. Troodon
4. Ankylosaurus
5. Ornithomimus
6. Saltasaurus
7. Triceratops
8. Leptoceratops
9. Acheroraptor
10. Dakotaraptor

Never Met a T. rex

Ten dinosaurs that *Tyrannosaurus rex* could never have encountered

These dinosaurs were all extinct by the time *T. rex* emerged:

1. Allosaurus
2. Archaeopteryx
3. Apatosaurus
4. Brachiosaurus
5. Diplodocus
6. Coelophysis
7. Stegosaurus
8. Iguanodon
9. Spinosaurus
10. Compsognathus

Tyrannosaurus rex

Leptoceratops

---

*Or more likely, have eaten. Who needs friends?

Comeback Kid

Five things scientists would need to do to clone a *Tyrannosaurus rex*

1. Find some *T. rex* blood

To clone an animal, modern scientists would need the DNA, or genetic code, found inside its cells. A good place to start looking for dinosaur DNA is in a sample of its blood or soft tissue, which could potentially be preserved in a fossil, inside a prehistoric bloodsucking insect, or within a frozen layer of soil called permafrost.

2. Extract its DNA

Next, they would need to find a complete sample of the *T. rex*'s DNA within those blood or tissue cells. This is very hard to do because not only is DNA easily damaged but it also breaks down over time. If scientists did discover some fully intact *T. rex* DNA, it would have to be extracted from the dinosaur's cells very carefully.*

3. Choose a host animal

The next challenge would be to pick a modern animal to give birth to the clone. They could choose a crocodile, which shares a common ancestor with dinosaurs. But the best animal would probably be a bird, as modern birds are directly descended from dinosaurs. And because the host animal would effectively be laying a dinosaur egg (i.e., a big one) it would be better to choose a large modern bird, such as an ostrich.

4. Help it survive and grow

However, even if scientists successfully cloned a *T. rex*, we don't know whether the animal could survive in the modern world. Everything, from the food it could eat to the amount of oxygen in the air, would be different from the Cretaceous Period. So they would potentially have to create a special environment for the dinosaur clone to live in, including a menu of food designed to simulate its prehistoric diet.

5. Clone more dinosaurs!

If the new *T. rex* clone was able to survive and thrive in our world, they might then want to create more clones to keep it company. Some scientists estimate that you need at least 5,000 animals to create a healthy long-term population of that species. So their next challenge would be working out how to feed 5,000 hungry *T. rex* clones . . .

*The oldest sample of DNA that scientists have been able to study is from a rhinoceros's tooth that is around 1.7 million years old. *Tyrannosaurus rex* DNA would be at least 66 million years old, and it is very unlikely that the DNA could survive intact for that long.

Speed Demons and Slowpokes

Some of the fastest—and slowest—dinosaurs on land»

Scientists use a combination of the size, weight, muscle strength, and fossilized footprints of a dinosaur to estimate how quickly it could run.*

Compsognathus—40 mph (64 km/h)

Gallimimus—31 mph (50 km/h)

Velociraptor—25 mph (40 km/h)

Allosaurus—21 mph (34 km/h)

Tyrannosaurus rex—18 mph (29 km/h)

Triceratops—16 mph (26 km/h)

Diplodocus—15 mph (24 km/h)

Ankylosaurus—6 mph (10 km/h)

Brachiosaurus—6 mph (10 km/h)

Euoplocephalus—5 mph (8 km/h)

Stegosaurus—4 mph (6 km/h)

Argentinosaurus—3 mph (5 km/h)

Stegosaurus

Compsognathus

» To find out about the fastest animals alive today, see pages 178–179.

*The sprinter Usain Bolt's fastest recorded running speed is around 27 miles per hour (44 km/h). The average human walking speed is around 2.5–3 miles per hour (4–5 km/h) so, were it alive today, an *Argentinosaurus* could stroll alongside us.

High Flyers

How the wingspans of pterosaurs and dinosaurs compare to modern birds»

Quetzalcoatlus (pterosaur) — 36 ft (11 m)
Almost three times larger than the wandering albatross, which has the largest wingspan of any living bird

Pteranodon (pterosaur) — 20 ft (6 m)
Twice as big as a trumpeter swan

Rhamphorhynchus (pterosaur) — 6 ft (1.8 m)
The same as a black vulture

Dimorphodon (pterosaur) — 4.5 ft (1.5 m)
The same as an osprey

Eudimorphodon (pterosaur) — 3.3 ft (1 m)
The same as a peregrine falcon

Pterodactylus (pterosaur) — 3.3 ft (1 m)
The same as an owl

Archaeopteryx (dinosaur) — 1.6 ft (50 cm)
The same as a dove

Ichthyornis (dinosaur) — 1.4 ft (40 cm)
The same as a common swift

Nemicolopterus (dinosaur) — 9.8 in (25 cm)
The same as a robin

Oculudentavis (dinosaur) — 2 in (5 cm)
Smaller than a bee hummingbird, the smallest bird alive today

Dove

Archaeopteryx

» For the wingspans of the largest airplanes, see page 318.

Quetzalcoatlus is the largest known flying animal ever to have lived.

Ready for Takeoff

Quetzalcoatlus in numbers

70 million The number of years since *Quetzalcoatlus* is thought to have first appeared on Earth.

15,000 The maximum height in feet (4,600 m) at which some scientists think *Quetzalcoatlus* was able to fly.*

12,000 The maximum distance in miles (19,000 km) that some scientists estimate *Quetzalcoatlus* could fly without stopping. That's almost halfway around the world!

1971 The year its first fossils were found, in Texas.

530 Its approximate weight in pounds (240 kg), which is about the same as two giant pandas, and 20 times heavier than the biggest modern flying birds.

80 Its estimated top flying speed in miles per hour (128 km/h).

26 The length of its body from beak to tail in feet (8 m). The beak alone was longer than a human being and when standing on the ground, *Quetzalcoatlus* was as tall as a giraffe.

*Scientists aren't sure whether *Quetzalcoatlus* took off by flapping its enormous wings or by gliding from the top of cliffs and other high places.

Taking Flight

The four stages of dinosaur
feather evolution

1. Hollow fiber

Dinosaur feathers weren't originally
designed for flying. Some dinosaurs used
them to stay warm, while others used them
to signal or show off to other dinosaurs. So
early dinosaur feathers were hollow fibers
more like thick hairs than birds' feathers.

2. Bundle of fibers

Feathers gradually evolved to become more
complex, with multiple fibers all attached
to a central point at the base.

3. Central spine

The next development was a central shaft
or spine running along the middle of the
feather, to which the individual barbs were
connected on either side.

4. Ready for liftoff

Over time, feathers evolved to become
better for flying. For example, the spines of
fully-developed dinosaur and bird feathers
are on one side of the feather rather than
in the middle. This new pattern helped to
create more lift for flying.

Stage 1

Stage 2

Stage 3

Stage 4

Eggstraordinary!

How the sizes of eight fully-grown dinosaurs compared to the size of their eggs

Most animals have to do lots of growing to develop from babies to adults. A full-grown human, for example, is roughly three to four times taller than a newborn baby. Some young dinosaurs grew even faster than human beings*—and ended up being many, many times bigger than the eggs that they hatched from.

Fully-grown *Argentinosaurus*

*Dinosaur fossils have growth rings inside the bone, which are similar to the rings you find inside trees. You can count these lines to estimate the age of the dinosaur when it died. You can also measure the distance between the lines to estimate how quickly or slowly the dinosaur grew. The bigger the distance, the faster it was growing at the time.

1. _Argentinosaurus_ 200 times bigger than its egg
Egg: 8 in (20 cm) long**
Full-grown dinosaur: 131 ft (40 m) long

2. _Titanosaurus_ 93 times bigger
Egg: 7.8 in (20 cm) long
Full-grown dinosaur: 61 ft (18.5 m) long

3. _Apatosaurus_ 75 times bigger
Egg: 12 in (30 cm) long***
Full-grown dinosaur: 75 ft (23 m) long

4. _Maiasaura_ 60 times bigger
Egg: 6 in (15 cm) long
Full-grown dinosaur: 29.5 ft (9 m) long

5. _Hypselosaurus_ 27 times bigger
Egg: 12 in (30 cm) long
Full-grown dinosaur: 27 ft (8 m) long

6. _Troodon_ 16 times bigger
Egg: 6 in (15 cm) long
Full-grown dinosaur: 8 ft (2.5 m) long

7. _Protoceratops_ 9 times bigger
Egg: 5 in (12.5 cm) long
Full-grown dinosaur: 6 ft (1.8 m) long

8. _Oviraptor_ 8 times bigger
Egg: 6 in (15 cm) long
Full-grown dinosaur: 6 ft (1.8 m) long

Argentinosaurus egg

Argentinosaurus is thought to be the largest land animal that has ever existed.

**An _Argentinosaurus_ had an egg roughly the same size as that of an ostrich, which produces the largest egg of any bird alive today.

***A baby _Apatosaurus_ would gain more than 30 pounds (14 kg) of weight each day as it grew to become a 100-ton (90-tonne) adult. This is a similar rate of growth to a modern whale.

Millions of Years in the Making

The eight main ways that fossils* form

1. Mineralization

When a dead organism is buried in a covering of rock, mud, or sand, minerals can slowly fill the spaces in its cells. When these crystallize, they gradually turn into rock. The parts of a creature's body most likely to become fossilized in this way are the hard parts: the bones, teeth, or shell.

2. Petrification

The same process of mineralization can also happen to plants and trees. Fossilized tree trunks are described as "petrified," which means "changed to stone."

3. External mold

Sometimes the body of the dead organism dissolves completely, leaving behind only the shape or impression of its body within the stone (which was originally mud or another sediment, such as sand) burying it. This fossil impression is called a mold.

4. Natural cast

A natural cast starts out the same as an external mold, with a hole in the stone left behind by an organism's body. Minerals can then start to crystallize inside the hole, eventually forming a solid fossil made of a rock such as flint.

5. Preserved in amber

If the body of a small animal or insect becomes covered in the sticky sap produced by some trees, it can be preserved for millions of years within fossilized tree resin, which is known as amber.

6. Freezing

This is the best way to preserve the body of an ancient organism but it only happens very rarely as an animal must stay frozen from the time it died right up until it is discovered by a lucky paleontologist.**

7. Mummification

An animal's skin and internal organs can also be preserved for thousands of years if they are completely dried out shortly after its death. This can happen naturally in hot and dry parts of the world and is known as mummification. Ancient Egyptians preserved human and animal bodies by drying them out and mummifying them.»

8. Carbonization

Sometimes organic material, such as the leaves of plants or the body parts of fish and reptiles, breaks down, leaving only the element carbon behind. This leftover carbon creates an impression in the rock, sometimes including fine details of the organism's original shape.

---

*An estimated one bone in every billion becomes fossilized. And less than 0.001 percent of all species that have ever lived have been turned into fossils.

**Paleontologists sometimes dig underground mineshafts into permafrost, which is frozen soil, rock, and sand held together by ice. Hundreds of dinosaur fossils have been found here.

» To find out how the ancient Egyptians mummified people and animals, see page 246.

This insect was trapped in sticky tree sap millions of years ago. Over time, the tree sap became amber, with the insect perfectly preserved inside.

Dino Detectives

The five trace fossils that paleontologists use to piece together the life of a dinosaur

As well as its fossilized bones, a dinosaur sometimes leaves behind other clues about what it looked like and how it lived. Here are five examples of these trace fossils and what we can learn from them.

1. Footprints and tracks Preserved dinosaur footprints, also known as ichnites, are left behind when a dinosaur walks on mud or soft ground. If the conditions are just right, the footprint hardens to rock and fossilizes. By studying the shape of its footprints, paleontologists can estimate how heavy the dinosaur was, whether it walked on two legs or four, and even how quickly it was moving.

2. Eggs and nests The first thing we can tell from a dinosaur egg* is the approximate size of the baby dinosaur inside. The number of eggs,** and how they were arranged within a nest or underground burrow, also give us an idea of how dinosaurs behaved as parents and what they did to protect and care for their young.

3. Poop By studying fossilized dinosaur poop,*** which are called coprolites, we can tell what kind of animal made them. Coprolites also contain clues about the animal's diet.

4. Bite marks These dramatic marks in dinosaur bones give us a more detailed understanding of how dinosaurs fought each other and how strong they were. Bite marks have also revealed that some carnivorous dinosaurs attacked and killed members of their own species.

5. Feathers Fossilized feathers reveal valuable information: what feathered dinosaurs looked like, how they kept warm, and whether they were able to fly. Paleontologists have also started to study microscopic "melanosomes," which are found inside fossilized feather cells and which hold information on the color of the feathers.

Right: Imprints of feathers can be seen around the limbs and body of this *Anchiornis huxleyi* fossil. Melanosomes in the fossil suggest that it might have had feathers of more than one color.

---

*As far as we know, every species of dinosaur reproduced by laying eggs.

**In 2019, a ten-year-old schoolboy named Zhang Yangzhe discovered a collection of 11 dinosaur eggs in Heyuan, China, after spotting what looked like a "strange stone" on the ground.

***George Frandsen from Florida has 1,277 coprolites, making him the proud owner of the world's largest collection of fossilized poop. Frandsen's biggest coprolite weighs 4.2 pounds (1.92 kg). He's even given it a name: "Precious."

Anchiornis huxleyi

Under the Hammer

Seven expensive dinosaur fossils sold at public auction

You might assume dinosaur fossils should be free. After all, they are just lying around in the ground. But complete (or almost complete) skeletons are very rare, so the finders can get a lot of money for them. Here are seven fossils that fetched shocking prices at auction.

1. Sue the *Tyrannosaurus rex*

Price tag: $13.4 million (equivalent to about 3,800 diamond rings)*

Buyer: The Field Museum in Chicago, where Sue is now on display

Profile: Sue, the most expensive dinosaur fossil ever sold at auction, is named after Sue Hendrickson, the paleontologist who discovered the beautifully preserved fossil.

2. Apollonia, Prince, and Twinky the *Diplodocuses*

Price tag: $9.2 million (equivalent to about 2,600 diamond rings)**

Buyer: The Lee Kong Chian Natural History Museum in Singapore, where they are on display

Profile: This trio of dinosaurs was discovered buried in a quarry. Scientists think that they could have been part of the same herd.

3. Battling *Allosaurus* and *Stegosaurus*

Price tag: $3.1 million (equivalent to about 890 diamond rings)

Buyer: An unnamed museum

Profile: When the fossils were found, the jaw of the *Allosaurus* was clamped around the leg of the *Stegosaurus*, leading some scientists to think that the two dinosaurs killed each other in a deadly fight before both were buried in mud.

4. The Mystery Dinosaur

Price tag: $2.4 million (equivalent to about 690 diamond rings)

Buyer: Anonymous***

Profile: Scientists first thought this dinosaur fossil was an *Allosaurus*, but when further investigations proved their theory wrong, it was given the name "Mystery Dinosaur." If the fossil is ever identified as a new type of dinosaur, the auctioneers said the owner might have a say in choosing a scientific name for the new species.

5. Misty the Dinosaur

Price tag: $700,000 (equivalent to about 200 diamond rings)

Buyer: Anonymous

Profile: This *Diplodocus* skeleton was given the nickname "Misty," short for the "mystery quarry" where she was discovered by paleontologist Raimund Albersdoerfer and his two sons Benjamin and Jacob.

---

*Prices are converted into the value of today's currency, and the equivalent values take an approximate cost of a diamond ring as being $3,500.

**Carnivorous dinosaurs (like the *T. rex*) tend to fetch more money at auction than the herbivores (such as the *Diplodocus*).

***Fossil-buyers at auction are not required to disclose their identity or declare what they intend to do with their purchase, so several of the world's dinosaur skeletons are untraceable, and probably lost to science.

6. Raptor nest with eggs

Price tag: $500,000 (equivalent to about 140 diamond rings)

Buyer: Anonymous

Profile: This dino nest contained 22 broken eggs, with some tiny raptors clearly visible inside.

7. Freya the *Hypacrosaurus*

Price tag: $149,324 (equivalent to about 40 diamond rings)

Buyer: Anonymous

Profile: This rare duck-billed dinosaur fossil measures around 23 feet (7 m) long and 10 feet (3 m) tall, almost as big as a *Tyrannosaurus rex*.

Freya the *Hypacrosaurus*

Can You Dig It?

Seven steps to unearthing your own dinosaur fossil and putting it on display

1. Survey the site Carefully examine areas of exposed prehistoric rock where dinosaur fossils are likely to be found. Look out for scraps of dinosaur bone and other clues.

2. Expose the fossil Once you've found part of a fossil, start digging away the surrounding rock so that the fossil is more fully exposed. Paleontologists' tools include hammers, drills, chisels, and trowels, as well as brushes to sweep away the dust.

3. Map it out Record the position each fossil was found in. You can do this by placing a 3.3-foot- (1-m-) square grid of strings over the excavation site. With the grid in place, photos of the site will show how big things are and the positions they were found in.*

4. Remove the fossil It can take days, or even weeks, to excavate a fossil from the rock that surrounds it. Once the dinosaur fossil is sufficiently exposed, cover it in a plaster cast to protect it as you remove the fossil from the rock and transport it back to the laboratory. Once there, you can use brushes and hand tools to help expose each bone.

5. Scan the fossil Take X-rays and CT scans of the inside of the fossilized bones. This helps to build a detailed 3D model of the fossil on a computer.

6. Mount the fossil If the fossil is going to be put on display in a museum, perhaps as part of a full dinosaur skeleton, you will then mount it on a strong metal frame called an armature. If there are bones missing from the dinosaur skeleton, you can make replacement bones to fill in the gaps.

7. Make a model For some museum displays, you will also need to create model versions of other parts of the dinosaur's body such as its muscles, skin, tongue, and eyes. You can do this using clues on the dinosaur's bones—such as where they were attached to its muscles—and by making comparisons with modern animals with similar anatomies. Congratulations, your DIY dinosaur reconstruction is now ready to go on display!

Left: A paleontologist carefully chips rock away from dinosaur bones in the Quarry Exhibit Hall at Dinosaur National Monument, Utah.

*Modern paleontologists also use a series of digital photographs to create a 2D or 3D model of the fossil and where it was found. This technique is called "photogrammetry."

Fake Fossils

Seven dinosaur fossils that weren't the real deal

1. Beringer's Lying Stones

When: 1725

What happened: Professor Johann Beringer, who worked at the University of Würzburg in Germany, liked to go walking on nearby Mount Eibelstadt looking for fossils. A group of his fellow teachers from the university decided to play a trick on him by carving fake fossils from limestone in the shape of lizards, frogs, and spiders and planting them on the mountainside to fool Professor Beringer into thinking they were real. The professor was completely taken in and even published a book about his amazing finds." Eventually, the truth came out and the fake fossils became known as "Beringer's Lying Stones." Some are still on display at the Oxford University Museum of Natural History in the UK.

2. *Hydrarchos*

When: 1845

What happened: A huge sea serpent was apparently discovered by the amateur fossil hunter and showman Albert Koch, who brought it to New York City to show it to the public. Koch named the spectacular creature *Hydrarchos* and eventually sold its 114-foot (35-m) skeleton to King Friedrich Wilhelm IV of Prussia (which is now Germany), who put it on display at a museum in Berlin. Unfortunately for King Friedrich, the *Hydrarchos* fossil was a fake. Koch had assembled it out of the bones of at least six different prehistoric whales and added in some ammonite fossils for good measure. The truth didn't come out until years later. The bones of *Hydrarchos* were destroyed during the bombing of Germany during the Second World War.

Koch's *Hydrarchos* skeleton, on display in 1845.

» For more cunning hoaxes, see page 292.

3. *Amphicoelias fragillimus*

When: 1877

What happened: Famous paleontologist Edward Drinker Cope thought that a piece of dinosaur bone that had been dug up in Colorado belonged to a huge new species of dinosaur that would have been "the biggest in history." The new dinosaur was named *Amphicoelias fragillimus*, and it was estimated to have measured 190 feet (58 m) long and to have weighed more than 100 tons (90 tonnes). However, the bone then mysteriously disappeared and, as no bone of a dinosaur that big has ever been found since, some experts think it was a fake—or maybe had never even existed at all.

4. Woody the *Aachenosaurus*

When: 1887

What happened: The naturalist Abbe G. Smets found two fossils in France that he thought came from a new kind of dinosaur, which he called *Aachenosaurus*. Smets was so confident about his discovery that he even created a full-scale recreation of what he thought an *Aachenosaurus* looked like. However, the paleontologist Louis Dollo and botanist Maurice Hovelacque disagreed with Smets' theory and, after investigating, proved that his "important dinosaur finds" were just bits of fossilized wood!

5. *Archaeoraptor*

When: 1999

What happened: An important new species of flying dinosaur was reported to have been found in China. It was said to be a missing evolutionary link between dinosaurs and birds and was named *Archaeoraptor*. However, expert paleontologists realized that the *Archaeoraptor* skeleton was a fake. The head and body belonged to a fossilized bird, while the tail had come from a flying dinosaur called a *Microraptor*.

6. *Ichthyosaurus*

When: 2000

What happened: One of the most impressive exhibits at the National Museum of Wales, in the UK, was the fossilized skeleton of a 200-million-year-old ichthyosaur which had been on display there for more than 100 years. However, when museum staff removed the skeleton from its display case to clean it, they were shocked to discover it wasn't an ichthyosaur at all. The skeleton contained the bones of two different animals and some artificial bones all stuck together to make it look like a dinosaur. In the end, the museum decided to keep the skeleton on display as an example of a fake dinosaur.

7. Spot the *Apatosaurus*

When: 2014

What happened: A news report claimed that scientists at a university in Liverpool, UK, had created a clone of a baby *Apatosaurus*, which had been successfully hatched by an ostrich. A photograph of the baby dinosaur, which the scientists had named Spot, was included in the report. However, experts soon realized that the article was made up and the picture was of a baby kangaroo, not a dinosaur.

Wipeout!

Thirteen strange and unlikely theories about why the dinosaurs became extinct

Most scientists now agree that the dinosaurs died out after a giant asteroid or comet collided with Earth 66 million years ago. Before scientists knew about this event—which is known as the K-T mass extinction*—people came up with other theories to explain why the dinosaurs all died out. Some of these theories are interesting—if also completely wrong.

1. Carnivorous dinosaurs ate too many other dinosaurs' eggs.

2. The caterpillars of the first moths and butterflies ate so many plants that there was no longer enough food for herbivorous dinosaurs to survive. In turn, this meant there weren't enough herbivores for the carnivores to eat.

3. The bright prehistoric sunlight gradually damaged dinosaurs' eyesight, so they could no longer find enough food or reproduce.

4. An exploding star sent harmful waves of energy crashing into Earth's atmosphere, drastically changing the climate.

5. Dinosaurs grew too big to survive.

6. Dinosaurs' brains got smaller until they became too stupid to survive.

7. Herbivores produced so much methane by passing gas that it made the Earth too hot.

8. The dinosaurs became bored with the prehistoric world and couldn't be bothered to go on.

9. A change in the chemical hormones inside dinosaurs' bodies caused their eggs' shells to become too thin.

10. Dinosaurs kept injuring their backs.

11. Carnivores ate all the other dinosaurs and then each other.

12. Depending on which scientist you asked, the Earth's climate became too hot, too cold, too dry, or too wet.

13. A rise in the number of flowering plants led to the extinction of the dinosaurs by hay fever.

*A "mass extinction" means that more than 50 percent of the animal species on Earth died out at one time. No land animal bigger than a dog survived the mass extinction that killed the dinosaurs.

Deadly Impact

The asteroid* that probably wiped out the dinosaurs in numbers

66,000,000 The number of years ago that the asteroid collided with Earth.

44,700 The asteroid's estimated speed as it hit the Earth in miles per hour (72,000 km/h), which is more than 100 times faster than a jet airplane. The impact of the collision created a giant crater in the surface of the Earth.**

2,000 The depth in feet (600 m) of the sedimentary sand and rock that lies on top of the crater today.

110 The width of the crater in miles (180 km).

75 The percentage of plant and animal species that became extinct after the asteroid's impact.

50 The maximum estimated diameter of the asteroid in miles (80 km).

*Scientists aren't sure whether the Earth was hit by an asteroid or a comet. But we can see and measure the huge effects of its impact, so we are 100 percent sure that something very big and heavy collided with Earth 66 million years ago. To find out the difference between an asteroid and a comet, see page 30.

**The crater created by the impact of the asteroid is known as the Chicxulub crater and it was discovered in the late 1970s in a region of Mexico called the Yucatán Peninsula. A large section of this huge crater is submerged beneath the sea.

Sole Survivors

All the types of dinosaur that are still
alive today

1. Birds*

*That's it. However, there are around 10,000
species of bird alive on Earth. So, if you want
to see a dinosaur, just look up the nearest tree.

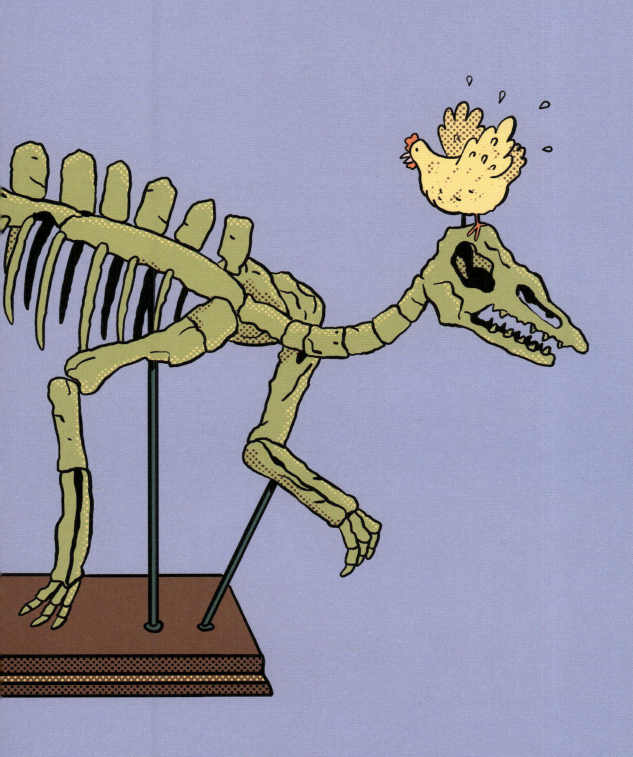

Chapter 4

Animals

A list of things you'll encounter in this chapter:

An immortal jellyfish

Loyal flatworms

A frog that can push its bones through its skin

Ferret electricians

Spider webs that trap bats

The loudest animal on Earth

A shape-shifting octopus

Animals with three eyelids

The mammal that can't pass gas

Fish that poop sand

A blood-sucking moth

Chimpanzee toothpicks

The brainiest dog breed

The fastest-moving animal on Earth*

A monster dragonfly

The world's tiniest shark

An unsinkable cat

*And it's not a cheetah.

Short and Sweet

Fourteen animals with short lifespans

1. **Adult mayfly**—2 days
2. **Gastrotrich**—3 days*
3. **Dragonfly**—2 weeks**
4. **Housefly**—4 weeks
5. **Dwarf pygmy goby fish**—2 months
6. **Labord's chameleon**—4–5 months
7. **Bee**—5 months***
8. **Monarch butterfly**—9 months
9. **Cockroach**—1 year
10. **Mosquitofish**—1 year
11. **Mouse**—1 year
12. **Pygmy shrew**—1 year
13. **Robin**—1 year
14. **Octopus**—1.5 years

*Gastrotrichs, also known as hairybellies or hairybacks, are tiny marine organisms that are no longer than 0.1 inch (3 mm).

**Although some dragonflies can live for up to a year.

***Queen bees live for up to five years.

Old-Timers

Thirteen animals with long lifespans

1. **Immortal jellyfish**—forever!*
2. **Ocean quahog clam**—507 years
3. **Greenland shark**—392 years
4. **Bowhead whale**—211 years
5. **Rougheye rockfish**—205 years
6. **Red sea urchin**—200 years
7. **Aldabra giant tortoise**—188 years**
8. **Galapagos tortoise**—177 years
9. **Shortraker rockfish**—157 years
10. **Lake sturgeon fish**—152 years
11. **Orange roughy fish**—149 years
12. **Eastern box turtle**—138 years
13. **Mediterranean spur-thighed tortoise**—127 years

*This species of jellyfish called *Turritopsis dohrnii* is a rare example of an animal that can develop from its young stage (a polyp) to its mature stage (a grown-up jellyfish) before returning to its young stage. It repeats the process in an apparently endless cycle. In reality, many immortal jellyfish will be eaten by predators or die from disease but, in terms of its own biology, there is nothing to stop one from living forever.

**The world's oldest known living terrestrial animal is an Aldabra giant tortoise called Jonathan, who is thought to have hatched in 1832. He lives on the island of Saint Helena in the Atlantic Ocean. Jonathan's tips for a long, healthy life include plenty of sleep, sun, and mushy bananas.

Aldabra giant tortoise

Between Meals

Ten animals that can go the longest without food

1. **Tardigrade**—30 years

2. **Olm***—10 years

3. **Crocodile**—3 years

4. **Swell shark**—1 year, 3 months

5. **Galapagos tortoise**—1 year

6. **Scorpion**—1 year

7. **Ball python**—6 months

8. **Humpback whale**—6 months

9. **Black bear**—3 months

10. **Emperor penguin**—3 months

Tardigrades are microscopic creatures that are famed for their ability to survive in extreme conditions, such as the pressure of the deep ocean and even the vacuum of space.

*Olms are a species of blind salamander that live in total darkness in caves for as long as 100 years. They can go without food for so long because they use up very little energy. In one study, scientists observed an olm that didn't move at all for seven years.

Two of a Kind

Twenty species of animal that pair for life

1. Albatrosses
2. Anglerfish*
3. Barn owls
4. Black vultures
5. Beavers
6. Condors
7. Coyotes
8. Gibbons
9. Golden eagles
10. Ospreys
11. Penguins
12. Prairie voles
13. Sandhill cranes
14. *Schistosoma mansoni* worms**
15. Seahorses
16. Shingleback skink lizards
17. Swans
18. Termites***
19. Turtle doves
20. Wolves

Extended Families

Ten animals that give birth to a large number of offspring at a time

1. **Ocean sunfish**—300 million eggs
2. **African driver ant**—4 million eggs*
3. **Atlantic sturgeon**—2.5 million eggs
4. **Seahorses**—2,000 babies**
5. **Puff adder**—156 babies
6. **Tailless tenrec**—32 babies***
7. **Naked mole rat**—28 babies
8. **Virginia opossum**—25 babies
9. **Gray partridge**—22 eggs
10. **Rabbits**—14 babies

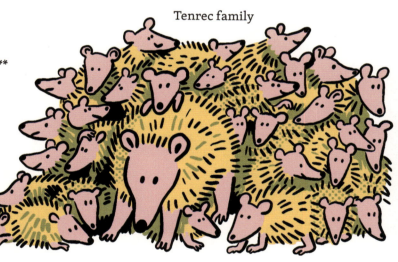

Tenrec family

*After some species of anglerfish mate, the males become permanently attached to the females and the happy couple stay physically connected for the rest of their lives.

**Schistosoma mansoni* are microscopic parasitic flatworms that live inside human beings and can cause diseases such as snail fever. This doesn't make them sound very romantic but they do form close bonds with their mates. Ahhhh.

***Unlike ants and bees, where multiple males pair with the queen, a termite queen and a single termite king stay together as a couple to produce the whole termite colony.

*Each month.

**Very unusual in the animal kingdom, it's the male seahorses that become pregnant and give birth.

***The tailless tenrec is a small hedgehog-like mammal that lives in Madagascar. If you haven't seen one before, it might be because it can hibernate for up to 75 percent of the year.

Do Me a Favor

Five examples of animal mutualism

Mutualism is a term used to describe a partnership between two organisms in which both species benefit.

1. Clownfish and sea anemones
Clownfish are often found swimming among the tentacles of sea anemones, which sting nearly all other fish. Thanks to a special mucus (slimy coating) on their skin, the clownfish aren't harmed. In return for a safe place to live, the clownfish chase away the anemone's main predator, the butterflyfish.

2. Rhinoceroses and oxpecker birds
Rhinoceroses allow these little birds to sit on their backs and eat ticks, flies, and other insects that live on their skin. The rhinos benefit by having annoying parasites removed while the oxpeckers get a free lunch.

3. Gray wolves and striped hyenas
These two predators have been known to hunt together. The hyenas benefit from the hunting ability of the wolf pack, while contributing their own great sense of smell and their ability to break up large bones.

4. Ants and aphids Some species of ant eat a substance called honeydew that is made by tiny insects called aphids. The aphids make honeydew from plant sap. In order to protect their honeydew supply, the ants will keep the aphids safe from predators. The ants also herd the aphids to new plants to find fresh sap. Some ants have even been known to "milk" honeydew from the aphids by stroking them with their antennae."

5. Remoras and sharks Remoras are small fish that attach themselves to sharks and other large marine animals. The remoras keep the sharks' skin free of parasites and are even allowed to swim around the sharks' teeth to remove bits of food that might otherwise become breeding grounds for harmful bacteria. In return, the remoras enjoy free meals while also hitching a ride.

»To find out about other jobs that ants do, see page 187.

Bird Sanctuary

Three amazing facts about sociable weaver bird nests

1. They are the biggest birds' nests on Earth at more than 20 feet (6 m) wide.

2. They have spiky straws at the entrance tunnels to protect the nest from predators.

3. The nests are used by multiple generations of birds for more than a hundred years. Four hundred individual birds can live in one nest at a time.

Going Undergound

Three amazing facts about prairie dog* towns

1. Prairie dog towns are networks of tunnels that run underground for miles in every direction.

2. They include lots of different rooms to store food, hide from predators, and house "nurseries" for baby prairie dogs.

3. One of these underground towns in Texas covered 25,000 square miles (65,000 km²) and was home to an estimated 400 million prairie dogs.

Tower of Strength

Three amazing facts about termite mounds

1. They are made of mud, chewed wood, termite poop, and saliva.

2. The largest mounds can soar up to 23 feet (7 m) high, which is taller than a giraffe.

3. All termite mounds have air-conditioning systems that circulate hot and cold air between the mound and the outside.

World Wide Web

Three amazing facts about communal spiderwebs

1. A certain species of spider called *Anelosimus eximius* is particularly sociable. They live in rain forests and their webs can hold as many as 50,000 spiders.

2. Some webs can cover whole trees and bushes and stretch for more than 1,000 feet (300 m).

3. Each spider in the web has a job to do: some are in charge of repairs, others find prey, and others look after the baby spiders, known as spiderlings. And the bigger the web the more food there is for the community to eat. Some webs are even large enough to trap birds and bats.

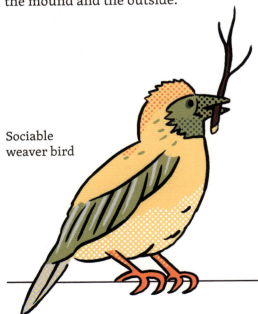

Sociable weaver bird

Right: This is the underneath of a sociable weaver bird's nest in Namibia, Africa.

*Prairie dogs are related to squirrels and marmots.

Noisy Neighbors

Ten animals that make amazingly loud sounds"

Sound is measured in a unit called the decibel. The quietest sound that can be heard by the human ear is 0 decibels. A whisper is 30 decibels, a normal conversation is 60 decibels, and a jet engine at takeoff is about 140 decibels. But some creatures from the animal kingdom produce sounds that are even louder . . .

1. Tiger pistol shrimp—200 decibels

The tiger pistol shrimp has a large claw that shoots out jets of water at such speed that they form air bubbles in the water. When each air bubble collapses, it creates a shock wave that is loud enough to kill other shrimps and fish up to 6.5 feet (2 m) away.*

2. Blue whale—188 decibels

Blue whales use a combination of loud noises to communicate and socialize with each other. The main types of sounds are clicks, whistles, and pulses, or rhythmic calls. Whales' loudest calls can be heard up to 500 miles (800 km) away, which is roughly the distance between San Francisco and San Diego.

3. Greater bulldog bat—140 decibels

Bats use sound to navigate and find food in the dark using a technique called echolocation.** The greater bulldog bat is the loudest member of the bat family and it uses its exceptionally loud sounds to track the movement of fish in pools of water. However, the bats' calls are too high-pitched for humans to hear.

4. Kakapo—132 decibels

The kakapo, a flightless member of the parrot family, is the loudest of all birds. Its booming mating calls are made using special air sacs in its chest and can be heard more than 4 miles (7 km) away.

5. Green grocer cicada—120 decibels

Cicadas are the loudest insects. They create their distinctive chirping sound by moving special membranes called "tymbals" on either side of their abdomens. The sound is then amplified by their hollow abdomens. Only male cicadas "sing" and they do it to attract a female.***

6. Lion—114 decibels

Lions roar for different reasons, including communicating with other members of their pride and to establish their territory. The loudest lion's roar can travel distances of up to 5 miles (8 km) across the African plains.

"To find out about humans that make amazingly loud sounds, see page 368.

*When the air bubble collapses, it also produces a tiny flash of light. For a moment, this raises the temperature inside the bubble to 8,492°F (4,700°C), which is almost as hot as the surface of the Sun.

**To echolocate, a bat sends out a sound wave from its mouth or nose. When the sound wave hits an object, it produces an echo. This returns to the bat's ears, helping it to build up a mental picture of the world around it.

***Cicadas often stay grouped close together because this makes their chirping sounds bounce around in a way that makes it difficult for birds to locate (and eat) them.

7. Elephant—103 decibels

African elephants use their trademark trumpeting to communicate with other members of the herd, who can be several miles away. If you're standing close enough, the sound of an elephant's roar will make your whole body vibrate!

8. Water boatman—99 decibels

Relative to their size, the small aquatic insects called water boatmen are the loudest animals on Earth. Male water boatmen "sing" to attract a mate. They create this sound by rubbing a part of their body against ridges on their abdomen, often "singing" in chorus with other males.

9. Coquí frog—95 decibels

Male coquí frogs make a loud chirping sound to impress and attract females. Their chirps come in two parts, which is how they got their name. The first "co" sound is used to warn off other competing males. The second "kee" sound helps females locate them.

10. Howler monkey—90 decibels

Howler monkeys deserve their name: When they howl together as a troop, their calls can be heard up to 3 miles (5 km) away. These intimidating group calls warn other monkeys to stay out of their territory.

Fantastic Beasts

Ten animals that seem to have superpowers

All animals are extraordinary but some have special features and abilities that you would usually only find in a superhero movie . . .

1. Electric eels can stun their prey with electric shocks of 600 volts.*»

2. Mexican salamanders, called axolotls, can regrow almost any part of their bodies, from muscles and bones to nerve cells and even their own internal organs.

3. Salmon can sense the currents of the Earth's magnetic field, using them like a map to navigate for hundreds of miles through oceans and rivers to reach their annual breeding grounds.

4. Pit viper snakes can "see" in the dark using special organs on their faces that sense heat. These allow them to find other animals (and potential prey) in total darkness.

5. Mimic octopuses can impersonate other animals, changing their shape and color to look like (and fool) lionfish, jellyfish, shrimp, crabs, and other prey.**

6. North American wood frogs can freeze their own blood to help them survive the intense cold as they hibernate through winter.

7. Sea cucumbers can turn their body tissue from solid to liquid and squeeze through small cracks between rocks. They then "re-form" into their original shape on the other side.

8. Lyrebirds can imitate almost any sound they hear, from chain saws and barking dogs to cell phones and even human voices.

9. Sardines can become invisible! By swimming in close formation and using reflective light crystals in their skin, they create an optical illusion that makes predators think they've disappeared.

10. Geckos can walk up a vertical pane of glass thanks to tiny electrostatic forces*** that are created between the surface of the glass and thousands of tiny hairs on their feet.

Left: As well as being able to walk up almost any surface, many geckos can also drop their tails to escape predators. They can then grow brand-new tails.

---

*This is just over five times the voltage contained within a standard electrical wall socket.

»For another example of electricity in nature, see pages 88–89.

**The mimic octopus also uses its color-changing powers as camouflage, allowing it to blend in with any background.

***Electrostatic forces are created by the buildup of electric charges on objects. These charges can cause the object to become attracted to other objects.

They've Got It Licked

Eight animals with supersized tongues

1. Blue whale—216 in (550 cm)

A blue whale's tongue can weigh up to 4.4 tons (4 tonnes), which is roughly the same as two hippopotamuses.

2. Chameleon—48 in (120 cm)

A chameleon's sticky tongue can be up to twice as long as its body. The chameleon uses it to grab insects and pull them into its mouth at lightning speed.*

3. Giant anteater—24 in (60 cm)

A giant anteater uses its tongue, which can be more than a third of the length of its body, to gobble up ants and other insects. Incredibly, it can flick its tongue in and out 160 times in a minute.**

4. Giraffe—20 in (50 cm)

Giraffes' strong, muscular tongues, which they use to grab and strip branches of their leaves, are a dark purple-black color. It is thought the dark color prevents sunburn.

5. Okapi—18 in (46 cm)

An okapi, which is a relative of a giraffe but looks like a cross between a horse and a zebra, has a tongue so long it's able to lick its own eyelids and ears.

6. Pangolin—16 in (40 cm)

A pangolin is a scaly mammal with a long, sticky tongue. Its tongue runs most of the way through its body and is attached near its pelvis.

7. Sun bear—10 in (25 cm)

Despite being the smallest species of bear, sun bears have the longest tongues. They use them to reach honey and insects inside tree trunks and other hard-to-lick places.

8. Tube-lipped nectar bat—3.4 in (9 cm)

This mouse-sized South American bat usually only grows to 2.3 inches (5.8 cm) and has the longest tongue relative to body size of any mammal. It uses its straw-like tongue to suck nectar from tropical flowers.

Chameleon

*As it leaves its mouth, a chameleon's tongue can travel at 60 miles per hour (100 km/h).

**So never offer an anteater a lick of your ice cream.

True Visionaries

Animals' eyes in numbers

1 million The number of light-sensitive cells in each square millimeter of an eagle's eye. Humans have 200,000.»

28,000 The number of lenses in each of a dragonfly's eyes.

350 How many times more sensitive to color a gecko's eyes are at night than a human being's.* (Humans can hardly see any color in the dark of night.)

150 The distance in feet (46 m) from which an owl can spot a moving mouse.

24 The number of eyes a box jellyfish has.

16 The number of types of color receptor a mantis shrimp has in its eyes. Humans have three (red, green, and blue).

11 The diameter in inches (27 cm) that the colossal squid's eyeball measures. This is roughly the size of a soccer ball and is the largest eye of any living animal.

3 The number of eyelids a camel has.** The first two stop desert sand blowing in, while the third sweeps across the eye to keep it clean.

2 The diameter in inches (5 cm) of an ostrich eye, the largest of any bird.***

2 The number of directions that a chameleon can look at once. A chameleon's eyes move independently, which gives it an almost 360-degree field of vision.

1 The number of eyes that a dolphin closes when it's asleep. The other one always stays open.

Ostrich

»To find out more about human eyes, see page 222.

*Geckos don't have eyelids, so they lick their eyeballs clean with their tongues.

**And it's not the only one. Many animals have a third eyelid, including cats, owls, and frogs.

***An ostrich's eye is bigger than its brain.

It Wasn't Me

Mammals that can't pass gas*

1. Sloths

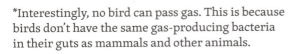

*Interestingly, no bird can pass gas. This is because
birds don't have the same gas-producing bacteria
in their guts as mammals and other animals.

No Way Out

The three animals that don't poop

1. Tardigrades Instead of pooping, some species of these microscopic creatures release unwanted substances from their bodies by shedding their skin.

2. Jellyfish Technically, jellyfish don't poop as they do not possess anuses. They do, however, release waste material through their mouths.

3. _Demodex_ mites These microscopic arthropods store a lifetime of bodily waste inside special cells in their intestines.

Doing Their Business

Five animals that poop in extraordinary ways

1. Caterpillars shoot flakes of digested plant matter out of their bottoms. They fire this waste, which is called "frass," to a distance of nearly 40 times the length of their bodies in order to conceal their location from predators.

2. Parrotfish mostly eat bits of coral. When they poop, it's almost entirely made of newly-formed sand.

3. Vultures poop on their own legs and feet so that as the liquid poop evaporates, it sucks heat away from their skin, cooling them down.

4. Sloths spend most of their time hanging around (and sleeping) in trees, but typically come down to the ground once a week to poop—which they always do in the same spot.

5. Sperm whales can fire out exploding clouds of poop to drive away and confuse potential predators.

Sweet Dreams

How long fourteen animals can sleep each day

1. **Koala**—22 hours*
2. **Brown bat**—20 hours
3. **Armadillo**—18 hours
4. **Opossum**—18 hours
5. **Python**—18 hours
6. **Owl monkey**—17 hours
7. **Tiger**—16 hours
8. **Tree shrew**—16 hours
9. **Squirrel**—15 hours
10. **Sloth**—14.5 hours
11. **Platypus**—14 hours
12. **Lion**—13.5 hours
13. **Gerbil**—13 hours
14. **Rhesus monkey**—12 hours

Koala

*Koalas sleep for up to 90 percent of the time because they aren't able to get much energy from their main source of food—the leaves of the eucalyptus tree. Eucalyptus is extremely difficult to digest and it takes their stomachs a long time to break it down and extract nutrients.

Bloodsuckers

Ten animals that drink other animals' blood

1. Female mosquitoes drink the blood of other animals, such as mammals, birds, and reptiles. They need the blood to make eggs.

2. Vampire bats use their razor-sharp teeth to make tiny cuts in their victims before licking the blood. Vampire bats are the only mammal known to have a diet that is solely based on blood.

3. Lampreys, which are strange, eellike sea creatures, use their sucker-shaped mouths to attach themselves to other fish before feeding off their blood.*

4. Fleas' only source of food is other animals' blood. Bites aren't all that fleas give their victims; they often infect them with diseases in the process. The bubonic plague, which killed more than a quarter of Europe's population in the Middle Ages, was initially spread by fleas.

5. Siberian vampire moths use their long, spiked tongues to drink the blood of large animals including cattle, rhinos, and elephants.

6. Vampire finches like to suck the blood of another bird found on the Galapagos Islands—the blue-footed booby. The finches will sneak a drink as they helpfully pick out parasites from the boobies' feathers.

7. Leeches are bloodsucking worms. In the 19th century, it was believed that, if applied to a patient, leeches would suck away "bad" blood and cure diseases. However, leeches are no longer used by doctors in this way.**

8. Oxpeckers, which are also called tickbirds, sit on the side of large "host animals" such as buffalo, where they remove flies, ticks, and maggots. This sounds nice and helpful but oxpeckers also drink the host animals' blood as they dig out the insects.

9. Bedbugs often live inside mattresses and wooden beds and usually bite at night while their human victims are asleep. They also release a special anesthetizing substance along with their bite, which makes the bite painless, although it can later become itchy.

10. Assassin bugs use a long straw-like part of their body called a rostrum to suck the blood from other animals. An assassin bug's victims include a variety of other insects and spiders—even bloodsucking vampire bats!

---

*Thankfully, lampreys don't have a taste for swimming humans.

**Although leeches are sometimes used by modern doctors to help improve patients' blood flow around areas of skin that have poor circulation following surgery.

Fighting Back

Ten animals with surprising methods of defense

1. Boxer crabs allow poisonous anemones, sponges, and corals to ride on their claws, creating scary "boxing gloves" to frighten away predators.

2. Malaysian ants sacrifice their own lives to defend the colony. The soldier ants can force their bodies to explode and spray a sticky poison over attackers.

3. Porcupines use their long, pointy quills to charge sideways or backward at predators.

4. Bombardier beetles spray attackers with a hot, foul-smelling fluid squirted from their bottom (which is as unpleasant as it sounds).

5. Texas horned lizards squirt jets of high-pressured blood from their eyes. The stream of blood can travel 5 feet (1.5 m) and is mixed with a foul-tasting chemical.

6. Hairy frogs (also known as the horror frog or Wolverine frog) can crack their own toe bones and push them through their skin to form sharp claws.

7. Spanish ribbed newts can push their ribs out through their skin to create two spiky ridges along their back. At the same time, their skin releases a poisonous substance onto the spikes to create an extra line of defense.

8. Hagfish release a slimy substance that expands when it mixes with water and can clog up the gills of other fish trying to attack them.

9. Sea cucumbers can fire their own internal organs out of their bottom at attackers. A sea cucumber's organs are sticky and contain a poison called holothurin.*

10. Opossums automatically "play dead" and emit a smell like rotting flesh when scared. They then curl up and don't move for several hours in the hope that predators will think they have actually died.

Porcupine

Leopard

*Amazingly, losing its internal organs isn't fatal to the sea cucumber—they regrow in around six weeks.

Masters of Disguise

Five animals that use clever tricks to fool other animals

1. Snake mimic caterpillar When it's threatened, this crafty caterpillar puffs up the front of its body so that it looks like a venomous snake, complete with a diamond-shaped "face" and large snakelike "eyes."

2. Potoo This nocturnal bird sleeps during the day and so, to avoid being spotted by predators, it stands completely still and pretends to be the branch of a dead tree.

3. Orchid mantis This meat-eating insect uses its disguise as part of a beautiful pink-and-white tropical flower to attract flies and bees, then gobbles them up.

4. Pygmy seahorse This tiny sea creature is camouflaged to look like a piece of coral. It is so hard to spot that it was only discovered by accident, hiding inside a piece of coral that scientists were studying in a laboratory.

5. Decorator crab This crab decorates its shell with bits of plants, seashells, and other objects it finds on the seafloor so that it perfectly blends in with its surroundings.*

Spot the Orchid mantis!

*Does this make it a snappy dresser?

Animal Smarts

Fourteen ingenious tools that animals use in the wild

1. Spears Chimpanzees use long sticks to hunt other primates and to collect army ants to eat.

2. Fishing rods Galapagos finches use the spines of cactuses to fish for insects in small pools of water.

3. Forks Crows use twigs, feathers, and other pointy objects to reach and grab insect larvae.

4. Hammers Sea otters use stones to crack open mollusk shells to get to the food inside.*

5. Helmets Bottlenose dolphins hold sea sponges in their mouths to protect their snouts as they search for food in the sand on the ocean floor.

6. Toothpicks Chimpanzees use twigs to clean their teeth.

7. Dental floss Some macaque monkeys have been known to use strands of hair to floss between their teeth.

8. Shields Octopuses pick up halved coconut shells and use them as protective shields to hide from predators.

9. Whistles Orangutans hold bunches of leaves to their lips and blow on them to make a high-pitched squeaking sound to scare away predators.

10. Burglar alarms Corolla spiders attach small pebbles to the entrance of their burrows, which may help alert them to vibrations made by nearby animals.

11. Rulers Gorillas use long sticks to measure how deep a pool of water is before deciding whether to cross it.

12. Umbrellas Orangutans use large leaves to shelter from the rain.

13. Toilet paper Orangutans sometimes also use leaves to wipe their bottoms.

14. Fly swatters Elephants pull branches from trees, strip them of leaves, break them down to the right length, and then use them to swat away annoying insects.

*Crows living in Japan have also learned an amazing strategy to crack open nuts. They drop them onto pedestrian crossings and wait until passing cars have driven over them. When the traffic stops, the crows dive down to collect the nuts from the cracked shells and gobble them up.

Clever Canines

Ten of the brainiest breeds of dog

An expert in dog psychology named Professor Stanley Coren created a series of tests to measure the intelligence of different breeds of dog. Coren's tests investigated three kinds of doggy intelligence. First, a dog's ability to perform tasks it was bred for, such as herding animals and fetching objects. Second, a dog's ability to solve problems on its own, such as retrieving food placed beneath an upturned bowl. Third, a dog's obedience in following instructions from humans. Overall, these are the dog breeds that came out on top.*

1. Border collie

2. Poodle

3. German shepherd

4. Golden retriever

5. Doberman pinscher

6. Shetland sheepdog

7. Labrador retriever

8. Papillon

9. Rottweiler

10. Australian cattle dog

*The three dog breeds that received the lowest scores on Coren's tests were the English bulldog, Basenji, and Afghan hound.

Working Like a Dog

Seven animals that do useful jobs

1. Mouse-hunting cats

Employed to: Keep mice and other rodents away from 10 Downing Street, the official home of the UK Prime Minister. The first Chief Mouser (its official title) was appointed to this key role in the 1500s during the reign of King Henry VIII.

2. Medical detecting dogs

Employed to: Use their extraordinary sense of smell to sniff out signs of various medical conditions in human beings. These include cancer, low blood sugar levels, and depression.

3. Land mine detection rats

Employed to: Find land mines, which are dangerous unexploded bombs hidden under the ground. It takes nine months to train a Gambian pouched rat to recognize a land mine—mostly by rewarding it with bananas. When it finds one, the rat is taught to freeze and make quick scratches on the ground to show its handlers where to find the mine. And because the rat is relatively light and small, there's no danger that it will set off the land mine if it steps on one.

4. Capuchin helper monkeys

Employed to: Help humans with restricted movement or physical disabilities by carrying out practical tasks, such as turning kitchen appliances on and off, dialing a phone, and even scratching a hard-to-reach itch. Training for capuchin monkeys to become human helpers lasts between three and five years.

5. Rooftop lawn-mowing sheep

Employed to: Cut the grass that covers the roofs of houses in the Faroe Islands, North Atlantic Ocean. The islanders line their roofs with layers of turf and grass to help them stay warm and dry. It's then the job of local sheep, not lawn mowers, to munch the grass when it gets too long and keep the roofs looking tidy.

6. Miniature guide horses

Employed to: Help visually impaired humans navigate the world, including guiding them as they walk through busy streets and cross the road. Dogs are better known for being guide animals but miniature guide horses are becoming increasingly popular. They are naturally calm, not easily distracted, and ideal for humans who are allergic to dogs but who are in need of guiding.

7. Ferret electricians

Employed to: Run long wires and cables through underground tunnels that are too small for humans to fit through. Specially trained ferrets have been used to help build oil pipelines, thread wires through narrow tubes at the Peterson Air Force Base in Colorado, and connect sound and lighting cables beneath a pop concert stage in London, UK.

Speed Merchants

Ten of the fastest animals on land

1. **Cheetah***—75 mph (120 km/h)

2. **Pronghorn antelope**—61 mph (98 km/h)

3. **Quarter horse****—55 mph (88 km/h)

4. **Springbok**—55 mph (88 km/h)

5. **Blue wildebeest**—50 mph (81 km/h)

6. **Indian antelope**—50 mph (81 km/h)

7. **Lion**—50 mph (81 km/h)

8. **Greyhound**—45 mph (72 km/h)

9. **Kangaroo**—44 mph (71 km/h)

10. **Hare**—43 mph (70 km/h)

*A cheetah can accelerate from 0 to almost 60 miles per hour (0 to 100 km/h) in three seconds, which is quicker than many sports cars.

**A quarter horse is an American breed of horse and is the world's fastest over short distances.

Endurance Athletes

Five animals that are excellent long-distance runners

Cheetahs may be the fastest sprinters in the animal kingdom, but other animals have better stamina, which means they can keep going at high speed for longer periods of time. These are the average speeds that certain animals can maintain over a distance of about 20 miles (30 km):

1. Ostrich—30 mph (48 km/h)

Could run a marathon* in: 53 minutes.

2. Pronghorn antelope—30 mph (48 km/h)

Could run a marathon in: 53 minutes.

3. Camel—25 mph (40 km/h)

Could run a marathon in: 1 hour and 3 minutes.

4. Alaskan husky sled dog—15 mph (24 km/h)

Could run a marathon in: 1 hour and 45 minutes.

5. Horse—11 mph (17 km/h)

Could run a marathon in: 2 hours and 30 minutes.**

*A marathon is a long-distance race run over 26.2 miles (42.2 km). The fastest ever recorded marathon time by a human being is 1 hour and 59 minutes by the Kenyan athlete Eliud Kipchoge. Kipchoge's average running speed during a marathon is approximately 13 miles per hour (21 km/h). For more incredible human physical feats, see pages 362–363.

**The town of Llanwrtyd Wells in Wales hosts an annual 22-mile (35-km) man-versus-horse race. Humans have only won the race twice; usually the best runners finish around 10 minutes behind the horses.

Feats of Strength

Six of the strongest animals relative
to their body weight

1. Oribatid mite

Can lift objects: 1,180 times its own weight.

Equivalent to: A human lifting
177,000 cans of soup.*

2. Dung beetle

Can pull objects: 1,141 times its own weight.

Equivalent to: A human pulling
171,150 cans of soup.

3. Rhinoceros beetle

Can lift objects: 850 times its own weight.

Equivalent to: A human lifting
127,500 cans of soup.

4. Leafcutter ant

Can lift objects: 50 times its own weight.

Equivalent to: A human lifting
7,500 cans of soup.

5. Gorilla

Can lift objects: 10 times its own weight.

Equivalent to: A human lifting
1,500 cans of soup.

6. Tiger

Can lift objects: Twice its own body weight.

Equivalent to: A human lifting
300 cans of soup.

Mighty leafcutter ants can carry
leaves and other creatures that
are much bigger than themselves.

*This calculation uses 137 pounds (62 kg) as the
global average human weight and a can of soup
weighing 14.5 ounces (415 g).

Liftoff

How far eight animals can jump relative to the size of their bodies

1. Flea—200 times its body length.

Equivalent to: A human jumping the length of 33 buses in a single bound.*

2. Tree frog—150 times its body length.

Equivalent to: A human jumping across two and a half soccer fields.

3. Jumping spider—100 times its body length.

Equivalent to: A human jumping the length of ten train cars.

4. Kangaroo rat—27 times its body length.

Equivalent to: A human jumping the length of two blue whales.

5. Grasshopper—20 times its body length.

Equivalent to: A human jumping the length of a basketball court.

6. Impala—8 times its body length.

Equivalent to: A human jumping the length of three cars parked end to end.

7. Kangaroo—6 times its body length.

Equivalent to: A human jumping the length of a bus.

8. Snow leopard—6 times its body length.

Equivalent to: A human jumping the length of nine shopping carts.

*The longest recorded jump by a human being is 29.36 feet (8.95 m), by the American athlete Mike Powell, which was around four and a half times his body length.

Fly Like the Wind

Ten of the fastest animals in the air

1. **Peregrine falcon**—
    200 mph (320 km/h)*

2. **Golden eagle**—150 mph (241 km/h)

3. **Gyrfalcon**—130 mph (209 km/h)

4. **White-throated needletail swift**—
    105 mph (170 km/h)

5. **Eurasian hobby**—100 mph (160 km/h)

6. **Mexican free-tailed bat**—
    100 mph (160 km/h)**

7. **Frigatebird**—95 mph (153 km/h)

8. **Pigeon**—93 mph (150 km/h)

9. **Spur-winged goose**—
    88 mph (142 km/h)

10. **Gray-headed albatross**—
    79 mph (127 km/h)

Peregrine falcon

*The peregrine falcon is the fastest-moving animal on Earth and travels at more than twice the speed of a cheetah.

**The birds at the top of this list achieve their fastest speeds when they are diving down vertically toward their prey, thanks to the force of gravity. It's thought that the record for fastest horizontal flying—in which an animal uses only its own muscles to generate speed—is held by the Mexican free-tailed bat, which is also the world's fastest mammal.

Follow the Crowd

Six animals that form giant swarms and how many are invited to the party

1. Desert locusts—billions

Desert locusts are usually solitary creatures. But when a lack of food forces them together, the locusts change color (from brown and green to black and yellow) and gather in billion-strong swarms that can munch through all the vegetation in a field in a matter of minutes.

2. Herring—billions

Lots of species of fish swim together in vast groups called "schools." A single school of red herring can contain several billion fish and occupy an area of sea measuring 1.2 cubic miles (5 cubic km).

3. Mexican free-tailed bats—millions

Giant colonies of Mexican free-tailed bats are usually found in caves. However, one colony of more than a million bats lives beneath a bridge in the city of Austin, Texas, where the bats have become a popular tourist attraction.

4. Monarch butterflies—millions

Each winter in America, tens of millions of monarch butterflies migrate south in search of warmer weather. Some populations of these butterflies migrate to Mexico, while others head towards the California coast.

5. Red crabs—millions

Each year on Christmas Island in the Indian Ocean, around 45 million red crabs emerge from the rain forest and scuttle on a 5-mile (8-km) journey to the sea, where they will mate to produce . . . even more red crabs!*

6. Starlings—thousands

Starlings often fly together in huge flocks at dusk, swooping across the sky in spectacular aerial displays. A flock of starlings can contain anything from a few hundred to tens of thousands of birds.**

*During the time of the red crab migration, some roads are closed on Christmas Island so that the crabs can cross without being disturbed (or run over).

**A flock of starlings is known as a "murmuration."

Globetrotters

Eight animals that go on long migrations across land, sea, and air"

A migration is a seasonal movement of animals from one part of the world to another. Animals migrate for a variety of reasons. These include finding food, mating, and giving birth to babies.

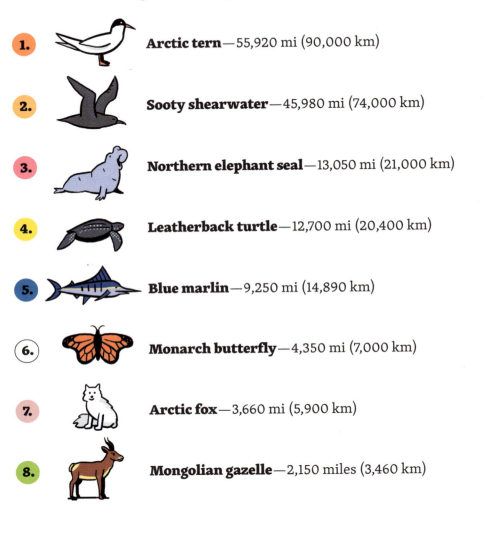

1. **Arctic tern**—55,920 mi (90,000 km)

2. **Sooty shearwater**—45,980 mi (74,000 km)

3. **Northern elephant seal**—13,050 mi (21,000 km)

4. **Leatherback turtle**—12,700 mi (20,400 km)

5. **Blue marlin**—9,250 mi (14,890 km)

6. **Monarch butterfly**—4,350 mi (7,000 km)

7. **Arctic fox**—3,660 mi (5,900 km)

8. **Mongolian gazelle**—2,150 miles (3,460 km)

Right: This world map shows the migration routes of the animals in the list. Match up the colors of the arrows with the colors of the circles next to each animal to find out where they travel.

" To find out about people who have been on extraordinary journeys, see pages 356–357. Or for the fastest journeys around the world using different machines, see page 306.

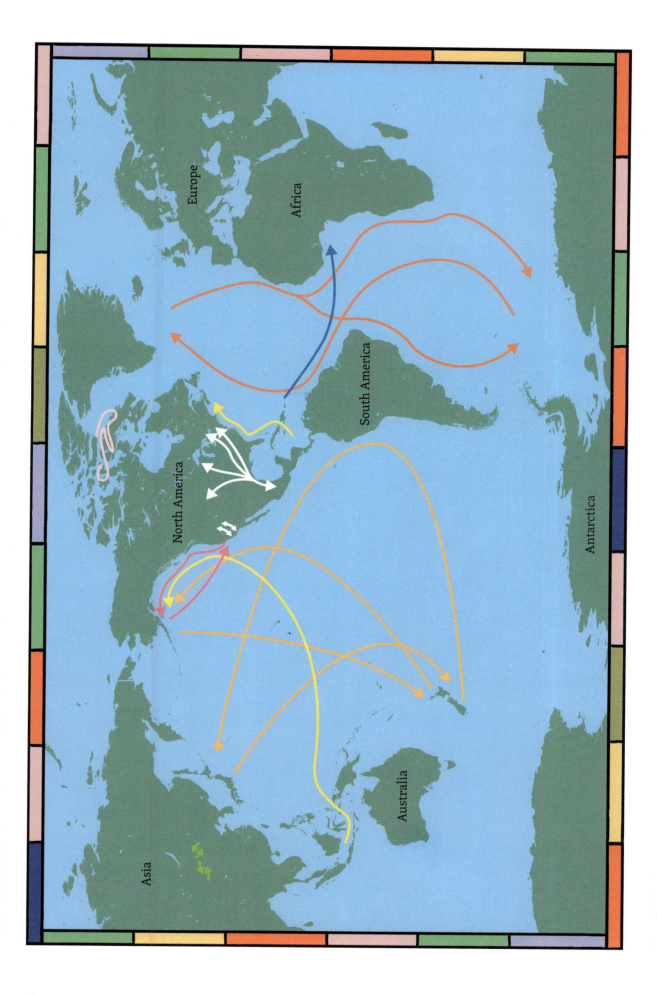

Bugging Out

The world of insects in numbers

1.4 billion The number of insects there are for every single human being on Earth.*

400 million The number of years that insects have been alive on Earth. This means that insects predate dinosaurs and flowering plants.

8 million The number of leafcutter ants that can live in a single colony.

2 million The number of flowers honeybees must visit to make roughly one pound of honey.

1.5 million The number of species of insect that have been discovered so far. Scientists estimate that there may be as many as 9 million more.

40,000 The number of eggs a queen termite can lay in a day, which is roughly one egg every two seconds.

10,000 The approximate number of species of ant on Earth.

40 The approximate percentage of insects that are beetles.

6 The number of legs all adult insects have.

Left: As bees fly through the air, their bodies become charged with static electricity. When they visit flowers this charge helps pollen to stick to them.

*The weight of all the insects in the world is around 70 times heavier than the weight of all the humans.

Team Players

The four types of ant and the different jobs they do

1. Queen ants lay eggs—up to 300,000 in just a few days.

2. Male drone ants mate with the queen (then die shortly afterward).

3. Female worker ants build and maintain the nest, find and gather food, take care of the queen and the larvae she produces, and defend the colony from attack.

4. Winged male and female ants fly away to form other colonies.*

*Some of the surviving flying female ants will become the queens of new colonies.

Beetlemania!

Soldier beetle

One hundred awesome beetles

The world is full of beetles—they are a great example of the amazing diversity of life on Earth. Between 300,000 and 400,000 species have been described so far and some scientists predict that there are more than 2.5 million species still waiting to be discovered.*

1. Acorn weevil
2. Alfalfa weevil
3. Ant beetle
4. Ant-like flower beetle
5. Bark beetle
6. Bark-gnawing beetle
7. Bess beetle
8. Billbug
9. Black oil beetle
10. Blister beetle
11. Bloody-nosed beetle
12. Blue fungus beetle
13. Boll weevil
14. Bombardier beetle
15. Borer beetle
16. Branch and twig borer
17. Carrion beetle
18. Case-bearing leaf beetle
19. Chafer beetle
20. Checkered beetle
21. Click beetle
22. Cobalt milkweed beetle
23. Colorado potato beetle

Colorado potato beetle

24. Comb-clawed beetle
25. Common asparagus beetle
26. Common furniture beetle
27. Common red soldier beetle
28. Confused flour beetle
29. Cucumber beetle
30. Darkling beetle
31. Deathwatch beetle
32. Dermestid beetle
33. Devil's coach horse beetle
34. Dogbane beetle
35. Dung beetle
36. Drugstore beetle
37. Eastern Hercules beetle
38. Feather-winged beetle
39. Firefly
40. Flat bark beetle
41. Flat grain beetle
42. Flea beetle
43. Flower chafer beetle
44. Fog-basking darkling beetle
45. Fruitworm beetle
46. Fungus weevil
47. Giraffe weevil**
48. Golden tortoise beetle
49. Grain weevil
50. Great diving beetle
51. Green June beetle
52. Ground beetle
53. Hairy fungus beetle

Scarab beetle

Dogbane beetle

Flower chafer beetle

Jewel weevil

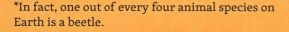

---

*In fact, one out of every four animal species on Earth is a beetle.

**The giraffe weevil has the longest neck of any insect. It takes up more than half of its 1-inch- (2.5-cm-) long body.

Bess beetle

54. Harlequin beetle	**84.** Spider beetle
55. Hister beetle	**85.** Spotted asparagus beetle
56. Japanese beetle	**86.** Spotted cucumber beetle
57. Jeweled frog beetle	**87.** Stag beetle
58. Jewel weevil	**88.** Tansy beetle
59. June beetle	**89.** Telephone-pole beetle
60. Larder beetle	**90.** Tiger beetle
61. Leaf beetle	**91.** Titan beetle
62. Leaf-rolling weevil	**92.** Tortoise beetle
63. Lizard beetle	**93.** True weevil
64. Long-horned beetle	**94.** Tumbling flower beetle
65. Mealworm beetle	**95.** Varied carpet beetle
66. Metallic wood-boring beetle	**96.** Violin beetle
67. Minotaur beetle	**97.** Water scavenger beetle
68. New York weevil	**98.** Wheat weevil
69. Oedemerid beetle	**99.** Whirligig beetle
70. Potato beetle	**100.** Yellow longhorn beetle
71. Powderpost beetle	
72. Predaceous diving beetle	
73. Red-spotted longhorn beetle	
74. Rhinoceros beetle	
75. Rove beetle	
76. Sap beetle	
77. Scarab beetle	
78. Seven-spotted ladybug	
79. Sexton beetle	
80. Shining leaf chafer beetle	
81. Silken fungus beetle	
82. Skin beetle	
83. Soldier beetle	

Blue fungus beetle

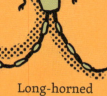

Long-horned beetle

Minotaur beetle

Cucumber beetle

Giraffe weevil

Checkered beetle

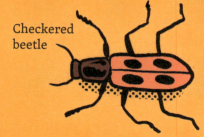

Meganeura

Creepy-Crawlies

Four supersized creatures that terrorized the Earth millions of years ago

At times in its prehistoric past, there was a lot more oxygen in Earth's atmosphere than there is today. Some scientists think this extra oxygen gave some types of animals, such as insects and crustaceans, the energy to grow far bigger than similar species that are alive now. Here are some truly monstrous examples.

1. *Anomalocaris* — 25 times bigger than a modern shrimp

Size: Almost 6 ft (2 m) long.

Lived: 490 million years ago.

Looking like a cross between a squid and a giant shrimp, *Anomalocaris* was a strange-looking underwater predator with big eyes. It used the two large stalks, or mandibles, that extended out in front of its mouth to pull its prey toward its razor-sharp teeth.

2. *Jaekelopterus* — 40 times bigger than a modern-day scorpion

Size: 8 ft (2.4 m) long.

Lived: 390 million years ago.

Jaekelopterus was a supersized sea scorpion that hunted its prey along the seabed. Scientists think that some prehistoric fish evolved bony armor just to protect themselves from this enormous predator.

3. *Arthropleura* — 100 times bigger than a modern-day millipede

Size: More than 8.5 ft (2.6 m) long.

Lived: About 300 million years ago.

Think of a centipede or millipede. Now imagine one as big as a crocodile. Meet *Arthropleura*, the largest known invertebrate* ever to live on land. You will probably be relieved to hear that this enormous millipede only ate plants.

4. *Meganeura* — 12 times bigger than a modern-day dragonfly.

Size: Its body was 17 in (43 cm) long, while its wings were even bigger, stretching to 2.3 ft (70 cm).**

Lived: 298 million years ago.

The monster dragonfly was probably the largest insect in history. It was so big that it may have eaten animals as large as frogs and squirrels.

*Invertebrates are animals that don't have a backbone, such as insects, crabs, and worms.

**Like a modern dragonfly, *Meganeura* could flap its front and back wings separately, which allowed it to hover and fly both forward and backward.

Jaws

Ten of the biggest species of shark

1. **Whale shark**—45 ft (13.7 m)*
2. **Basking shark**—40 ft (12.3 m)
3. **Greenland shark**—24 ft (7.3 m)
4. **Pacific sleeper shark**—23 ft (7 m)
5. **Great white shark**—21 ft (6.4 m)
6. **Great hammerhead shark**— 20 ft (6.1 m)
7. **Thresher shark**—20 ft (6 m)
8. **Tiger shark**—18 ft (5.5 m)
9. **Cow shark**—16 ft (4.8 m)
10. **Bigeye thresher shark**—15 ft (4.6 m)

Jaws Junior

Ten of the smallest species of shark

1. **Dwarf lanternshark**—7 in (17 cm)
2. **Green lanternshark**—9 in (23 cm)
3. **African lanternshark**—10 in (24 cm)
4. **Broadnose catshark**—10 in (24 cm)
5. **Spined pygmy shark**—10 in (24 cm)
6. **Pygmy shark**—11 in (27 cm)
7. **Thorny lanternshark**—11 in (27 cm)
8. **Granular dogfish**—11 in (27 cm)
9. **Longnose pygmy shark**—11 in (27 cm)
10. **Short-tail lanternshark**—17 in (42 cm)

Whale shark

*The whale shark is the largest shark in the world and about as long as a school bus. Don't be scared if you meet one, though. It only feeds on tiny marine animals called plankton.

Deep Blue

Blue whales in numbers

40 million The number of shrimp-like krill a blue whale can eat in a day.

350,000 The blue whale's total weight in pounds (160,000 kg), which is roughly the same as 2,200 human beings or 17 African elephants.

25,000 The approximate number of blue whales living in the wild.

1,320 The amount of air in gallons (5,000 l) that blue whales can breathe into their lungs. An adult human's lungs can hold 1.6 gallons (6 l).

400 The weight of a blue whale's heart in pounds (180 kg).*

200 The weight in pounds (90 kg) that a baby blue whale gains each day as it grows, which is more than the weight of some adult humans.

100 The length of a blue whale in feet (30 m), which is about as long as a Boeing 737 airplane.

80–90 The lifespan of a blue whale in years.

*A blue whale's blood vessels are so wide you could swim through them.

Absent Friends

One hundred species of animal that have become extinct in recent times

Wildlife organizations check on endangered species to see how many are still alive.* However, it is difficult to find and keep track of insects, fish, birds, and other smaller animals. So although lists of endangered and extinct species are based on researchers' best estimates, they can sometimes be proved wrong by later studies. Here are just 100 of the animals that we think are now extinct.

1. Ainsworth's salamander
2. Alagoas foliage-gleaner (bird)
3. American chestnut moth
4. Atlas bear
5. Bali tiger
6. Barbary lion
7. Big-eared hopping mouse
8. Blackfin cisco (fish)
9. Blue walleye (fish)
10. Bonin pipistrelle (bat)
11. Bramble Cay melomys (rodent)
12. Broad-faced potoroo (marsupial)
13. Bubal hartebeest (antelope)
14. Bulldog rat
15. Candango mouse
16. Cape lion
17. Cape Verde giant skink (lizard)
18. Captain Cook's bean snail
19. Caribbean monk seal
20. Carolina parakeet
21. Cascade funnel-web spider
22. Caspian tiger
23. Castle Lake caddisfly (insect)
24. Catarina pupfish
25. Christmas Island pipistrelle (bat)
26. Corquin robber frog
27. Crescent nail-tail wallaby
28. Cryptic treehunter (bird)
29. Dark flying fox (bat)
30. Desert rat-kangaroo
31. Durango shiner (fish)
32. Eastern elk
33. Eastern hare-wallaby
34. Falklands wolf
35. Giant vampire bat
36. Golden toad
37. Graceful priapella (fish)
38. Gravenche (fish)
39. Great auk (bird)
40. Gunther's streamlined frog
41. Harelip sucker (fish)
42. Heath hen
43. Hula bream (fish)
44. Indefatigable Galapagos mouse
45. Indochinese warty pig
46. Japanese sea lion
47. Javan tiger
48. Kawekaweau (lizard)
49. Kona giant looper moth

*It is estimated that around a quarter of all mammal species on Earth are currently at risk of extinction.

50. Lake Pedder earthworm
51. Laughing owl
52. Laysan honeycreeper (bird)
53. Lesser bilby (marsupial)
54. Levuana moth
55. Maiden rocksnail
56. Mauritius wood pigeon
57. Mount Glorious day frog
58. Mount Matafao different snail
59. Navassa rhinoceros iguana
60. Nearby pearly mussel (mollusk)
61. New Zealand grayling (fish)
62. Norfolk starling (bird)
63. Northern gastric-brooding frog
64. O'ahu tree snail
65. Paradise parrot
66. Passenger pigeon
67. Peñasco least chipmunk
68. Pig-footed bandicoot (mammal)
69. Pinta Island tortoise**
70. Puerto Rican hutia (rodent)
71. Pyrenean ibex
72. Quagga (zebra-like mammal)
73. Rabbs' fringe-limbed tree frog
74. Ridley's stick insect
75. Rocky Mountain locust
76. Rodrigues giant tortoise
77. Round Island burrowing boa
78. Sandhills crayfish

79. Sardinian pika (mammal)
80. Schomburgk's deer
81. Selmunett lizard
82. Siamese flat-barrelled catfish
83. Silver trout
84. Sloane's urania (butterfly)
85. Sooty crayfish
86. Spectacled cormorant (bird)
87. Southern gastric-brooding frog
88. Stephens Island wren
89. Saint Helena giant earwig
90. Syrian wild ass
91. Tasmanian tiger
92. Tecopa pupfish
93. Thicktail chub (fish)
94. Toolache wallaby
95. Vietnamese Javan rhinoceros
96. Western black rhinoceros
97. White-footed rabbit-rat
98. Xerces blue (butterfly)
99. Yellowfin cutthroat trout
100. Yunnan lake newt

**The last known purebred Pinta Island tortoise died in captivity in 2012, at the age of 100. He was known as Lonesome George.

Celebrity Creatures

Ten animals that won a place in history

1. Incitatus the horse (41 CE)

According to some historians, the Roman emperor Caligula tried to appoint his horse Incitatus to the role of consul—one of the most important political jobs in the Roman Empire.

2. Clara the rhinoceros (1740s)

Given as a pet to the head of a Dutch trading company, Clara later became famous across Europe as one of the first rhinoceroses to be widely seen by the public there.*

3. Wolfgang Amadeus Mozart's starling (1780s)

The Austrian composer taught the starling to sing some of his pieces of music.

4. Lord Byron's bear (1800s)

Byron took a tame bear with him to study at Cambridge University in the UK because they wouldn't allow him to bring his dog.

5. Poll the parrot (1840s)

President Andrew Jackson's pet parrot was known for repeating rude words.

6. Mrs. O'Leary's cow (1870s)

For many years this unfortunate animal was blamed for starting the Great Chicago Fire of 1871 by kicking over a lantern and setting its stall on fire.**

7. Cher Ami the pigeon (1910s)

Cher Ami saved the lives of a stranded group of American soldiers in the First World War by flying a message through enemy lines to US headquarters with details of the soldiers' location. Cher Ami was awarded the French Croix de Guerre medal for its bravery.

8. Hachikō the dog (1920s)

This remarkably loyal Japanese Akita dog would walk to the station each day to meet its owner as he returned from work. After the owner's death, Hachikō continued visiting the station for the next nine years, hoping to meet him there.

9. Unsinkable Sam the cat (1940s)

According to a popular story told during the Second World War, Sam the cat had the misfortune of being on board three different warships that were each sunk by the enemy (the first ship was German and the other two were British). The story says that Sam managed to float to safety on pieces of wreckage all three times." Sam's portrait is on display at the National Maritime Museum in London, UK.***

10. Tardar Sauce, aka "Grumpy Cat" (2010s)

This frowning feline became world-famous when her picture was shared millions of times on the Internet. Her expression was actually caused by two medical conditions—an underbite and feline dwarfism. It is likely that she was actually a perfectly happy cat.

---

*Clara was so popular she even started a fashion trend in Paris, with women styling their hair *à la rhinocéros* by adding a ribbon or feathers to look like a rhinoceros's horn.

**However, historians now think a man called Daniel "Peg Leg" Sullivan was responsible for starting the fire, and in 1997 the Chicago City Council officially apologized for the mistake.

"To learn about an unsinkable human, see page 359.

***After being saved from his third sunken ship, Sam was described by his rescuers as being "angry but quite unharmed."

Grumpy Cat

Animal Fantasies

Fifteen popular myths about animals—debunked

1. Dogs only see in black and white. False! They can't see the full range of colors that humans can but they can see yellows, blues, and grays.

2. When they're threatened, ostriches hide by burying their heads in the sand. False! Ostriches can't nest in trees, so instead they dig holes in the ground for their eggs. They sometimes stick their heads into the holes to move their eggs around, which is probably what started the myth.

3. Bats are blind. False! Although they use echolocation to navigate, they can also see.

4. Anteaters suck up ants through their long noses. False! They lap them up with their sticky tongues.

5. Humans accidentally swallow eight spiders per year while they're asleep. False! It can happen, but it's very unlikely that a spider would want to jump into your mouth while you're asleep any more than it would while you're awake.

6. Earwigs lay their eggs inside people's ears. False! Despite the name, earwigs prefer to lay their eggs in moist soil or under the bark of trees.

7. Mice love cheese. False! They will eat it but they much prefer sweet foods.

8. Bulls get angry when they see the color red. False! This myth is connected to the tradition of Spanish bullfighting, where matadors twirl a red cape in front of the bull. Studies suggest that it is the quick movement of the cape, rather than the color, that causes the bull to charge. Bulls, like most mammals, can't see the color red.

9. All bees die after inflicting a single sting. False! This is true of honeybees but not of other species.

10. Turkeys can't fly. False! They don't usually travel farther than 300 feet (90 m) but they can fly at speeds of 55 miles per hour (88 km/h).

11. Wolves howl at the Moon. False! They do howl at night simply because that's when they're most active.

12. Camels carry water in their humps. False! Their humps store fat instead, allowing a camel to survive for days in the desert without eating any food.

13. Owls can spin their head around a full 360 degrees. False! They can, however, rotate their heads a long way— about 270 degrees.

14. Goldfish can't remember things that happened longer than a second ago. False! In fact, goldfish have relatively good memories and have been taught by scientists to operate tiny levers, recognize the presence of their owners, and remember the way out of underwater mazes.

15. Cats only purr when they're pleased. False! Cats also purr when they're hungry, unhappy, or recovering from injury. Researchers think that the low frequency of a cat's purr may work as a self-healing mechanism that improves the strength and health of its bones.

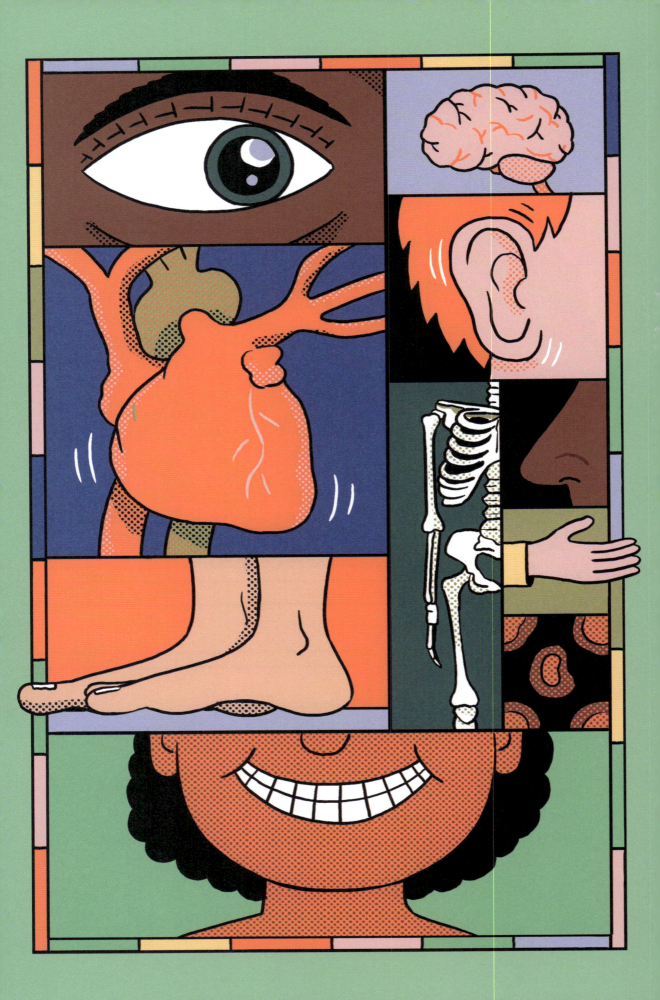

Chapter 5

The Body

A list of things you'll encounter in this chapter:

The longest human fingernail

Golden blood

Dreams about flying

Brain cleaning

Fruit DNA*

People who see music as colors

Red eyes

Earwax ingredients

Popping joints

Goosebumps

Outie belly buttons

Tricks of the mind

Toe-print patterns

*You have more in common with a banana than you might think!

This Is Your Life!

An average human spends . . .

24 years sleeping

15 years sitting down

14 years working

7 years using a smartphone

4 years eating

4 years walking

18 months going to the bathroom

9 months getting dressed

6 months exercising

6 months in the shower

3 months brushing their teeth

Human Factory

Over your lifetime, your body will make about . . .

4,000,000,000,000,000* red blood cells

9,000 gal (40,000 l) of urine

7,000 gal (26,500 l) of saliva

2,800 gal (10,500 l) of sweat

2,500 lb (11,400 kg) of poop**

45 lb (20 kg) of skin

40 ft (12 m) of hair

Let It Grow

How long different parts of your body can grow in a year

Hair on your head—6 in (15.6 cm)

Your hair doesn't grow at a consistent speed: It grows quicker during summer than it does in winter.

Body—5 in (12 cm)

The body grows at different rates depending on how old you are. On average, boys grow fastest at age 14, and girls grow fastest at age 12.

Fingernails—1.5 in (4.2 cm)*

The speed each fingernail grows is related to the length of the finger, so the nail on your index finger grows faster than the nail on your little finger.

Toenails—0.7 in (1.9 cm)

Scientists think that fingernails grow faster than toenails because they receive a better supply of blood, oxygen, and nutrients.

---

*This is four quadrillion.

**That is roughly the weight of two Asian elephants!

*The longest human fingernail ever recorded was the left thumbnail of Shridhar Chillal from India, which was almost 6 feet (2 m) long.

Sticky Fingers

Eight common* fingerprint patterns

Although every individual fingerprint is unique, human fingerprints can still be divided into these eight general patterns.

1. Plain arch

5. Tented arch

2. Radial loop

6. Ulnar loop

3. Double loop

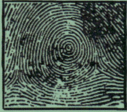

7. Plain whorl

4. Central pocket loop whorl

8. Accidental whorl

Handy Information

The percentage of people who are left- or right-handed, or both*

Right-handed—90 percent

Left-handed—9 percent

Cross-dominant (when the left hand is preferred for some tasks and the right hand for others)—about 1 percent

Ambidextrous (when tasks can be performed equally well with either hand)—less than 1 percent

---

*It is estimated that 65 percent of human fingerprints have loop patterns, 30 percent have whorl patterns, and 5 percent have arch patterns. Have a look at your fingerprints: do they have arches, loops, or whorls?

*Some studies show that you can tell whether a baby will be left- or right-handed in the womb by seeing which thumb it prefers to suck.

High Five!

The human hand in numbers

120 The approximate number of ligaments (tough bands of connective tissue) in a human hand.

100 How many touch receptors* you have in each fingertip.

48 The number of named nerves in the hand, including three major ones—the median, ulnar, and radial nerves.

34 The number of muscles you use to move your fingers: 17 in the palm of your hand and 18 in your forearm.**

30 The number of arteries in the hand, which supply it with blood.

29 The number of joints in the hand.

27 The total number of bones in each hand.

25 The percentage of the motor cortex used to control the muscles in your hands. The motor cortex is the part of the brain that controls the movement of your body.

9 The number of muscles that control the movement of your thumb.

7 The length in inches (18 cm) of the average adult human hand.

Foot Feats

Human feet in numbers

125,000 The number of sweat glands on each foot.

80,000 The number of miles (128,000 km) the average human walks in a lifetime.

7,000 The number of nerve endings in each foot, which explains why they're so ticklish.

127+ The number of ligaments and tendons* in each foot.

75 The percentage of time that your toes are touching the ground while you're walking.

33 The number of joints in each foot.

26 The number of bones in each foot.

19 The number of muscles in each foot.

8 The volume of sweat in fluid ounces (240 ml) that your feet produce in a day.

4 The number of years it takes for your feet to double in length from the time you are born.

---

*Touch receptors are a type of sensory neuron found in the skin. They transmit information to the brain about what the hands feel.

**These muscles are connected to your fingers by tendons. There are no muscles inside your fingers.

*Ligaments connect bones to other bones. Tendons connect muscles to bones.

It's Elementary

The chemical elements that make up your body

Everything in your body—from muscles and organs to bones and blood—is made from combinations of chemical elements. These are the most common elements in your body as an approximate percentage of your total weight:

Oxygen—65 percent

Carbon—18 percent

Hydrogen—10 percent

Nitrogen—3 percent

Calcium—1.4 percent

Phosphorus—1.1 percent

Sulfur—0.3 percent

Potassium—0.25 percent

Chlorine—0.2 percent

Sodium—0.2 percent

Magnesium—0.1 percent

Aluminum*—less than 0.1 percent

Arsenic—less than 0.1 percent

Copper—less than 0.1 percent

Gold—less than 0.1 percent

Iron—less than 0.1 percent

Lead—less than 0.1 percent

Mercury—less than 0.1 percent

Silver—less than 0.1 percent

Uranium—less than 0.1 percent

A Number Two

What poop is made of

Water—75 percent

Dead bacteria—7.5 percent

Food your body can't digest—7.5 percent

Fats—3.5 percent

Minerals and salts—3.5 percent

Bodily Fluid

How much of the human body is made of water

Babies—78 percent

Male adult—60 percent

Female adult—55 percent*

---

*From aluminum onward is a selection of interesting trace elements found in the body. These are present only in tiny amounts.

*One of the reasons that female bodies contain less water than male bodies is due to the type of tissue that they contain. Female bodies have more fat tissue than male bodies, and fat tissue contains less water than other types of tissue.

Breaking Point

How long the human body can survive without . . .

Food—6-8 weeks

A human can go without food for several weeks, as long as they have a regular intake of water to stay hydrated.

Water—3-4 days

The exact length of time depends on how active the person is, how much they sweat, and how much food (which also contains water) they eat.

Oxygen—3 minutes*

The average person can hold their breath for between 30 seconds and 3 minutes. However, some people, such as deep-sea divers, train their bodies to use oxygen more efficiently and so can hold their breath for longer.

Are You a Banana?

The percentage of DNA you have in common with other animals (and fruit)

DNA is found inside the cells of all living things. It's a set of genetic codes that tells an organism how to develop and grow.

Other humans—99.9 percent

Chimpanzees—96 percent*

Cats—90 percent

Mice—85 percent

Dogs—84 percent

Cows—80 percent

Fruit flies—61 percent

Bananas—60 percent

Honeybees—44 percent

Rice—24 percent

* The record for holding a single breath is 24 minutes and 3.45 seconds. The record is held by the Spanish freediver Aleix Segura.

*Among other animals, chimpanzees and bonobos are humans' closest genetic relatives.

Express Yourself

Seven universal facial expressions

Human beings can make up to 10,000 individual facial expressions. However, scientists believe that there are only seven universal ones, each used to communicate one of the seven basic human emotions. This means the seven facial expressions below are used and understood by human beings everywhere, no matter which country or culture they come from.*

1. Happiness

4. Surprise

7. Anger

2. Contempt

5. Sadness

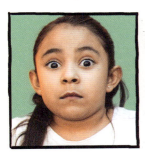

3. Fear

6. Disgust

*To prove that these seven facial expressions are truly universal, a psychologist named Dr. Paul Ekman went to find an isolated tribe in Papua New Guinea that had never met people from the outside world before. He wanted to see if they used the same facial expressions as everyone else. They did!

A Familiar Face?

Five facial features you may have inherited from your parents

1. Hairline shape Look in the mirror at your hairline, which is where the top of your forehead joins your hair. Is the boundary between the two a straight line? Or does it form the shape of a "V"? Hairlines with a V-shape are known as a "widow's peak," and whether you have one depends on whether one or both of your parents do too.

2. Eye color The iris, which is the part of the eye that surrounds the black pupil at the center, gets its color from natural substances called pigments, which are controlled by a person's genes.

3. Freckles Freckles are tiny dots of darker skin, which some people have all the time and others develop after they have spent time in the sun. Freckles can be caused by a combination of inherited genes and the environment.

4. Earlobe attachment Are the sides of your earlobes attached to the sides of your head, or are they dangling free? This is another feature that you've inherited from your parents, which means that if both your parents have attached earlobes, you almost certainly will too.

5. Dimples Look at your cheeks. Do you have small indents in either of them? How about when you smile? If you do, these indents are called dimples. It is common for several members of one family to have dimples and so it is thought to be an inherited feature.

Widow's peak

Widow's peak

Growth Spurts

How babies get bigger inside the womb

A baby typically spends about nine months growing and developing inside its mother's womb. Here's the approximate size of the baby at each stage of the process:

1–3 weeks—so tiny it can only be seen through a microscope

4 weeks—the size of a poppy seed

5 weeks—the size of a sesame seed

6 weeks—the size of a lentil

7 weeks—the size of a blueberry

8 weeks—the size of a kidney bean

9 weeks—the size of a grape

10 weeks—the size of a green olive

11 weeks—the size of a fig

12 weeks—the size of a lime

14 weeks—the size of a lemon

15 weeks—the size of an apple

16 weeks—the size of an avocado

18 weeks—the size of a bell pepper

20 weeks—the size of a large grapefruit

28 weeks—the size of an eggplant

29 weeks—the size of a butternut squash

34 weeks—the size of a cantaloupe

39–42 weeks—this marks the end of the average nine-month human pregnancy, by which time the baby is usually ready to be born

Early Starters

Things babies can do inside the womb

6 weeks The baby's heart has started beating and pumping blood. Its heart beats around 100 times a minute.

8 weeks The baby starts to pee, which means it is swimming around in a mixture of a liquid that includes its own pee. (After 10 weeks, it starts drinking it!) Babies also now have a sense of touch—the first human sense to develop.

9 weeks The baby starts to practice breathing, even though it is still getting all the oxygen it needs from its mother through the umbilical cord.

10 weeks The baby can kick and move its limbs.

11 weeks The baby can taste the food that its mother has been eating, though the baby's sense of taste becomes stronger as its taste buds develop.

12 weeks Some babies can hiccup inside the womb.

13–16 weeks The baby can suck its own thumb, stretch, and yawn.

16 weeks The baby can hear sounds, such as the mother's heartbeat, breathing, and stomach gurgling. The baby can also clasp its hands together.

24 weeks The baby is able to make facial expressions, such as raising and lowering its eyebrows.

27 weeks The baby can open its eyes and see light, although its vision is still blurry. It is at this stage of the pregnancy that babies also start to smile.

28 weeks Scientists think that babies are able to cry if they are startled or upset.

33–36 weeks The baby can use its hands to grip things firmly. It is also able to recognize its mother's voice.

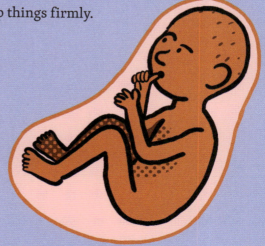

Gray Matter

The human brain in numbers

86 billion The number of neurons (nerve cells) in your brain.

1 billion The number of connections (called synapses) between nerve cells found in a piece of brain tissue the size of a grain of sand.

100,000 The length in miles (160,000 km) of all the blood vessels in the brain.

12,000 The number of brain neurons that adults lose each day that are never replaced.

1,000 The number of nerve impulses a neuron can transmit every second.

268 The maximum speed in miles per hour (431 km/h) that information can travel through the brain.

60 The percentage of your brain that is made of fat.

25 The age at which your brain is fully formed.

23 The amount of power in watts that the brain can generate—that's enough to power a light bulb!

20 The percentage of your body's total energy that your brain uses up.

4 The age at which your spinal cord, which sends messages from your brain to the rest of your body, stops growing.*

0.01 How many seconds it takes a nerve impulse to travel from your spinal cord to your big toe.

Right: These false-color Magnetic Resonance Images (MRIs) show cross sections of a healthy human head. In the bottom image, you can see the spinal cord running up through the neck and into the brain stem, which is the light-blue area in the center.

*As the rest of your body grows, new nerve cells grow and connect to the spinal cord lower down the back. This means that the spinal cord is still the right size for your body.

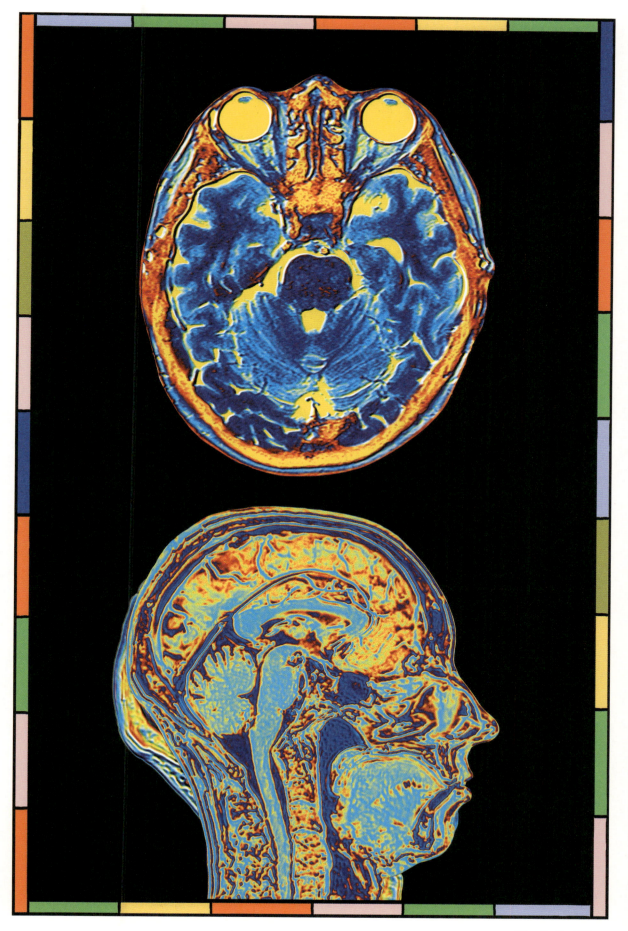

Chasing the Dream

Fifteen common human dreams

Human beings have dreams whenever they go to sleep, even if they can't always remember them. We can also have the same dreams or similar dreams as other people. These are some of the things that humans* often dream about:

1. Falling
2. Being chased
3. Being late or unprepared for an exam
4. Flying
5. Being naked in public
6. Their teeth falling out
7. Missing a bus, train, or plane
8. Meeting a famous person
9. Being in school
10. Getting lost
11. Moving in slow motion
12. Discovering a secret room
13. Seeing spiders, snakes, or other creepy creatures
14. Finding money
15. Going on vacation

The Power of Sleep

Important things that happen to your body while you're snoozing

Brain-tidying Your brain organizes and stores new information as memories.

Emotions The brain regulates your emotions. So, if you don't get enough sleep, your moods the next day can be more extreme.

Detox The body gets rid of the unwanted proteins that build up in the brain while you're awake.

Muscle freeze Your muscles are paralyzed or frozen for some of the time that you're asleep. Some scientists think this is to stop your body from moving while you're dreaming.

Fewer bathroom breaks Your body releases hormones that make you less hungry and stop you from needing to go to the bathroom so often.

Running repairs The body restores energy and helps your cells to repair and grow, by fueling them with a type of sugar called glucose.

Germ-fighting Your immune system releases proteins called cytokines that fight infection and inflammation. It also creates antibodies and immune cells, which destroy harmful germs. This is why it is important to sleep if you are sick.

*Scientists have discovered that some animals also enter a dreamlike state while they're sleeping, including monkeys, dogs, cats, rats, and elephants. However, we have no idea what they dream about.

Mind Games

Four fun optical illusions and how they trick the brain

Sometimes we see things that aren't really there. This is because the brain has to decode the information that it receives from the eyes. When the brain is confused by something, it sometimes changes the way we see it in order to make sense of it. These illusions show how the brain can be tricked.

1. Hermann Grid

What to do: Look at the grid of white lines. Focus on one of the meeting places or intersections where two white lines cross.

What you see: Smudgy gray dots seem to appear at the other intersections of the white lines, although never at the intersection that you are looking at directly. If you try to look straight at one of the gray dots, it will disappear.

How it works: The sharp contrast between the squares and white lines fools your brain into thinking there must be bits of gray in between. The gray bits don't appear in the intersections you focus on because your eyesight is more detailed and accurate when you look at something directly.

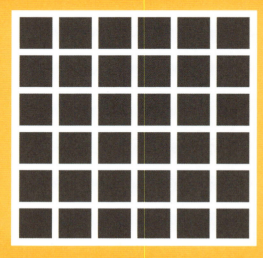

2. Adelson Checker Shadow

What to do: Look at the two squares marked 1 and 2 in Picture A. Decide which square is brighter.

What you see: Most people see square 2 as looking lighter and brighter than square 1. In fact, they are the same color. This is illustrated in Picture B, where a gray line connects square 1 to square 2.

How it works: The picture fools your brain into thinking that the apple is casting a shadow over square 2, and therefore the brain accounts for this shadow by making square 2 appear a lighter color than it really is.

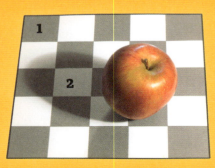

Picture A

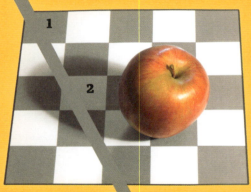

Picture B

3. Shepard Tables

What to do: Look at this picture of two tables. Decide which of the two tabletops is longer.

What you see: At first glance, the tabletop at the top seems to be longer and thinner than the tabletop at the bottom. Now, take some tracing paper and trace the outline of the tabletop at the top. Move the tracing paper so that your drawing is directly on top of the tabletop at the bottom. You'll see that the two tabletops are actually the same shape!

How it works: The table legs fool your brain into thinking the tables are three-dimensional objects. The brain therefore assumes that the end of the table at the top is farther away from the eye, so it must be longer. The brain then perceives the tabletop at the top as longer than it is.

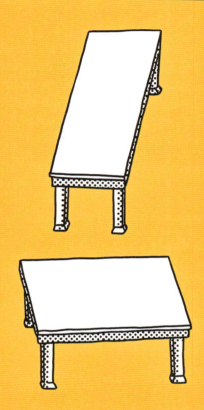

4. Blind-spot illusion

What to do: Hold the book at arm's length and look at the cross and dot below, with your nose pointing in between them. Cover or close your left eye and stare at the cross with your right eye. Now move your face slowly towards the page while still staring at the cross with your right eye.

What you see: At some point as you move closer to the page, the black spot will disappear.

How it works: The black spot disappears because the human eye has a blind spot or "hole" in the retina where the optic nerve enters the eye. This blind spot is always there and your brain automatically fills it in for you with the surrounding colors.

Fear Factor

Thirty phobias

A phobia is an intense fear of an object or situation. Phobias come in many different forms and can affect the body in numerous ways, often making the person feel as if they are in danger. Here are just some of the phobias that people suffer from.

1. Ablutophobia is a fear of having a bath or washing.

2. Acrophobia is a fear of heights.

3. Aerophobia is a fear of flying.

4. Agoraphobia is a fear of public places or large open spaces.

5. Anthophobia is a fear of flowers.

6. Apeirophobia is a fear of infinity.

7. Arachnophobia is a fear of spiders.

8. Astraphobia is a fear of thunder and lightning.

9. Bananaphobia—go on, take a guess!

10. Bibliophobia is a strong dislike or fear of books. As you are reading this, you probably don't suffer from bibliophobia.»

11. Chaetophobia is a fear of hair.

12. Chromophobia is a fear of colors.

13. Coulrophobia* is a fear of clowns.

14. Cynophobia is a fear of dogs.

15. Decidophobia is a fear of making decisions.

16. Genuphobia is a fear of knees or the act of kneeling.

17. Globophobia is a fear of balloons. Some people are scared of the balloons themselves, whereas others are scared of the sound balloons make when they burst. Other people are scared of the squeaking sound made by two balloons rubbing together.

18. Hippopotomonstrosesquippedaliophobia is the fear of long words. It would've been nicer to people who suffer from hippopotomonstrosesquippedaliophobia to pick a shorter word for it.

19. Koumpounophobia is a fear of buttons on clothes.

20. Mysophobia is a fear of germs and bacteria.

21. Nomophobia is a fear or worry about being without your cell phone, or being unable to use it.

22. Ophidiophobia is a fear of snakes.

23. Peladophobia is the fear of going bald or of bald people.

24. Pogonophobia is a fear of beards or bearded people.

25. Scolionophobia is a fear of school.

26. Social phobia is a fear of being at a social event with lots of other people.

27. Somniphobia is a fear of falling asleep.

28. Taphophobia is a fear of being buried alive.

29. Trypanophobia is a fear of injections and hypodermic needles.

30. Turophobia is a fear of cheese.**

»If you do have bibliophobia, definitely DO NOT turn to pages 280–281.

*A famous sufferer of coulrophobia is Daniel Radcliffe, the actor who played Harry Potter.

**If reading about all these phobias has made you worried about developing one, you may have a case of phobophobia, which is a fear of phobias.

Boo!

Five ways your body reacts when you're afraid

Your body's reaction to fear is called the "fight or flight" response.* This is because when you're faced with something scary, you have two choices: confront it (fight) or run away (flight). To prepare you to either face your fear or run away from it, the body automatically does the following things:

1. Your heart beats faster to pump more blood to your muscles and brain.

2. You start breathing faster so that your lungs can take in more oxygen to help your muscles and brain work better. This surge of oxygen and glucose to your muscles can make your arms, legs, and knees feel wobbly. Your body is actually preparing for action.

3. The pupils of your eyes get bigger so you can see and focus better on whatever is making you afraid.

4. You start to sweat. Sweat caused by stress—which is sometimes called nervous sweat—is different from the sweat your body produces to cool down in heat or during exercise. Some scientific studies suggest that the smell of nervous sweat makes people more alert.

5. Your digestive and urinary systems slow down so you can save energy and concentrate on dealing with the thing that's scaring you. Now is not the time for a bathroom break!

*Your body's first reaction to fear is to release a hormone called adrenaline, which activates the body's other physical responses.

Hair-Raising Information

Human hair in numbers

100,000–150,000 The average number of strands of hair on a human head.

100 The average number of hairs that are lost and replaced each day.

90 The percentage of your hair that is growing at any one time. The other 10 percent is "resting."

30 The percentage that your hair can stretch when it is wet.

13 The number of tons (12 tonnes) in weight that all the hair on a human head could support if it was gathered together. That's about the same weight as 18 cows!

10 The number of miles (16 km) the new hair you grow each year would stretch if you laid all the strands in a line.

5 The average lifespan in years of a single strand of hair.

0.02 The average number of inches (0.4 mm) a hair on your head grows each day.

Luscious Locks

The most common hair colors*

Black/Very dark brown hair—85 percent

Brown—11 percent

Blond—3 percent

Red—1 percent

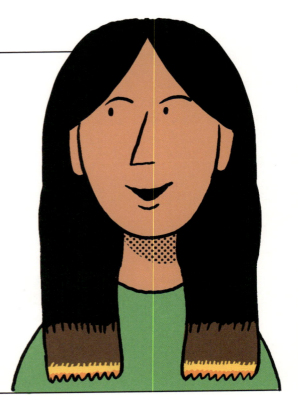

*The color of your hair is largely determined by a natural substance called melanin. As humans get older, we stop producing so much melanin, which causes our hair to turn gray and then white.

Sensational!

The five basic human senses—and five others you might not realize you have

Information about the world outside and the workings of the body is collected and transmitted to the brain through the senses. Scientists think that human beings could have more than 20 different senses.» These are some of the most important:

1. Touch Touch is thought to be the first sense a human develops, after just eight weeks in the womb. The areas of your body that are most sensitive to touch include your lips, tongue, and fingers.

2. Sight The human eye contains more than 100 million light-sensitive cells and can tell the difference between 10 million different colors.*

3. Hearing Your ears are still working even while you're asleep. During sleep, your brain ignores most sounds, only reacting to loud or unexpected noises.

4. Smell You have around 400 types of smelling receptors in your nose and can detect at least a trillion different smells. Humans can also identify other people's emotions, such as fear and disgust, by the smell of their sweat.

5. Taste Adult humans have between 2,000 and 10,000 taste buds, although each one is only alive for between ten and 14 days.

6. Proprioception This is the sense you have of the position and movement of your body. Proprioception enables you to touch the end of your nose with your finger while your eyes are closed.

7. Equilibrioception This allows you to balance, move, and accelerate.

8. Thermoreception This is the way that your body senses heat and cold. Thermoreception applies to the body's awareness of both the temperature of the outside world and its own internal temperature.

9. Interoception Close your eyes for a moment. What can you feel happening inside your body? Is your heart beating fast? Are you hungry or thirsty? Interoception is your awareness of the different sensations and processes happening inside your body.

10. Chronoception When you're really interested in something—such as a fascinating book, like *Listified!*—it sometimes feels as if time is passing more quickly. When you're bored, things can feel like they're taking longer to happen, almost as if time itself is slowing down. This is chronoception: your own personal awareness of time.

» To find out about some amazing animals with super senses, see page 165.

*Synesthetes have a rare condition called synesthesia, in which a person experiences the blending of two senses. For example, some synesthetes can see music as colors.

Color Vision

The estimated percentage of humans with different eye colors

Brown—80 percent

Blue*—8 percent

Amber—5 percent

Hazel—5 percent

Green—2 percent

Gray—less than 1 percent

Red/Violet* *—less than 1 percent

More than one color—less than 1 percent

Eye Caramba!

The human eye in numbers

100 million The number of light-sensitive cells in the eye.

2 million The number of working parts in the eye.

256 The number of patterned ridges and folds in the iris that make it unique.

70 The percentage of the body's sensory receptors (structures in the body that react to stimulus, such as light) contained in the eye.

18 The percentage of the eyeball that is visible.

15–20 The average number of times a person blinks every minute.

5 The average lifespan of one eyelash in months.

3 The number of colors a human eye can see—red, blue, and green. All the other colors are a combination of these three.

1.6 The distance in miles (2.74 km) from which someone with good eyesight can see a candle flame.

Right: The iris is a ring of muscle that controls how much light enters the eye. Eye color is determined by the color of the iris.

*Blue eyes were caused by a random genetic mutation that first appeared in a single human around 10,000 years ago. That one person is the ancestor of everyone who has blue eyes today.

**A very small number of people with a medical condition called albinism—which means they have no coloring in their hair, skin, and eyes—can look as if they have red or violet eyes. This is because the lack of eye coloring allows the red of the blood vessels to show through.

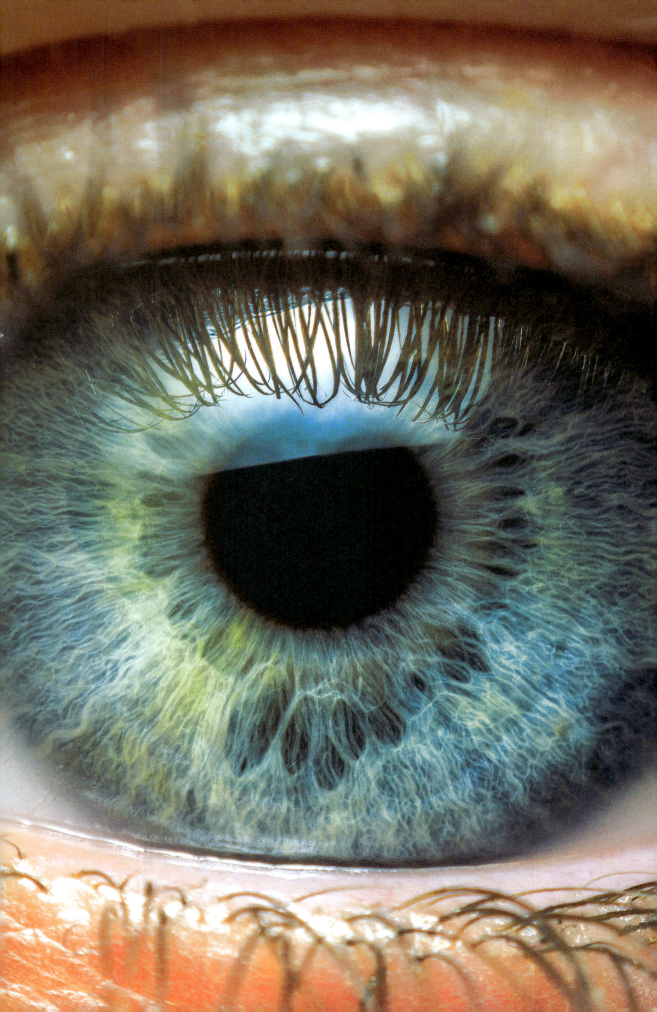

Big Mouth

The mouth and teeth in numbers»

6 billion The estimated average number of individual bacteria living inside your mouth.

5,000 How many years archaeologists estimate human beings have been using toothbrushes, or something that works as a toothbrush, to clean their teeth.

66 The percentage of your teeth that is hidden beneath your gums.

44 The percentage of people who suffer from untreated tooth decay, making it the second-most common human disease after the common cold.

32 The total number of adult teeth.

20 The total number of baby teeth, which often start coming through when a baby is six months old and are gradually replaced by adult teeth between the ages of five and 14.

4 The number of wisdom teeth or third molars that people usually have (although some people have fewer, or even none!).

2 The number of minutes dentists recommend you spend brushing your teeth (twice a day).

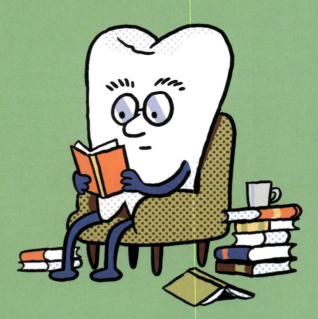

» To find out about the biggest dinosaur teeth, see page 126.

Power Players

The strongest* muscles in the body

Masseter The masseter is the muscle that pulls your jaw shut when you are chewing. If all the muscles in the body were exactly the same size and weight, the masseter would be the most powerful.

Eye muscles The six key muscles that control the position of your eyes have a lot of work to do. For example, if you spend an hour reading this book, your eyes will have made almost 10,000 separate movements.

Tongue The tongue, which is made of eight different muscles, helps you eat and swallow food. It also moves into different shapes when you speak. Your tongue even works while you're asleep, helping to push saliva down your throat.

Heart The heart is the hardest-working muscle in your body. Even when resting, the heart muscles work twice as hard as the muscles in the legs of a person sprinting. Each day your heart pumps more than 1,500 gallons (7,000 l) of blood around the body. In a human lifetime, the heart can beat more than 2 billion times.

Myometrium The uterus, or womb, is the organ in a female body in which a baby starts to grow and develop. The myometrium muscle cells in the walls of the uterus have to be very strong to push the baby through the birth canal when it is born.

Gluteus maximus The gluteus maximus may sound like the name of a Roman gladiator, but it is actually one of the muscles in your butt. It is also the biggest muscle in the human body. It helps your body to stand upright and maintain a good posture. You can feel your gluteus maximus working when you walk up a flight of stairs.

Soleus The soleus muscle is the biggest muscle in your calf, which is the lower part of your leg between your knee and ankle. It is the muscle in your body that can pull with the greatest force.

---

*It is not possible to say with certainty which one part of your body is the strongest because there are different ways to measure muscle strength. These include what scientists call "absolute strength," which means how much force a muscle can create; "dynamic strength," which is how well a muscle can repeat the same movement lots of times; "elastic strength," which is a muscle's ability to move quickly; and "strength endurance," which is a muscle's ability to keep moving for a long time.

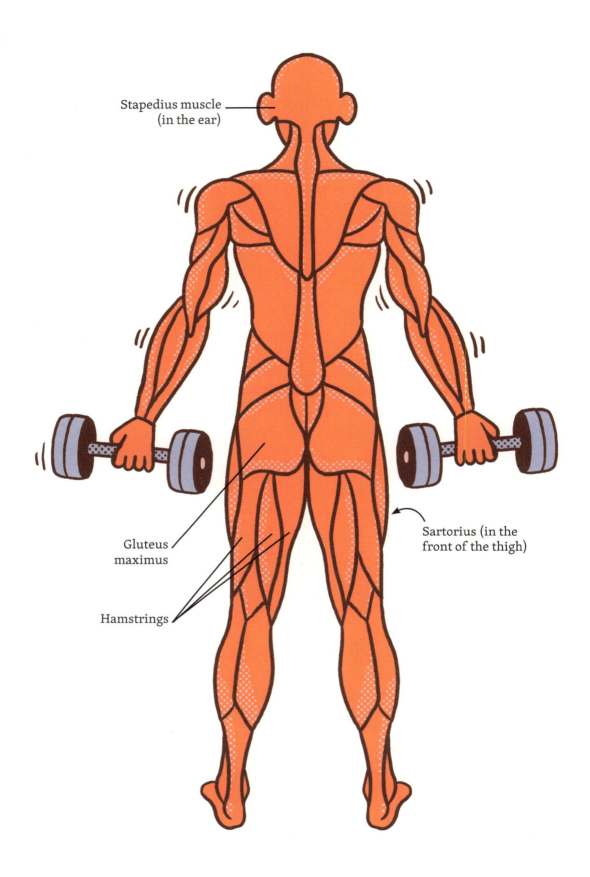

Stapedius muscle
(in the ear)

Gluteus
maximus

Hamstrings

Sartorius (in the
front of the thigh)

Extreme Muscles

Extraordinary muscles that stand out from the crowd

Largest—gluteus maximus

You have one gluteus maximus muscle in each of your buttocks, which is why together they're sometimes called your "glutes."

Longest—sartorius

The sartorius muscle runs diagonally down your thigh from the outer side of the hip bone to the inside of the knee. Depending on how tall you are, the sartorius muscle can be more than 20 inches (50 cm) long.

Smallest—stapedius

The stapedius muscle is in your ear and its job is to support the smallest bone in your body, which is called the stapes. The stapedius muscle is approximately 0.04 inches (1 mm) long.

Most injured—hamstring

Three hamstring muscles run down the back of your thigh between your hip and your knee; they are called the semimembranosus, semitendinosus, and biceps femoris. Injuries to these muscles are thought to be the most common among people who play sports.

Get a Move On

How many muscles your body uses to do things

200—taking a step

The human body has more than 600 muscles and you use about a third of them taking a single step.

100—speaking

You use muscles in lots of different parts of your body to speak, including in your chest, neck, jaw, lips, and tongue.

100—swallowing

You use around 50 pairs of muscles to chew, swallow, and move your food down from your mouth, through your esophagus, and into your stomach.

10—smiling

To make the smallest smile possible—only raising the corner of your lips and your upper lip—takes five pairs of muscles.

8—blinking

The two main pairs of muscles in each upper eyelid that allow you to blink are the orbicularis oculi, which close the eye, and the levator palpebrae superioris, which open the eye. Your eyes blink more than 10 million times a year.

6—frowning

You need just six muscles to make the smallest frown possible, one pair to drop the lower lip and two pairs to lower the corners of your mouth.

Left: Our bodies have more than 600 muscles. The muscles that help us move around are called skeletal muscles.

Pump It Up

The most common* blood types

A blood type, or group, is a way of classifying different types of blood and is something you inherit from your parents. The letters used—A, B, and O—refer to different substances on the surface of the red blood cells. The percentages listed are of the world population.

O positive—38.67 percent

A positive—27.42 percent

B positive—22.02 percent

AB positive—5.88 percent

O negative—2.55 percent

A negative—1.99 percent

B negative—1.11 percent

AB negative—0.36 percent

Seeing Red

Human blood in numbers

4 million–6 million The number of red blood cells in a drop of blood the size of a pinhead.

120 The average number of days a red blood cell circulates in your body.

20–60 The number of seconds it takes a drop of blood to travel from your heart through your body and back around to your heart again.

42 The number of days donated blood lasts in storage.

7 The length of a red blood cell in microns. A micron is 0.000039 inches (one millionth of a meter).

1.5 The average number of gallons (5.7 l) of blood an adult human has in their body.

0.04 The average length of a capillary (a small blood vessel) in inches (1 mm).

0.000007 The number of ounces (0.2 mg) of gold contained in your body, most of which is found in your blood. Don't spend it all at once!

---

*The rarest blood type in the world is called Rhnull. It was first discovered in an Aboriginal Australian in 1961, and since then there have been fewer than 50 people who are known to have had it. The Rhnull blood type is so rare that it is sometimes called "golden blood."

Going with the Flow

Eight useful things carried in the bloodstream*

1. Oxygen The heart pumps blood to the lungs, where it collects oxygen breathed in from the air. The oxygen is then carried by red blood cells back to the heart, where it is pumped throughout the body.

2. Carbon dioxide Blood also collects waste products from around the body—one of which is carbon dioxide. The blood carries this gas to the lungs so that it can be breathed out.

3. Glucose This sugar is one of the main sources of energy for our cells. It's created in the digestive system from the carbohydrates in food.

4. Amino acids These are the building blocks that make up proteins such as antibodies (see below).

5. Antibodies Proteins called antibodies fight off viruses and bacteria by sticking onto these unwanted invaders so they can't do the body any harm.

6. Hormones These chemical messengers tell the body to carry out specific tasks. Insulin, for example, is a hormone that controls the amount of glucose in the body.

7. Urea When the body breaks down protein, one of the waste products is a chemical called urea. It is filtered out of the bloodstream by the kidneys.

8. Minerals Elements such as sodium, potassium, calcium, and magnesium are all carried in the bloodstream. They help to maintain the right blood pressure and stop your blood from becoming too acidic.

It's in the Blood

The four key ingredients that make up human blood

1. Red blood cells These transport oxygen to and from the lungs. The human body produces between 2 and 3 million red blood cells every second.

2. White blood cells These cells help to protect the body from disease and infection. White blood cells make up less than 1 percent of your blood.

3. Platelets The main job of platelets is to stop the body from bleeding. They are called platelets because under a microscope they look like tiny plates.

4. Plasma Plasma is the liquid part of the blood and is about 90 percent water.

Red blood cell   White blood cell

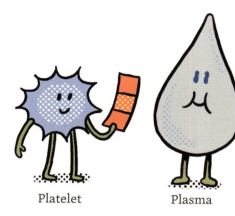

Platelet   Plasma

*Blood is pumped around the body by the heart through a complex network of arteries, veins, and blood vessels called the circulatory system.

Big Bones

The ten longest bones* in the body

1. **Femur (thigh bone)**—
   20 in (50 cm)

2. **Tibia (shin bone)**—
   17 in (43 cm)

3. **Fibula (in the lower leg)**—
   16 in (40 cm)

4. **Humerus (in the upper arm)**—
   14.5 in (37 cm)

5. **Ulna (in the lower arm)**—
   11 in (28 cm)

6. **Radius (in the lower arm)**—
   10 in (26 cm)

7. **Seventh rib**—
   9.5 in (24 cm)

8. **Eighth rib**—
   9 in (23 cm)

9. **Innominate bone (hip bone)**—
   7 in (18.5 cm)

10. **Sternum (breastbone)**—
    6.5 in (17 cm)

Skeleton Crew

Four remarkable bones and
what they're known for

1. Petrous—toughest bone

The petrous, which forms part of the
temporal bones on each side of your skull,
is widely considered to be the densest or
hardest section of bone in the body. Its
main job is to protect the inner ear.

2. Stapes—smallest and lightest

The stapes, which is shaped like a horse
stirrup, is one of the three bones in the
middle ear collectively known as the
ossicles. The stapes is just 0.1 inch (3 mm)
long, so it would easily fit on the tip of
your finger.

3. Hyoid—loneliest

The hyoid bone, which is in your throat, is
one of the only bones in the body that isn't
closely connected to another bone. It holds
your tongue in place so that you can talk,
breathe, and swallow.

4. Femur—biggest and strongest

The largest, longest, and strongest bone
in your body is your femur, or thigh bone.
It connects your hip to your knee.

---

*These are average lengths for each bone of an
adult human. The length of bones in your body
will depend on how tall you are.

Ouch!

The most commonly broken parts of the body

Collarbone Your collarbones are the two long bones that connect your arms and shoulder joints to the breastbone in the middle of your chest. People—and children especially—typically break their collarbones by falling onto one of their shoulders.

Arm There are three bones in your arm—the humerus, the ulna, and the radius. People commonly break the radius and the ulna, which connect the elbow joint to the wrist, when they fall over heavily.

Wrist When you trip, you are likely to put your hands out in front of you to cushion the impact. If you still land heavily, this can break one or more of the 13 small bones in your wrist.

Ankle People typically break their ankle when the joint is twisted or rolled as they stumble or trip.

Feet and toes You can break the bones in your feet and toes with a sudden impact or by putting them under too much strain for a long period of time. The most commonly broken toe is the little toe.

X-rays allow doctors to look inside the body to see if bones are broken. This arm is broken in two places.

Tipping the Scales
The ten heaviest human organs

5. Heart
Average weight: 0.6 lb (300 g)
The approximate weight of: a can of soup

4. Lungs
Average weight of both together: 2.7 lb (1,250 g)
The approximate weight of: a large pineapple

3. Brain
Average weight: 3.3 lb (1,500 g)
The approximate weight of: a steam iron

2. Liver
Average weight: 3.4 lb (1,560 g)
The approximate weight of:
a two-slice toaster

1. Skin
Average weight: 10 lb (4,535 g)
The approximate weight of:
a large bag of potatoes

10. Eye
Average weight: 0.017 lb (7.5 g)
The approximate weight of: a pencil

9. Thyroid
Average weight: 0.04 lb (20 g)
The approximate weight of: a mouse

8. Pancreas
Average weight: 0.15 lb (70 g)
The approximate weight of: a tennis ball

7. Spleen
Average weight: 0.4 lb (175 g)
The approximate weight of: a baseball

6. Kidneys
Average weight of both together: 0.5 lb (260 g)
The approximate weight of: a grapefruit

Spare Parts

Six organs your body can survive without* and why

1. Stomach If the stomach needs to be removed, surgeons can connect the esophagus directly to the small intestine, so that food can still pass through the digestive tract.

2. Spleen The role the spleen plays in storing and recycling red and white blood cells can be managed by the liver and other organs.

3. Colon The colon, which is also called the large intestine, can be removed from the digestive tract in the same way as the stomach.

4. Gallbladder The gallbladder stores extra amounts of a substance called bile, which helps to break down fats. However, your liver can still produce enough bile even if the gallbladder is taken out.

5. Appendix The appendix is a small, worm-shaped organ that is thought to store useful bacteria. However, most people who have their appendix taken out don't notice any difference.

6. Reproductive organs Although humans need reproductive organs to have children, they are not essential to survival.

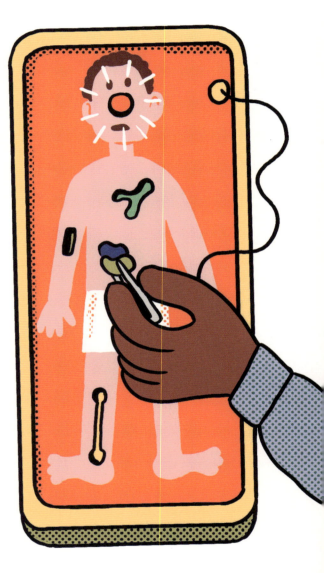

*Most humans have two lungs and two kidneys, but in both cases it is possible to survive using just one.

What's That Stuff?

Nine types of gunk your body produces

1. Sweat Your sweat is mostly made of water and, on its own, doesn't smell like anything. But the bacteria that live on your skin break sweat down into acids that cause the stale smell called "body odor."

2. Rheum (or "sleep") The sticky mucus that can gather in the corner of your eyes while you're asleep is called rheum, and is made of dried-up tears. When you're awake, your eye's automatic blinking spreads the tears around so that the fluid drains away. But when you're asleep, your eyes stop blinking, so the tears collect and dry out in the corner of your eyes.

3. Mucus Also known as snot, mucus is produced in the lining of cells that run from the inside of your nose down to your lungs. It defends the body by trapping bacteria, viruses, and tiny particles carried in the air.

4. Earwax Doctors call this mixture of oil, sweat, hair, and dead skin cerumen, but it is more commonly called earwax. It's formed at the outer part of your ear canal and slowly moves toward the opening of your ear as you move your jaw to chew and talk. Its job is to moisturize the ear and stop unwanted particles from getting inside.

5. Saliva One of the jobs of saliva is to combat tooth decay by reducing the growth of bacteria in your mouth. Another job that saliva does is to help break down food, making it easier to swallow.

6. Pus The thick white ooze that can form inside a pimple on your skin or in a wound is called pus. It's a combination of dead and dying white blood cells, fluid, bacteria, and decomposing body tissue.

7. Vomit Vomiting or "throwing up" happens when your body wants to get rid of the contents of your stomach and the contents of part of your intestines. It typically contains a mix of half-digested food, saliva, and acids your stomach uses to break down food.

8. Feces The digestive system gets rid of all the solid waste matter that the body doesn't need in the form of feces. Other words for feces are "excrement" and "poop."

9. Urine The body collects liquid waste in your bladder, before releasing it as urine (pee).

Hic!

**Ten sounds the body makes
and why they happen**

1. Ringing in your ears A constant ringing sound in your ears is called tinnitus. A common cause is damage to the hair cells inside your inner ear. This can make your brain think that sound waves are entering the ear even when they're not.

2. Whistling in the nose That high-pitched whistling sound you can sometimes hear as you breathe through your nose happens when there is too much mucus—or snot—blocking the flow of air. Blow your nose and the whistling sound should disappear!

3. Sneezing From bright lights to dust, lots of things can make you sneeze. Sneezing is an automatic reflex and, when triggered, a muscle in your chest called the diaphragm forces you to take in a breath of air and then breathe it out very fast. The air from a sneeze can travel at more than 100 miles per hour (160 km/h).

4. Snoring The sound of snoring is caused by your tongue, mouth, throat, and the airways in your nose vibrating as you breathe. It happens because these parts of your body relax while you're asleep, making it more difficult for the air to get out."

5. Burping A burp is the sound of air escaping from your stomach. Burping is often an effect of swallowing large gulps of air while eating or drinking too quickly.

6. Hiccuping Hiccups are caused when your diaphragm pulls down, forcing you to inhale sharply. The "hic" sound is made by your vocal cords, which close suddenly and stop more air from entering. Hiccuping is an automatic reflex that can be the result of lots of things, including eating too much food, drinking soft drinks, stress, excitement, and sudden changes in temperature.

7. Coughing A cough protects your body by clearing your lungs and windpipe of anything that doesn't belong there, like mucus, dust, and fumes. The movement of air being expelled from the lungs creates the sound of a cough. A "wet" sound typically means that the cough has brought up some mucus.

8. Joints popping When you flex or move your joints, they can sometimes make a popping sound. It's nothing to worry about, and some scientists think it is simply caused by a bubble forming in the fluid that lubricates the joint, which then goes pop.

9. Stomach rumbling A rumbling tummy is usually the result of gas and fluid moving through your digestive tract. This is why your stomach can make rumbling sounds both when it's empty and after you've eaten a big meal.

10. Passing gas Flatulence is a release of gas from your digestive tract. The gas comes from air that has been swallowed when you drink soft drinks or eat foods that are difficult to digest. On average, people pass gas between five and 15 times a day.

» Want to know what makes humans stop snoring? Then turn to pages 40–41.

Survival of the Fittest

**Useful body features and abilities that
helped humans thrive and survive**

These brilliant body features and abilities gave ancient
human beings an advantage over other animals.

Sweating Lots of animals produce sweat, but only
a few use it to cool down as humans do. This ability
meant ancient humans could settle in hot climates. It
also prevented them from overheating when hunting
animals over long distances.

Brainpower The human ability to develop tools,
remember useful information, communicate,
and solve complicated problems is all thanks
to our impressive brain.

Throwing No other animal can throw objects with
the same power and accuracy as a human being.
Being able to aim and hurl weapons, such as rocks
and spears, made ancient humans successful hunters.

Opposable thumbs Human thumbs are opposable,
which means that they can be placed opposite the
fingers of the same hand and touch each finger in
turn. Having opposable thumbs gave ancient humans
the ability to make and use tools.

Walking upright Walking on two legs uses just
a quarter of the energy that a chimpanzee uses to
"knuckle-walk" on all fours. It also helped ancient
humans to travel long distances," leaving their arms
and hands free to gather food and hold weapons,
tools, and their babies.

Running long distances Compared to other
animals, human beings are very good at running
long distances. It is thought that ancient humans
used this special ability to chase large animals for
hours, and even days, until their prey eventually
collapsed and died from heat exhaustion.

» To learn about humans that have walked some
really long distances, see pages 356–357.

Completely Useless!

Five things on the body that humans no longer need

All species have unnecessary parts and features of their bodies left over from an earlier time in their evolutionary history. These are called "vestigial features" and humans have more than a hundred. Here are some of the easiest to spot:

1. Third eyelid Look in the mirror at the inside corner of your eye, next to your nose. Can you see a small fold of skin? This is called the plica semilunaris. Scientists think it is the last remaining part of a third eyelid that other animals, such as gorillas, use to keep their eyes clean and well protected.

2. Ear muscles Many mammals such as dogs and horses have muscles in their outer ears to move them toward the source of a sound. Humans still have these ear muscles but are mostly unable to use them.»

3. Wisdom teeth Ancient humans needed lots of teeth to eat raw meat and vegetables. But as human diets changed, our jaws became smaller. This means that often there is not enough room for our wisdom teeth to grow into the jaw alongside the other molars.

4. Tailbone While a human embryo is inside the mother's womb, it develops a tiny tail. The tail usually disappears before the baby is born, and all that remains is a useless stubby bone at the bottom of the spine called the coccyx, or tailbone.

5. Goose bumps If you feel cold or scared, little bumps called goose bumps form on your skin. Ancient humans had thick body hair, which would stand on end when they got goose bumps. This would have trapped a layer of air close to the skin to keep it warm, or could have helped to scare predators away, in the same way that cats puff up their fur to appear larger. But without our ancestors' thick body hair, goose bumps are pretty pointless.

» To find out more about one of these muscles, turn the page and read entry three in Odd Ones Out.

Odd Ones Out

Eight body parts that not everyone is born with

1. Double eyelashes

What they are: An inherited condition called distichiasis causes a person to form a second row of eyelashes immediately below the first.

How common they are: Distichiasis is probably quite rare, but we can't be sure. This is because you can have it and never notice!

2. Preauricular sinus

What it is: A small hole at the top of the ear where the ear cartilage meets the side of the face. The hole is harmless, although it can become infected.

How common it is: Around 1 percent of people have a preauricular sinus, although it is more common in people from certain parts of the world, including Africa and Asia.

3. Occipitalis minor muscle

What it is: A muscle at the back of the skull that once helped our ancient human ancestors move their ears to detect sounds. Now it doesn't really have a function.

How common it is: The percentage of people with an occipitalis minor muscle varies in different parts of the world. Most people from Malaysia, roughly half of people from Japan, and a third of Europeans are born with one. People who have this muscle can wiggle their ears.

4. Cervical rib

What it is: An extra rib that forms above the first rib from a bone in the neck called the seventh cervical vertebra. People can have cervical ribs on the left, right, or both sides of their body. There are usually no noticeable effects.

How common it is: Around 1 in 500, or 0.2 percent of people, have a cervical rib.

5. Sternalis muscle

What it is: A muscle that runs along the edge of the chest.

How common it is: Scientists don't know what the sternalis muscle is for, which is perhaps no bad thing because only 8 percent of people have one.

6. Pyramidalis muscles

What they are: Two triangle-shaped muscles inside your abdomen.

How common they are: Around 80 percent of people have pyramidalis muscles, although they don't serve any important function.

7. Outie belly button

What it is: Belly buttons are formed when the umbilical cord that connects the mother to her baby drops off after birth. A belly button that sticks out is sometimes known as an "outie." Several things, including the shape of the belly button and the fat that sits beneath it, determine whether you have an "outie" or an "innie."

How common it is: One scientific survey found that just 4 percent of people have "outies."

8. Palmaris longus muscles

What they are: These thin muscles, which run between the wrists and the elbows, are so weak that if they're cut or removed from the body, it doesn't make any noticeable difference to your mobility or strength of grip.

How common they are: Most people (or around 85 percent) are born with them.

Going Down

Six things that happen to the body when you dive deep underwater without a diving suit*

1. Diving reflex—at the surface

As soon as your face comes into contact with cold water, it triggers a diving reflex. This sends more oxygen to the vital organs—the heart and brain—and less oxygen to the hands and feet.

2. Heart slows—3 ft (1 m) deep

The diving reflex makes your heart beat between 10 and 25 percent slower. A slower heartbeat helps to preserve oxygen, which is carried in the blood. This is useful because there is no new oxygen to breathe in.

3. Eardrums may burst—13 ft (4 m) deep

You start to feel the water pressure in your ears at a depth of 1 foot (30 cm). At depths of 13 feet (4 m) and more it is possible that the increased pressure will cause your eardrums—a thin membrane in each ear—to burst.

4. Lungs shrink—33 ft (10 m) deep

As you go deeper, pressure squeezes your lungs and compresses the air inside. At a depth of 33 feet (10 m), your lungs are half the size they were at the surface.

5. Body sinks—66 ft (20 m) deep

Once you have reached a depth of about 66 feet (20 m), you start to sink instead of float. This is because the air in your lungs is becoming so squeezed by the pressure of the water.

6. Tricks of the mind—100+ ft (30+ m) deep

At this depth you can experience "nitrogen narcosis"—a feeling of sleepiness and mixed-up thinking also known as the "rapture of the deep." Deep-sea divers sometimes think they see things that are not there—even mermaids!

*When a human dives underwater, the weight of the water presses down on the body. Divers wear what is called an "atmospheric diving suit" to protect against these effects.

Going Up

Six things that happen to the body at high altitude

When climbing a mountain, the higher you go, the "thinner" the air becomes because the oxygen molecules are more spread out. Here's how traveling to great heights can affect the body:

1. Heavy breathing Above 5,000 feet (1,500 m) your body responds to the reduced amounts of oxygen by automatically breathing more quickly and deeply, and by pushing air to parts of the lungs that aren't normally used.

2. Red blood cell production Your heart beats faster and your body produces more red blood cells, which transport oxygen, as well as an enzyme that helps oxygen make its way into body tissues.

3. Bathroom breaks To make room in the body for new red blood cells, the kidneys start working faster to flush out fluids from the body as pee.

4. Weaker muscles Because less oxygen is reaching the muscles, exercise and physical effort are more difficult at this height.

5. Altitude sickness At about 8,000 feet (2,500 m) the body can suffer serious symptoms of altitude sickness.* These include headaches, nausea, and a loss of appetite and coordination. The only cure is rest and giving the body time to get used to the change in oxygen levels.

6. High-altitude sickness At about 18,000 feet (5,500 m), fluid can build up in the lungs and, even more seriously, inside the brain. This is caused by higher blood pressure forcing fluids out of the blood vessels into other parts of the body. High-altitude sickness is very dangerous and can be fatal if not treated immediately by returning to a lower altitude, taking special medicine, or using bottled oxygen.

*You don't suffer from altitude sickness when flying in an airplane because the air pressure and oxygen levels inside the plane are controlled.

Myth Busted!

The truth behind twelve popular myths about the body

1. Your head *doesn't* give off more heat than the rest of your body.

2. Humans *do not* use only 10 percent of their brains. All the different parts of the brain are used at some point during the day.

3. Your eyesight *doesn't* get worse if you read in the dark. Though your eyes can get tired more quickly.

4. Watching TV screens *doesn't* hurt your eyes.

5. Carrots *do not* improve your vision at night.

6. Your stomach *isn't* beneath your belly button. It's higher up the body, behind your ribs.

7. It *doesn't* take seven years to digest a piece of chewing gum. It will pass out of your body in your poop in a couple of days.

8. Dust in your home *isn't* mostly made of dead human skin cells. More than 60 percent of it comes from outside.

9. Hair, fingernails, and toenails *do not* continue growing after death.

10. Sugar *doesn't* make children more excited or energetic.

11. You *won't* catch a cold from going out in the rain. The common cold and flu are both viral infections, so you need to be near someone else who has the virus to become infected yourself.

12. Vitamin C *doesn't* stop you from catching a cold.

You Are One in Seven Billion

Fifteen features of the body that are unique to every human

1. The shape of your skull.*

2. The shape of your ears.

3. The ridges and folds in your irises.

4. The pattern of blood vessels within your retina.**

5. The patterns of your lip print.

6. The shape and positioning of your teeth.

7. The patterns of your tongue print.

8. The sound of your voice.

9. The patterns of your fingerprints.

10. The tiny ridges in the surface of your fingernails.

11. The shape of your bottom when you sit down.

12. The patterns of your toe prints.

13. The order of the genetic codes in your DNA.

14. The smell of your body odor.

15. The way you walk.

*One way scientists can measure this is by seeing how sounds make the skull vibrate.

**The retina is the light-sensitive layer of tissue at the back of the eyeball.

It's a Wrap

How to make an Egyptian mummy

The ancient Egyptians mummified dead bodies* to prepare them for the afterlife. If you were an ancient Egyptian, this is the process that you would follow to make a mummy.

1. Clear your schedule The entire process of mummification can take up to 70 days.

2. Wash the body Clean and purify the dead body—preferably in the River Nile.

3. Mash the brain Make a hole in the skull. Poke a long tool through the hole and wiggle it around to mash up the brain inside. Allow the liquefied brain to drain out through the nose.

4. Take out the organs Make a cut on the left side of the body. Remove the lungs, liver, stomach, heart, and intestines.

5. Wash the organs Now wash the organs in a special type of salt, called natron, to dry them out.

6. Store them in jars Next, place the lungs, liver, stomach, and intestines into separate containers called canopic jars (keep the heart to one side). Each of the jars should have the head of a different Egyptian god on it.

7. Replace the heart Now is the time to put back the cleaned heart.**

8. Stuff the body Fill the body with dried grass, straw, sawdust, and mud so it keeps its shape.

9. Salt the body Cover and fill the body with natron to absorb the moisture and prevent decay.

10. Dry the body Change the natron daily. Do this for 40 days.

11. Clean the body When the body has completely dried out, wipe away the salt and clean it with wine, oils, and scented waxes.

12. Glue any holes Use a sticky resin to seal up the hole that was made to take out the internal organs.

13. Add lucky charms Place a piece of jewelry over the closed wound to stop evil spirits from entering the body.

14. Wrap the mummy First, wrap the head and neck in linen bandages. Then move on to the fingers and toes. Lastly, wrap the arms, legs, and body, using a sticky resin to glue the bandages together. Make sure you have enough bandages— you'll probably need a few hundred yards (meters) at least.

15. Add a mask Place a ceremonial mask over the mummy's face.

16. The mummy is ready Put the finished mummy inside a wooden coffin. Then place the coffin inside a sarcophagus, which is a large stone coffin decorated with sculptures.

17. Add accessories Once the sarcophagus is inside the tomb, surround it with clothes, jewelry, furniture, food, and drink so your mummy can use them in the afterlife.

---

*The ancient Egyptians mummified humans as well as animals that they believed were sacred, including cats, mice, birds, and crocodiles.

**The Egyptians left the heart inside the mummy because they believed that it—and not the brain— was the center of human thought and feeling.

Right: This sarcophagus and mummy date back to about 640 BCE.

Chapter 6

Being Human

A list of things you'll encounter in this chapter:

Pogo-stick-related injuries

A language with 123 words

A bank that stores cheese

Armpit sniffers

A donkey sleeping in the bathtub*

A spaghetto

Faked fairies

A lady wearing size 879 shoes

An ancient lighthouse

The country that eats the most chocolate

A Santa hat

A 159-day chess match

Shakespeare's lost play

*If you do see one, it might be time to call the cops . . .

What Are the Chances?

The odds of fifteen improbable things ever happening to you*

1. Winning the lottery" —around 1 in 300 million**

2. Being killed by a falling coconut—1 in 50 million

3. Being made a saint—1 in 20 million

4. Becoming a parent to identical quadruplets***—1 in 15 million

5. Becoming a billionaire—1 in 2.6 million

6. Winning a gold medal at the Olympics—1 in 662,000

7. Going to the hospital with a pogo-stick-related injury—
    1 in 115,000

8. Finding a pearl in an oyster—1 in 12,000

9. Being injured by a toilet—1 in 10,000

10. Finding a lucky four-leaf clover—1 in 5,076

11. Tossing a coin ten times in a row and it landing heads-side up
    every time—1 in 1,024

12. Being born with 11 fingers or toes—1 in 1,000

13. Cracking open an egg and finding two yolks inside—1 in 1,000

14. Being born with one kidney—1 in 750

15. Being left-handed—1 in 10

---

*This list contains estimated general probabilities. In most cases, the specific probability of these things happening to you will also depend on other factors, such as where you live. For instance, if you live in a country where the plant clover doesn't grow, it is very, very unlikely that you will be able to find a four-leaf clover!

" To find out about someone who was *not* lucky enough to win the lottery (when the rest of his village did!), see page 359.

**This depends on the number of tickets sold in the lottery.

***Quadruplets are four children who are all born to the same mother at the same time.

Lost for Words

Eleven endangered languages that are now spoken by only one person

There are 7,111 languages currently used around the world. Of these, 41 percent are endangered, which means that they are spoken by so few people that they are in danger of becoming extinct.* According to the latest studies, the languages below are spoken by only a single human being.

1. Apiaká, Brazil**
2. Chaná, Argentina***
3. Diahói, Brazil
4. Kaixána, Brazil
5. Patwin, United States
6. Suena, Papua New Guinea
7. Taushiro, Peru
8. Tinigua, Colombia
9. Tolowa, United States
10. Volow, Vanuatu
11. Yámana, Chile

Language Lovers

The ten countries where the largest number of different languages are used

1. Papua New Guinea—840*
2. Indonesia—710
3. Nigeria—524
4. India—453
5. United States—335
6. Australia—319
7. China—305
8. Mexico—292
9. Cameroon—275
10. Brazil—228

*It is estimated that between 50 and 90 percent of the 7,111 languages used today will be extinct by 2100.

**Five of the languages on this list are from the Amazon rain forest of South America, home to more than 300 indigenous cultures with their own languages.

***Blas Wilfredo Omar Jaime from Argentina is the only known speaker of Chaná, a language that was used for centuries by the Chaná people living in modern-day Argentina and Uruguay. Jaime is known as Tató Oyendén, which means "keeper of the ancestral memory" in Chaná.

*Approximately 12 percent of the world's languages are from Papua New Guinea, despite the southwestern Pacific country having a relatively small population of 8.8 million people. This is partly because different waves of settlers have introduced new languages to Papua New Guinea over the last 40,000 years. It is also due to the country's geography. High mountain ranges, dense jungles, and big, fast-flowing rivers have created natural barriers between communities, so that they independently developed their own languages.

Word Power

Eight languages with extraordinary features

1. Silbo Gomero, Spain

Silbo Gomero is used only on the small island of La Gomera, in the Canary Islands. It's a unique language because it's based entirely on whistles. La Gomera has lots of mountains with steep valleys, and using different types of whistles in place of words and phrases is a good way to communicate over long distances.*

2. Archi, Russia

Archi is spoken by around 950 people who live in the village of Archib in southern Russia. In Archi, you can conjugate verbs (words that describe actions) in up to 1.5 million ways. Conjugation is a way in which verbs can be changed to fit different situations. For example, in English, you would conjugate the verb "to eat" as "eat," "eating," "was eating," "have eaten," and so on, depending on the situation you are describing. In Archi, there are many other factors that affect the verb; for example, the verb will change depending on who is doing the eating.

3. Pawnee, United States

Spoken by the indigenous Pawnee people, Pawnee commonly uses words with lots of syllables. For example, the Pawnee word for phone (which is one syllable in English) is: rarácawakataku (which is seven syllables). Some Pawnee words have more than 30 syllables.

4. Rotokas, Papua New Guinea

Spoken by around 4,000 people, Rotokas is thought to have the fewest sounds of any language on Earth. Also, its alphabet has only 12 letters.

5. Nicaraguan Sign Language, Nicaragua

Nicaraguan Sign Language is one of the few languages to have been invented spontaneously, without being influenced by other languages. It was created by children with hearing loss, who were studying together at the Melania Morales Special Education Center in 1979. Unlike other sign languages, which are based on existing spoken languages, the words, grammar, and syntax of Nicaraguan Sign Language were developed by children as they found a shared way to communicate with each other in the playground.

6. Taa, Southern Africa

Taa is an African language that is thought to have more phonemes, or sound units, than any other language. Most of the sound units in Taa are click sounds.

7. Pirahã, Brazil

Pirahã is spoken by fewer than 400 people, all of whom live in the Amazon rain forest. It has only three vowel sounds and eight consonant sounds. It also contains no numbers or words for colors, and verbs in Pirahã have no past tense.

8. Toki Pona, mostly used online

Toki Pona is a new language of cartoonlike symbols created in 2001 by Canadian language expert Sonja Lang. Its aim is to make communication simpler and so it contains only 123 words, the fewest of any language. It is currently used by a few thousand people in online chat groups and on social media.**

---

*Whistling islanders on La Gomera can exchange messages with people up to 3 miles (5 km) away.

**Toki Pona takes around two days to learn.

Ka-ching!

Eight unusual things that have been used as money

1. Cocoa beans These beans, which are used to make chocolate, were sometimes exchanged as currency by the Maya peoples in the 8th century in parts of Mexico and Central America.*

2. Stones Giant disc-shaped limestone rocks called rai stones were used as a form of money on the tiny Pacific island of Yap possibly as early as 500 CE. Each stone can be up to 12 feet (3.7 m) across and some of them weigh more than 5 tons (4.5 tonnes).**

3. Bottle caps In 2005, a beverage company in Cameroon launched a competition in which people could win prizes in exchange for special tokens placed under bottle caps. The prizes ranged from a free beverage to cars and cell phones. When other beverage companies launched similar competitions, bottle caps became so valuable people started to use them like money to pay for taxi rides.

4. Tea Bricks made from compressed tea leaves were used as a form of money in China and other parts of Asia from the 19th century until the 1930s. The value of each brick depended on the quality and rarity of the tea leaves inside.

5. Salt During the early years of the Roman Empire, it was common to pay for things with salt. Salt was rare and expensive because it was difficult to extract from seawater and transport around the world. Salt was used to flavor and preserve food and also as an antiseptic to treat wounds.***»

6. Shells Archaeologists think that humans have been using shells as currency for more than 3,000 years. They still have monetary value in the Solomon Islands in the Pacific Ocean. Here, shells are cut into small discs and collected on necklaces called strings, which are used as payment or gifts. One string is equivalent to approximately 1,000 Solomon dollars, or $125.

7. Playing cards In 1914, the start of the First World War led to a shortage of the metals used to make coins in Germany. To get around this problem, individual towns were allowed to print Notgeld or "emergency money" on materials including playing cards, silk, linen, and pieces of wood.

8. Fish In the 1600s, when the first settlers from England were making their homes in Newfoundland on the east coast of Canada, there was so little money available that people started paying for things with dried cod.

---

*Another financially useful food is Parmigiano-Reggiano cheese, which you can give to the Italian bank Credito Emiliano as a deposit when you borrow money from them. The bank then stores the cheese safely and will give it back only after you've repaid all the borrowed money. Each cheese has its own unique serial number so it can be traced by the police if it is stolen by bank robbers. Or mice.

**The value of each rai stone is determined not by its size but by its history. So the more difficult the stone was to carve and transport, the more valuable it is.

***The modern English word "salary" (which is the fixed amount of money that a worker earns) comes from the Latin *salarium* based on *sal*, the Latin word for salt.

» To find out about a protest that involved a march to collect salt, see page 370.

Odd Jobs

Twelve of the world's most unusual jobs

1. Teddy bear surgeon Some skillful craftspeople are experts in repairing broken or injured teddy bears. These "teddy bear surgeons" can be found working in toy shops or specialist "medical" facilities such as the Leith Toy Hospital in Edinburgh, Scotland.

2. Professional sleeper Hotels in several countries around the world, such as China and Finland, pay people to sleep in one of their rooms for a night and then file a report on how comfy the bed is.

3. Swan counter All the mute swans* in the UK are legally the property of the reigning king or queen. It is the unusual job of two people—the Warden of the Swans and the Marker of the Swans— to count all the mute swans on the River Thames each year, in a 900-year-old tradition called swan upping.

4. Professional line sitter People who don't want to wait in busy lines can pay someone to line up in their place for all kinds of things, from film premieres to the opening of new shops. Once professional line sitters approach the front of the line, they give the person who's paid for their time-saving services a call so they can swap places.

5. Armpit sniffer Professional "odor judges" have the eye-watering job of sniffing people's armpits to test how effective different types of deodorant are in controlling sweaty smells. If you have a sensitive nose, there are similar careers available in sniffing bad breath and stinky feet.

6. Iceberg mover When icebergs break off from polar ice caps, they usually melt slowly into the saltwater ocean. French engineer Georges Mougin had the ingenious idea of towing the icebergs across the ocean with a tugboat so they can be used in hotter parts of the world as drinking water. In what would be a world first, Mougin and a team of glacier scientists are currently working out how to tow an iceberg from Antarctica to the South African city of Cape Town, which often suffers from water shortages.**

7. Waterslide tester Some travel companies fly a specific person around the world to test how fun the waterslides are at different vacation spots. British waterslide tester Tommy Lynch did it for four years, describing it as the "best job in the world."

*There are three species of swan native to the UK: mute swans, Bewick's swans, and whooper swans.

**Mougin estimates that the perfect iceberg for towing would be 3,280 feet (1,000 m) long, 1,640 feet (500 m) wide, and 820 feet (250 m) deep. A glacier of this size contains enough fresh water to supply the whole of Cape Town for two and a half months.

8. Passenger pusher At subway stations in Japan, members of staff wearing white gloves and crisp uniforms have the job of shoving as many passengers as possible into the cars of each train.***

9. Dog food taster Because dogs aren't very good at filling in surveys, it's left to humans to try new flavors of dog food to see how they taste. Pet food tasters are usually experts in food science and write reports on each new recipe's nutritional value as well as saying if it's yummy (from a dog's point of view).

10. Funeral mourner Known officially as a "moirologist," a professional mourner can be hired to attend the funeral of someone they don't know. A moirologist can cry during the service and interact with the other guests. There are many reasons why a moirologist might be called upon, one of which is to give that impression that the deceased was popular and well-liked.

11. Snake milker Snake venom is a valuable substance used in a variety of medicines. But aside from asking the snake politely, how can you get venom from it? The answer is to hire a snake milker, who carefully holds the snake's head while encouraging it to bite down on the edge of a glass beaker. The snake will then release its venom into the beaker, as if it's biting its prey.

12. Bicycle fisher Amsterdam in the Netherlands is a city famous for two things: canals and bicycles. So it's not surprising that more than 10,000 bikes end up in the canals each year. It is someone's full-time job to sail a boat up and down, fishing them out.

***They are known as *oshiya*, which in Japanese means "pushers" or "stuffers." *Oshiya* have to politely let the passengers know before they start pushing them and are only allowed to push their backs or shoulders. Training to become an *oshiya* takes six months.

Big Countries

The ten largest countries in the world, by surface area

1. **Russia***—6.6 million sq mi (17.1 million km²)

2. **Canada**—3.9 million sq mi (10 million km²)

3. **China**—3.7 million sq mi (9.7 million km²)

4. **United States**—3.6 million sq mi (9.3 million km²)

5. **Brazil**—3.2 million sq mi (8.5 million km²)

6. **Australia**—3 million sq mi (7.7 million km²)

7. **India**—1.3 million sq mi (3.3 million km²)

8. **Argentina**—1.1 million sq mi (2.8 million km²)

9. **Kazakhstan**—1 million sq mi (2.7 million km²)

10. **Algeria**—0.9 million sq mi (2.4 million km²)

Small Countries

The ten smallest countries in the world, by surface area

1. **Vatican City***—0.16 sq mi (0.4 km²)

2. **Monaco**—0.8 sq mi (2 km²)

3. **Nauru****—8.1 sq mi (21 km²)

4. **Tuvalu**—10 sq mi (26 km²)

5. **San Marino**—24 sq mi (61 km²)

6. **Liechtenstein*****—62 sq mi (161 km²)

7. **Marshall Islands**—70 sq mi (181 km²)

8. **Saint Kitts and Nevis**— 105 sq mi (272 km²)

9. **Maldives**—115 sq mi (298 km²)

10. **Malta**—122 sq mi (316 km²)

Right: This world map shows the largest countries and the locations of the smallest.

*Russia covers around 11 percent of all the land on Earth.

*Despite being just an eighth of the size of New York City's Central Park, Vatican City has its own stamps, passports, flag, and national anthem.

**Nauru, which is found in the Pacific Ocean relatively near Australia and Papua New Guinea, is the world's smallest island country. For a brief period in the 1960s, it was also the world's richest country in terms of average wealth per person, after valuable underground deposits of phosphate rock were found there.

***To celebrate Liechtenstein's national day on August 15, the reigning prince and princess invite the whole country to a party at Vaduz Castle. Entertainments include a free fireworks display and a festival.

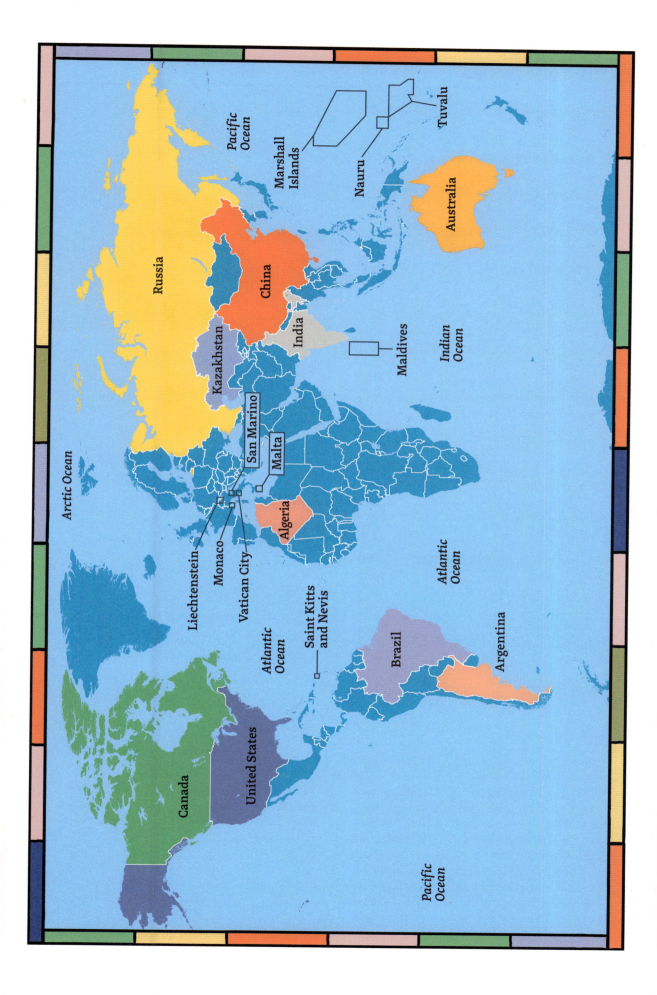

Unusual Rules

Twenty-four unlikely laws from around the world

Most places around the world have sets of laws for residents to follow. Some of these rules were written centuries ago and are no longer relevant today, while others are not commonly known. Other laws may have been passed to tackle a problem unique to the place.

1. In the city of Gainesville, Georgia, it has been illegal to eat fried chicken with anything but your hands since 1961. No knives, forks, or spoons are allowed.*

2. In the UK, the Salmon Act of 1986 states that it is illegal to hold salmon "under suspicious circumstances." This means that it is against the law for a person to receive a salmon that has been illegally fished. The maximum penalty is two years in prison.

3. In Switzerland, it is forbidden to go hiking naked.

4. At least 35 percent of all music played on radio stations in Canada must be by Canadian musicians.

5. In several Caribbean countries, including Barbados, Saint Vincent, and Saint Lucia, you are not allowed to wear clothing featuring a camouflage print.

6. In the UK, it is illegal to die in the Houses of Parliament.

7. In Thailand, it is forbidden to step on money. This is because it implies a lack of respect to the king of Thailand, whose portrait appears on banknotes.

8. On the Spanish island of Majorca, anyone caught building an "unauthorized sandcastle" faces a €100 (US $120) fine.

9. In Equatorial Guinea on the west coast of Africa, it is illegal to name a child "Monica."

10. In the city of Milan, Italy, it is a legal requirement to smile at all times.**

11. In South Africa, you are not allowed to wrestle a bear.

12. In the city of Mobile, Alabama, it is against the law to throw confetti or spray silly string.

13. On the Pacific island of Samoa, it is illegal to forget your wife's birthday.

14. In Germany, it is illegal to run out of gas on the highway.

15. In Western Australia, you are not allowed to own more than 110 pounds (50 kg) of potatoes.

---

*The last person to fall "fowl" of this law was Ginny Dietrick in 2009. As a joke set up by a friend, she was arrested by Gainesville police chief Frank Hopper for eating fried chicken with a fork on her 91st birthday. Hopper told her not to get up from her table until she had mastered the art of eating the fried chicken without cutlery "down to and including the licking of the fingers" afterward. Dietrick was pardoned and released as soon as she'd finished her chicken.

**However, the law does list occasions when you don't have to smile, such as if you work in a hospital, need to look after a sick family member, or are attending a funeral.

16. The city of Turin, Italy, passed a law in 2005 saying that dog owners must walk their pets at least three times a day—or face a €500 ($594) fine.

17. In Madagascar, pregnant women are not allowed to wear hats.

18. In Florida, it is illegal to pass gas in a public place on Thursdays after 6 o'clock in the evening.

19. In Scandinavia, car headlights have to be switched on at all times—including during the day.

20. It is illegal to deliberately disturb a wedding in South Australia. If you do, you could face two years in prison or an AU$10,000 (US $7,371) fine.

21. In Mexico, you're not allowed to take your feet off the pedals while cycling.

22. In Portugal, peeing while swimming in the sea is banned. (Though it would take a very clever detective to catch you.)

23. In Piazza San Marco, Venice, Italy, it is illegal to feed a pigeon.

24. In the state of Arizona, it is against the law to let a donkey sleep in your bathtub after 7 o'clock in the evening.***

***This law, passed in 1924, was aimed at a local merchant in Kingman, Arizona, who did allow a donkey to sleep in his bathtub. When a local dam broke and the city was flooded, the donkey was washed a mile down the valley. The donkey (and tub) survived but the local people spent so much time and effort rescuing it that they passed a law to stop the same thing from happening again.

Reaching For the Sky

A history of the world's tallest buildings

Humans are always trying to build things bigger and better than before. This list features some of the tallest human-made structures ever built. The dates below are the years in which each building was completed, making it the tallest in the world—for a time!

1. **Tower of Jericho**, modern-day Palestine (8000 BCE)—28 ft (8.5 m)

2. **Anu Ziggurat**,* modern-day Iraq (4000 BCE)—40 ft (13 m)

3. **Step Pyramid of Djoser**, Egypt (2648 BCE)—205 ft (62.6 m)

4. **Meidum Pyramid**, Egypt (2610 BCE)—307 ft (93.5 m)

5. **Bent Pyramid**, Egypt (2605 BCE)—332 ft (101.1 m)

6. **Red Pyramid**, Egypt (2600 BCE)—344 ft (105 m)

7. **Great Pyramid of Giza**, Egypt (2570 BCE)—481 ft (146.6 m)

8. **Old St. Paul's Cathedral**, England (1221 CE)—489 ft (149 m)

9. **Lincoln Cathedral**, England (1311 CE)—524 ft (159.7 m)

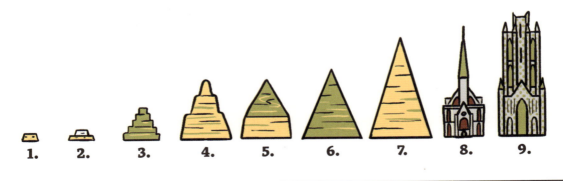

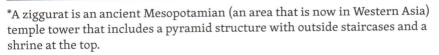

*A ziggurat is an ancient Mesopotamian (an area that is now in Western Asia) temple tower that includes a pyramid structure with outside staircases and a shrine at the top.

10. Washington Monument, United States (1884)—555 ft (169 m)

11. Eiffel Tower,** France (1889)—934 ft (300 m)

12. Chrysler Building, United States (1930)—1,046 ft (318.9 m)

13. Empire State Building, United States (1931)—1,250 ft (381 m)

14. North Tower of the Twin Towers, United States (1972)—1,368 ft (417 m)

15. Sears Tower (now called Willis Tower), United States (1973)—1,450 ft (443 m)

16. Petronas Towers, Malaysia (1998)—1,483 ft (451.9 m)

17. Taipei 101, Taiwan (2003)—1,671 ft (509.2 m)

18. Burj Khalifa,*** United Arab Emirates (2010)—2,722 ft (829.8 m)

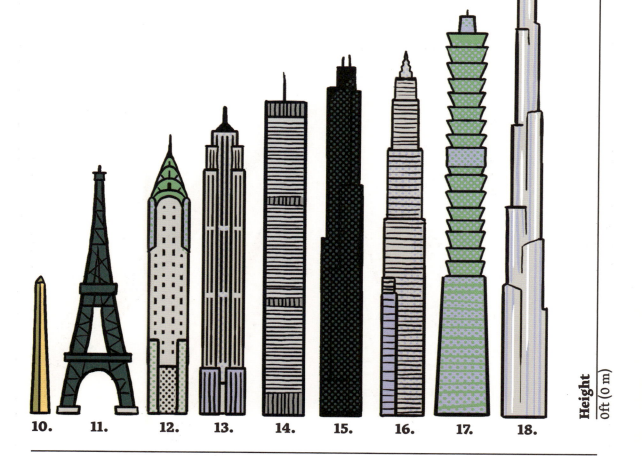

2,800 ft (853 m)

Height
0 ft (0 m)

10. **11.** **12.** **13.** **14.** **15.** **16.** **17.** **18.**

**The Eiffel Tower sways 2–3 inches (6–7 cm) in high winds.

***The Burj Khalifa has 163 stories. So if you're in a hurry, don't take the stairs. There are 2,909.

Tunnel Vision

Ten of the world's longest tunnels

1. Gadara Aqueduct,*
Jordan—106 mi (170 km)

This Roman tunnel once supplied water to several ancient cities including Adraha (which is known today as Dera'a in Syria) and Gardara (which is Umm Qais in modern-day Jordan).

2. Delaware Aqueduct,
United States—85.1 mi (137 km)

This carries New York City's main supply of water.

3. Päijänne Water Tunnel,
Finland—74.6 mi (120 km)

This tunnel supplies water to the Finnish capital, Helsinki.

4. Emisor Oriente Tunnel,
Mexico—38.5 mi (62 km)

The world's longest sewage tunnel, this flushes away the waste water of around 20 million people who live in Mexico City.

5. Guangzhou Metro Line 3,
China—37 mi (60 km)

Line 3 connects 30 different stations and includes the world's longest continuous metro tunnel.

6. Gotthard Base Tunnel,
Switzerland—35 mi (57 km)

The longest railway tunnel in the world runs deep beneath the Swiss Alps.

7. Channel Tunnel,
England/France—31 mi (50 km)

Dug beneath the English Channel, this is the longest tunnel connecting two countries.

8. Northern Line,
England—17.3 mi (28 km)

Started in 1890, this is one of the oldest metro lines in the world and the longest railway tunnel in the UK.

9. Large Hadron Collider tunnel,
Switzerland/France—16.7 mi (27 km)

This giant underground loop is used to smash together tiny particles smaller than atoms for scientific experiments.»

10. Lærdal Tunnel,
Norway—15.2 mi (25 km)

Connecting the towns of Lærdal and Aurland, this is the world's longest road tunnel.

Left: Engineers examine a completed section of the Channel Tunnel.

---

*An aqueduct is a human-made tunnel or channel that carries water.

» For more on the Large Hadron Collider and other giant machines, see pages 308–309.

Monumental

Fifteen of the world's most visited* buildings and monuments

1. Forbidden City, Beijing, China—19 million annual visitors

2. Sydney Opera House, Sydney, Australia—10.9 million annual visitors

3. Great Wall of China, Badaling**, China—10 million annual visitors

4. Palace of Versailles, Versailles, France—10 million annual visitors

5. Great Pyramid of Giza, Giza, Egypt—8.3 million annual visitors

6. Lincoln Memorial, Washington, DC, United States—7.8 million annual visitors

7. Colosseum, Roman Forum and Palatine Hill, Rome, Italy— 7.7 million annual visitors

8. Taj Mahal, Agra, India— 7.5 million annual visitors

9. St. Peter's Basilica, Vatican City— 7 million annual visitors

10. Eiffel Tower, Paris, France— 6.2 million annual visitors

11. Cologne Cathedral, Cologne, Germany—6 million annual visitors

12. Peterhof Palace, Saint Petersburg, Russia—5.2 million annual visitors

13. Statue of Liberty,*** New York City, NY, United States—3.5 million annual visitors

14. Christ the Redeemer statue,» Rio de Janeiro, Brazil—2 million annual visitors

15. Parthenon, Athens, Greece— 1.8 million annual visitors

Right: the Taj Mahal

*All figures are estimates based on recent yearly data.

**Badaling is where the Great Wall's main visitor center is located. It is the most visited section of the wall because it is close to Beijing, the capital city of China.

***The Statue of Liberty's official name is "Liberty Enlightening the World." The female figure holding the famous torch represents Libertas, the Roman goddess of freedom. She is wearing size 879 shoes!

» On which moon in our solar system could you jump as high as this statue? See page 37 to find out.

The Magnificent Seven

The Seven Wonders of the Ancient World

This famous list dates back to the 1st or 2nd century BCE, when the "Seven Wonders" were used as a kind of early travel guide for Greek sightseers. Seven were chosen because the Greeks believed the number seven represented perfection.

1. The Great Pyramid of Giza, Egypt

Made: About 2560–2540 BCE.

Built as a mausoleum, or tomb, for the Egyptian pharaoh Khufu, the Great Pyramid was the tallest human-made structure on Earth for more than 4,000 years. It is thought to weigh 6.5 million tons (5.9 million tonnes) and is the only one of the Seven Wonders of the Ancient World that exists today.

2. The Hanging Gardens of Babylon, modern-day Iraq

Made: 605–562 BCE.

These beautiful gardens, made up of a series of layered stone terraces, were supposedly built by the Babylonian ruler Nebuchadnezzar II for his wife, Amytis of Media. According to legend, Amytis missed the mountains and forests of her homeland, so Nebuchadnezzar ordered that a mountain covered in greenery should be built in her new home, the city of Babylon.*

3. The Temple of Artemis at Ephesus, modern-day Turkey

Made: 550 BCE.

The famously wealthy King Croesus of Lydia paid for the construction of this vast and impressive temple, the roof of which was supported by 127 60-foot- (18-m-) high pillars. It took more than 120 years to build but just one day to ruin. On July 21, 356 BCE, a man named Herostratus set fire to the temple with one aim: becoming famous.**

4. The Statue of Zeus at Olympia, Greece

Made: About 430 BCE.

This statue of Zeus, the leader of the Greek gods, was 40 feet (12 m) tall and carved by Phidias, the greatest Athenian sculptor of his day. It was initially placed in a temple at Olympia, the site of the ancient Olympic games, but was later moved to the city of Constantinople (now called Istanbul, in Turkey), where it is thought to have been destroyed by a fire in around 476 CE.

5. The Mausoleum at Halicarnassus, modern-day Turkey

Made: About 353 BCE.

A 135-foot- (41-m-) tall structure, this spectacular tomb was built entirely in white marble for Mausolus, the ruler of Caria, by his wife, Artemisia II. It was later destroyed by a series of earthquakes, but Mausolus's name lives on in the word "mausoleum," which is now used to describe any impressive building that houses a tomb.

---

*Several ancient sources claim that the gardens were destroyed by an earthquake in the 1st century CE but archaeologists have so far found no evidence of this. Most modern historians think that although they sound wonderful, the Hanging Gardens of Babylon were a popular myth.

**So that Herostratus wouldn't get his way, the Ephesians declared that his name should never be written down or remembered. (So to any Ephesians reading this, sorry.)

6. The Colossus of Rhodes, Greece

Made: About 294–282 BCE.

This towering 108-foot- (33-m-) tall bronze statue of the Greek sun god Helios stood at the entrance of the harbor of Rhodes. It later became the main inspiration for New York's Statue of Liberty, which is sometimes called the "modern Colossus."

7. The Lighthouse of Alexandria, Egypt

Made: About 280 BCE.

The flaming beacon at the top of this ancient lighthouse (electric light bulbs were not available back then, unfortunately) was so bright it could be seen 35 miles (56 km) out at sea. The lighthouse as damaged and then destroyed by earthquakes, but original pieces have been found at the bottom of the River Nile.

The Lighthouse of Alexandria

Grow Your Own

The world's five biggest crops and how much is produced in a year*

A crop is a plant that is grown on a large scale by humans. Crops can include vegetables, fruits, and grains. These five crops are all major sources of the world's food.

1. Sugar cane—2 billion tons (1.9 billion tonnes)
The stalks of this plant contain sugar, which is used to sweeten food and drinks.

2. Corn—1.2 billion tons (1.1 billion tonnes)
Varieties of corn are eaten as a vegetable, ground into cornmeal and corn starch, and processed to make the sweetener corn syrup.

3. Rice—863 million tons (783 million tonnes)
Grains of rice are the seeds of grasses commonly grown in Asia.**

4. Wheat—771 million tons (700 million tonnes)
Wheat is mostly ground to make flour for bread, pasta, pastry, and other foods.

5. Potatoes—408 million tons (370 million tonnes)
Potatoes can be baked, boiled, or fried and turned into lots of types of food, including chips and French fries.

*All numbers are estimates based on recent yearly data.

**Rice provides around 20 percent of all the calories, or food energy, consumed by humans around the world.

Humans' Best Friends

When various animals were domesticated by humans

Domesticated animals are those that have been trained or bred over multiple generations to be kept on a farm or as a pet.

Dogs—15,000+ years ago*

Cows—10,500 years ago

Sheep—10,500 years ago

Goats—10,000 years ago

Honeybees—10,000 years ago

Cats—9,500-12,000 years ago

Pigs—8,000 years ago

Chickens—7,000-10,000 years ago

Yaks—7,000-10,000 years ago

Llamas—6,500 years ago

Donkeys—6,000 years ago

Guinea pigs—6,000 years ago

Horses—6,000 years ago

Bactrian camels (camels with two humps)—5,500 years ago

Silkworms—5,500 years ago

Dromedaries (camels with just one hump)—5,000 years ago

Ducks—4,500 years ago

Water buffalo—4,500 years ago

Geese—3,500 years ago

Reindeer—2,000 years ago

Turkeys—2,000 years ago

Ostriches—150 years ago

*Every breed of dog is descended from an ancient species of wolf. Scientists aren't sure whether humans actively domesticated wolves, or whether wolves accidentally domesticated themselves by moving closer to humans to eat leftover food. Then, over multiple generations, wolves became tamer and slowly evolved into dogs.

Animal Farm

The world's six most common farm animals

1. **Chickens**—22.8 billion*

2. **Cows and oxen**—1.5 billion

3. **Ducks**—1.2 billion

4. **Sheep**—1.2 billion

5. **Goats**—1 billion**

6. **Pigs**—967 million***

*There are almost three times more chickens on Earth than human beings.

**Around the world more people drink milk from goats than from any other animal, including cows.

***Nearly half the world's pigs live in China.

Making Shapes

Twenty-four types of pasta and how to spot them

Pasta dough is typically made from flour, water, and sometimes egg. It is crafted into different shapes, then cooked by boiling or baking. All of these shapes have different names in Italian, because that is where pasta originated. Here are some of the translations.

1. **Acini di pepe**—pieces of pepper

2. **Alfabeto**—alphabet

3. **Ballerine**—dancers

4. **Cannelloni**—large reeds

5. **Cavatappi**—corkscrews

6. **Cavatelli**—little hollows

7. **Conchiglie**—shells

8. **Farfalle**—butterflies

9. **Fiori**—flowers

10. **Funghetti**—little mushrooms

11. **Gomiti**—little elbows

12. **Linguine**—little tongues

13. **Nuvole**—clouds

14. **Occhi di Passero**—sparrow eyes

15. **Orecchiette**—small ears

16. **Penne**—pens

17. **Radiatori**—radiators*

18. **Rigatoni**—ridged

19. **Rotelle**—wheels

20. **Spaghetti****—thin strings

21. **Stellette**—stars

22. **Tortellini**—little pies

23. **Trottole**—spinning tops

24. **Ziti**—short for *maccheroni della zita,* which means "macaroni of the bride"

---

*It is said that the ribbed shape of radiatori pasta is based on the front radiators of classic cars made by the famous Italian manufacturer Bugatti.

**A single strand of spaghetti is called a spaghetto.

Hot Stuff

How certain peppers rank on the Scoville scale of spiciness

The Scoville scale is a way of measuring how spicy or "hot" chili peppers taste when you eat them. It is named after Wilbur Scoville, the American pharmacist who invented the scale in 1912. The higher the number on the scale, the spicier the chili pepper. The numbers here are the highest ratings currently known to be possible for each type of pepper.

Carolina Reaper*—2.2 million**

Trinidad Moruga Scorpion—2 million

7 Pot Douglah—1.9 million

7 Pot Primo—1.5 million

Trinidad Scorpion Butch T—1.5 million

Naga Viper—1.4 million

Infinity—1.2 million

Ghost pepper—1 million

Habanero—350,000

Bird's eye—225,000

Cayenne—125,000

Chiltepin—100,000

Hungarian Wax—15,000

Jalapeño—10,000

Piment d'Espelette—4,000

Poblano—2,000

Sweet paprika—500

Bell pepper***—0

*The Carolina Reaper is officially the hottest chili pepper. In 2016, Gregory Foster from the United States set a new world record by eating 4.2 ounces (120 g) of Carolina Reaper chilies in one minute.

**There are hotter chilies currently under development, but they have yet to be officially tested.

***Capsaicin is the chemical compound in chili peppers that creates the spicy sensation of heat when you eat them. Bell peppers are related to chili peppers but do not contain any capsaicin, which is why they don't taste spicy.

Chocolate Eaters

The twenty countries that consume the most chocolate per person

This list shows how much chocolate the average person in each country eats in a year.*

1. Switzerland—176 bars**
2. Austria—162 bars
3. Germany—158 bars
4. Ireland—158 bars
5. United Kingdom—152 bars
6. Sweden—132 bars
7. Estonia—130 bars
8. Norway—116 bars
9. Poland—114 bars
10. Belgium—112 bars
11. Finland—108 bars
12. Slovakia—104 bars
13. The Netherlands—102 bars
14. New Zealand—100 bars
15. Australia—98 bars
16. Czech Republic—98 bars
17. Denmark—98 bars
18. Russia—96 bars
19. United States—88 bars
20. France—86 bars

*These calculations are based on an average bar of chocolate that weighs 1.76 ounces (50 g).

**For comparison, the average person in China eats just two bars of chocolate each year.

Sweet Spot

Chocolate in numbers

Eaten on their own, cocoa beans have a strong, bitter taste. But when they have been correctly prepared, their insides can be ground into cocoa, the key ingredient of chocolate.

4.8 million The approximate weight in tons (4.4 million tonnes) of all the cocoa produced each year.

12,770 The weight in pounds (5,792.5 kg) of the world's heaviest chocolate bar, which is the same as three pickup trucks. The gigantic bar was 13 feet 2 inches (4 m) long, 13 feet 2 inches (4 m) wide, and 1 foot 2 inches (35 cm) thick.

1,200 The average number of cocoa beans produced by one cacao tree in a year.

1847 The year the world's first chocolate bar was made. It was produced by the English company Fry's, which later became part of Cadbury.

1941 The year candy-coated M&M's were first produced by Forrest Mars Sr. He had the idea during the Spanish Civil War, when he saw soldiers eating small chocolates with sugary shells. The coating stopped the chocolate from melting in their hands.

50 The number of cups of hot chocolate the Aztec emperor Montezuma II drank each day from a golden cup.*

45 The number of cacao beans it takes to make a 1.76-ounce (50-g) bar of chocolate.

30 The percentage of the world's cocoa beans that come from the Ivory Coast, Africa.

*The Aztec Empire was an ancient civilization established between the 14th and 16th centuries in modern-day Mexico. The English word "chocolate" comes from the Aztec word *xocoatl*. Pronounced sho-KWA-til, it means "bitter water" and was used to describe a drink the Aztecs made from cocoa beans.

Celebrate in Style

Eleven unique ways birthdays are celebrated around the world

1. Canadians grab the person celebrating their birthday and coat their nose in butter to ward off bad luck.

2. At birthday parties, Mexicans hit a papier-mâché piñata with a stick while wearing a blindfold. After repeated hits, the piñata breaks open and the candy and toys stashed inside fall to the ground.

3. Jamaicans throw flour all over the person celebrating their birthday in a tradition called "antiquing."*

4. Argentinians pull the ears of the person celebrating their birthday: one tug for each year of their life.

5. In Ireland, children celebrating their birthdays are held upside down by family and friends and then gently "bumped" on the floor once for every year of their life—with an extra bump at the end for good luck.

6. In the Netherlands, people celebrate particular birthdays more than others. These special years are called Crown Years and happen when you turn five, ten, 15, 20, and 21.

7. In Ghana, instead of celebrating birthdays with a cake, children are given a special breakfast treat called *oto*, which is made from fried yams.

9. In Russia, instead of a birthday cake, the person celebrating a birthday receives a homemade pie with a personal message carved in dough on the top.

10. In China, people eat a bowl of long noodles on their birthdays. The noodles represent long life and the aim is to slurp the noodles into your mouth as far as possible before taking a bite.**

11. Australians prepare a special treat called fairy bread on birthdays, which is buttered bread covered in colored sugary sprinkles.

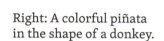

Right: A colorful piñata in the shape of a donkey.

---

*In Brazil, antiquing gets even messier because it also includes eggs.

**In China, people also "skip" certain birthdays because they are considered bad luck. Some women avoid celebrating their 30th, 33rd, and 66th birthdays, while some men don't celebrate their 40th. Instead, they simply stay 29, 32, 65, or 39 for two years in a row.

All Together Now

The eighty musicians that typically make up a symphony orchestra

A symphony orchestra can have between 60–90 musicians. So, if you want to start your own, here's who you'll need (the colored dots in the list match the colors of the musicians' shirts):

- **24** violin players*
- **12** viola players
- **10** cello players
- **8** double bass players
- **2** flute players
- **1** piccolo player
- **2** oboe players**
- **2** clarinet players
- **2** bassoon players
- **4** French horn players
- **3** trumpet players
- **2** trombone players
- **1** bass trombone player
- **1** tuba player
- **2** percussionists
- **1** timpani player
- **1** harp player
- **1** piano/celesta*** player
- **1** conductor

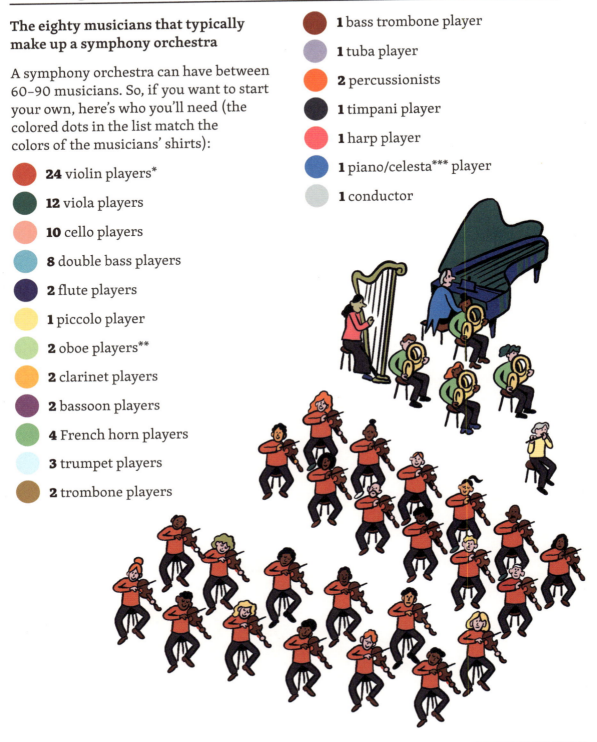

*Violin players in orchestras are usually split into two groups, the first violins and the second violins, which each play different parts of the musical score.

**One oboist should also be able to play the lower-pitched English horn.

***A celesta is a percussion instrument that looks like a small upright piano.

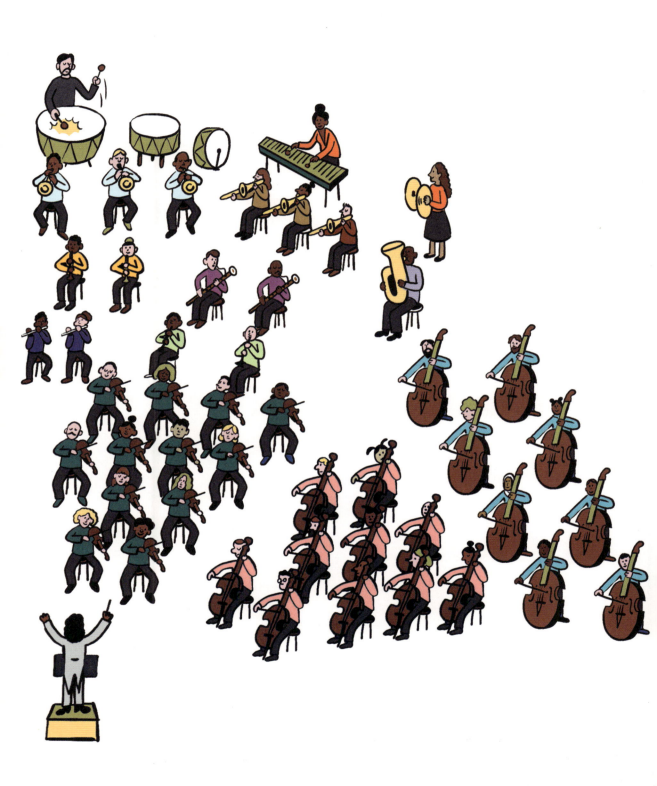

Read All About It

The thirteen books that have sold the most copies

1. The Holy Qur'an—more than 3 billion copies

First published: 650 CE

The Qur'an* is the sacred book of the religion of Islam. It was first memorized and then written down in the Arabic language more than 1,300 years ago.

2. The King James Bible—more than 2.5 billion copies

First published: 1611

It took a team of some 50 experts seven years to translate this English version of the Christian Bible from the Hebrew and Greek languages. It includes more than 788,000 words.

3. Quotations from Chairman Mao Tse-tung—800 million copies

First published: 1964

This book contains the thoughts of Mao Tse-tung, who was the Chairman—or leader—of China between 1954 and 1976. It is often called the *Little Red Book*.

4. Don Quixote by Miguel de Cervantes—500 million copies

First published: 1512

This 500-year-old Spanish story is about an old knight who goes on a series of adventures. It has been translated into more than 50 languages.

5. A Tale of Two Cities by Charles Dickens—200 million copies

First published: 1859

The two cities mentioned in the title are London, England, and Paris, France. It is the only one of Dickens's books that is set outside England.

6. The Lord of the Rings by J.R.R. Tolkien**—around 150 million copies

First published: 1954–1955

It took J.R.R. Tolkien more than 16 years to write his fantasy trilogy about the adventures of Frodo the hobbit and his companions. If you wanted to read Tolkien's three-volume novel out loud without stopping, you'd need more than two full days.

7. The Little Prince by Antoine de Saint-Exupéry—140 million copies

First published: 1943

This French children's story is about a young prince who visits different planets in space, including Earth. It has been translated into more than 300 languages.

---

*Qur'an means "recitation," which is the act of saying something aloud from memory.

**J.R.R. Tolkien knew more than 30 different languages, including Danish, Gothic, Greek, Italian, Latin, Middle and Old English, Norwegian, Old Norse, Spanish, Swedish, and Welsh. He also invented several new languages of his own that are spoken by characters in his books.

8. *Harry Potter and the Sorcerer's Stone* by J.K. Rowling*** — 120 million copies

First published: 1997

This is the first of seven books in the hugely popular wizarding series. In total, the seven Harry Potter books contain 1,100,086 words.

9. *Dream of the Red Chamber* by Cao Xueqin — 100 million copies

First published: 1754

Dream of the Red Chamber tells the story of a young boy named Jia Baoyu. It is one of the most popular books written in Chinese. It has 30 main characters and more than 400 minor ones.

10. *Alice's Adventures in Wonderland* by Lewis Carroll — 100 million copies

First published: 1865

Lewis Carroll's imaginative children's story is named after a real girl. She was the daughter of Carroll's boss, a man named Henry Liddell.

11. *The Hobbit* by J.R.R. Tolkien — around 100 million copies

First published: 1937

This children's story about Bilbo the hobbit's adventures, in which he finds a magic ring and helps recover a treasure hoard from a dragon, is set in the same fantasy world as *The Lord of the Rings*.

12. *And Then There Were None* by Agatha Christie — 100 million copies

First published: 1939

Agatha Christie is the author of numerous detective novels, and she has sold more than two billion books in total. This exciting mystery story that is set on a remote island is her most popular.

13. *The Lion, the Witch and the Wardrobe* by C.S. Lewis — 85 million copies

First published: 1950

C.S. Lewis, the author of this magical children's story with talking animals, was good friends with J.R.R. Tolkien, the writer of *The Hobbit* and *The Lord of the Rings*. They were both professors at Oxford University.

***Harry Potter and J.K. Rowling share the same birthday: July 31.

Brushstrokes

Ten of the most expensive paintings ever sold

1. *Salvator Mundi* by Leonardo da Vinci*—$469.7 million

Painted: Around 1500

This portrait is of Jesus Christ and its title means "the savior of the world."

2. *Interchange* by Willem de Kooning—$324 million

Painted: 1955

This abstract painting** was bought by American businessman Kenneth C. Griffin, who purchased Jackson Pollock's *Number 17A* (see entry 5) at the same auction.

3. *The Card Players* by Paul Cézanne—$284 million

Painted: around 1895

The two men shown playing cards in this painting were farmhands who worked on Cézanne's estate. It's one of a series of five similar paintings of people playing cards.***

4. *Nafea Faa Ipoipo* by Paul Gauguin—$227 million

Painted: 1892

This painting features two indigenous women on the Pacific island of Tahiti. The title is in Tahitian and means "When Will You Marry?".

5. *Number 17A* by Jackson Pollock—$216 million

Painted: 1948

Pollock's original ways of creating his colorful abstract paintings included pouring and dripping the paint onto the canvas from above.

6. *Wasserschlangen II* by Gustav Klimt—$201.7 million

Painted: 1904–1907

This painting of female mythological creatures called water nymphs features Klimt's most famous artistic technique: covering parts of his paintings with thin layers of gold.

---

*Leonardo da Vinci didn't sign any of his paintings. This has proved annoying to modern art historians, some of whom are still arguing about whether *Salvator Mundi* was painted by Leonardo at all.

**An abstract painting doesn't attempt to create an accurate picture of an object or scene.

***Cézanne's paintings of card players inspired American artist C. M. Coolidge to paint a similar series. However, Coolidge's paintings were different from Cézanne's in one significant detail: the card players were all dogs.

7. *No. 6 (Violet, Green and Red)* by Mark Rothko—$201 million

Painted: 1951

This painting simply features three rectangular blocks of color. Rothko thought that colors on their own express "basic human emotions."

8. Pair of portraits of Marten Soolmans and Oopjen Coppit by Rembrandt—$194 million

Painted: 1634

These portraits of a wealthy man and woman from Amsterdam in the Netherlands have always been bought and sold together because they were painted as wedding portraits.

9. *Les femmes d'Alger ("Version O")* by Pablo Picasso—$193.5 million

Painted: 1955

This was the last of 15 different versions of the painting Picasso created of the "women of Algiers." They were painted as a tribute to the French artist Henri Matisse, who died shortly before Picasso started work on them.

10. *Twelve Landscape Screens* by Qi Baishi—$146.9 million
Painted: 1925

Each of these screens shows one of a dozen landscapes at different times of the year. Each screen also features calligraphy, which is a beautifully styled form of handwriting.

Nafea Faa Ipoipo by Paul Gauguin

Hats Off

Twenty-four distinctive hats and where they come from

1. **Beret**—Basque region of Spain and France

2. **Bowler hat**—UK

3. **Breton**—France

4. **Chef's hat***—France

5. **Cloche**—France

6. **Ushanka**—Russia

7. **Cork hat**—Australia

8. **Deerstalker**—Scotland, UK

9. **Fez**—Morocco

10. **Gat**—Korea

11. **Hennin**—France

12. **Kufi**—Nigeria

13. **Panama hat****—Ecuador

14. **Picture hat**—UK

15. **Pillbox hat**—UK

16. **Rastacap**—Jamaica

17. **Rice hat**—China

18. **Santa hat**—United States***

19. **Sombrero**—Mexico

20. **Stetson**—United States

21. **Top hat**—UK

22. **Tricorn**—Spanish Netherlands (now Belgium and Luxembourg)

23. **Turban**—India

24. **Upe**—Bougainville, Papua New Guinea

---

*White chef's hats traditionally have 100 pleats or folds that are said to represent the supposed 100 different ways an egg can be prepared.

**Panama hats were invented in Ecuador, South America, but then became famous and were widely exported from nearby Panama, which is how they got their geographically inaccurate name.

***Santa's hat was first seen in drawings by American cartoonist Thomas Nast in the late 1800s.

Faithful Followers

The religions followed by the largest numbers of people*

Christianity—2.5 billion people
Founded: 1 CE.
Christians believe in one God and follow the teachings of Jesus Christ, who they believe is the son of God. Christianity's holy book is the Bible.

Islam—1.9 billion people
Founded: 7th century CE.
Islam was founded by the prophet Muhammad in Arabia. Muslims believe in one God, Allah, and their sacred book is called the Qur'an.

Hinduism—1 billion people
Founded: More than 3,000 years ago.
Hindus believe in many gods and consider one of them, Brahma, to be the creator of the Earth. There are many important Hindu texts. The oldest are called the Vedas. They were written in the ancient language of Sanskrit.

Buddhism—550 million people
Founded: Around 500 BCE.
Buddhists follow the teachings of Siddhartha Gautama, or the Buddha, who lived in India.» The goal of Buddhism is to reach a state of spiritual enlightenment and peace called nirvana. A sacred text of Buddhism is the Tripitaka.

Sikhism—28 million people
Founded: 1500 CE.
Sikhs believe in one God and follow the teachings of the Indian spiritual teacher Nanak, which are written down in the sacred Guru Granth Sahib.

Judaism—15 million people
Founded: As early as 4,000 years ago.
Jews believe in one God. They follow texts including the Torah, the Talmud, and Midrashic commentaries.

Falun Gong—about 10 million people**
Founded: 1992.
A relatively new religion, Falun Gong was founded in China and combines ritual exercises and meditation techniques.

---

*It's estimated that there are 880 million non-religious people in the world, which represents around 11 percent of the global population. Non-religious people include atheists, who do not believe in a god or gods; agnostics, who believe that the ultimate reality of the universe is unknowable; and people who have no connection to a system of religious thought.

» The biggest hand-painted portrait in the world is of the Buddha. To find out exactly how big, see page 380.

**Reliable estimates have been used for all entries in this list from this point onwards, but there is no confirmed number for each.

Taoism—about 9 million people

Founded: More than 2,000 years ago.

Believers of this Chinese religion try to act in harmony with the world and follow the Tao ("the way").

Baha'i Faith—about 5–8 million people

Founded: 1863.

Followers of the Baha'i Faith believe in one God and the ultimate unity of all people and all religions.

Confucianism—about 5–6 million people

Founded: 600–500 BCE.

Confucianism was founded in China around the teachings of the great philosopher Confucius.

Jainism—about 4 million people

Founded: 600 BCE.

A primarily Indian religion, Jainism does not include gods or spiritual beings. Instead, Jains believe in non-violence and the eternal human soul.

Shinto—about 3–4 million people

Founded: 500s CE.

Founded in Japan, Shintoism has no known founder or single sacred text. Believers communicate with spirits called *kami*.

Wicca—about 1–3 million people

Founded: Early 20th century CE.

Built around nature worship and witchcraft, Wicca was first developed in England.

Cao Dai—about 2.5 million people

Founded: 1926.

Cao Dai is a religion that has brought together ideas from other religions, including Buddhism, Taoism, Confucianism, and Roman Catholicism.

Rastafarianism—about 1 million people

Founded: 1930s.

Developed on the Caribbean island of Jamaica, Rastafarianism is both a religious and a political movement.

Tenrikyo—about 1 million people

Founded: 1800s.

Founded in Japan, Tenrikyo is based on Shintoism. Followers believe in one god called Tenri-O-no-Mikoto.

Zoroastrianism—about 190,000 people

Founded: 6th century BCE.

Believers in Zoroastrianism worship the supreme god Ahura Mazda.

Brief Battles

Six of the shortest wars

1. Anglo-Zanzibar War, 1896—40 minutes

The shortest war in history was fought between Britain and Zanzibar, an island state off the coast of East Africa. War broke out at 9 o'clock in the morning on August 27, when the British Navy attacked the sultan of Zanzibar's palace. It ended less than an hour later when the palace's flag was shot down, and British troops stopped firing.

2. Invasion of Anjouan, 2008—2 days

The government of Comoros, a small island nation off the coast of East Africa, invaded the rebelling island of Anjouan. Their ambition was to remove its president, Colonel Mohamed Bacar, who was said to have held an illegal election so that he could stay in power. Eleven people were injured during the invasion before Bacar fled Anjouan on a speedboat and the fighting stopped.

3. Soccer War, 1969—4 days

This brief conflict between the neighboring Central American countries of Honduras and El Salvador is known as the Soccer War because it was partly caused by a qualifying match for the World Cup. El Salvador won 3–2, but the result started rioting between rival fans. A few weeks later, a military war broke out that lasted exactly 100 hours before a cease-fire was agreed.

4. Six-Day War, 1967—6 days

This war was fought between Israel and the surrounding countries of Egypt, Syria, and Jordan. It lasted less than a week but led to political tensions between the countries that continued for decades.

5. War of the Stray Dog, 1925—11 days

According to some accounts, this war between Bulgaria and Greece was caused by a dog running across the border between the two European countries. A Greek soldier then ran after his dog but was shot by a Bulgarian soldier, which led to a brief conflict.

6. Norman Conquest, 1066—88 days

William of Normandy (the powerful Duke of a part of Northern France) and his invading army landed on the south coast of England at Pevensey on September 28, 1066. Just over two weeks later, they famously defeated King Harold II's forces at the Battle of Hastings.* Other English nobles surrendered to William (who became known as William the Conqueror) at the town of Berkhamsted, before he was then crowned William I of England at Westminster Abbey in London, on Christmas Day.

*The magnificent 230-foot- (70-m-) long Bayeux Tapestry tells the story of William's conquest of England. It is now on display in a museum in France.

Keeping the Peace

The fifteen countries that don't have an army

It is expensive for a country to pay for and equip its own army. So some smaller countries have decided not to have one at all. Some also have agreements with larger neighboring countries that have promised to defend them in a time of war.

1. **Solomon Islands**—population 674,900

2. **Samoa**—population 200,000

3. **Saint Lucia**—population 180,700

4. **Kiribati**—population 124,100

5. **Grenada**—population 113,300

6. **Saint Vincent and the Grenadines**—population 110,500

7. **Micronesia**—population 105,700

8. **Andorra**—population 76,900

9. **Dominica**—population 72,700

10. **Marshall Islands**—population 55,900

11. **Liechtenstein**—population 38,600

12. **Palau**—population 18,000

13. **Nauru**—population 12,800

14. **Tuvalu**—population 10,500

15. **Vatican City***—population 825

The Swiss Guard

*It is the job of the famous Pontifical Swiss Guard to protect the Pope, the leader of the Roman Catholic Church, who lives in Vatican City. Founded in 1506, the Swiss Guard has only 135 soldiers, making it the world's smallest army. However, Vatican City itself doesn't have an army and remains neutral during any war.

The Long Game

**Five games that took longer
than expected**

1. Marathon—54 years, 8 months, 6 days,
5 hours, 32 minutes

Japanese runner Shizo Kanakuri started
history's slowest ever marathon in 1912, at
the Stockholm Olympics. Running in very
hot weather, Kanakuri collapsed during
the race and was taken in by a local family.
He felt so ashamed of his performance that
rather than admit that he'd failed to finish,
Kanakuri decided to travel home to Japan
in secret. According to Swedish records,
Kanakuri was still officially missing until
1967, when, at the age of 75, he returned
to Stockholm to finish the marathon he'd
started more than half a century earlier.*

2. Chess—159 days

When two Soviet grand masters, Anatoly
Karpov and Garry Kasparov, contested the
World Chess Championship final in 1984,
the rules seemed clear: the winner would
be the first to win six games. However,
five months later, after 48 games,
including 40 draws and with Karpov
leading five wins to three, the organizers
abandoned the Championship. The
officials were worried about the players'
health after such a marathon contest,
although both Karpov and Kasparov
said they wanted to keep playing.**

3. Table tennis—59 hours

One of the longest ever competitive table
tennis matches was between Poland's
Alojzy Ehrlich and Romania's Farkas
Paneth in 1936. It was played at the World
Championships in Prague in what is now
the Czech Republic. The first rally alone
lasted for 2 hours and 12 minutes and
involved an estimated 12,000 shots.***

4. Cricket—43 hours, 16 minutes

This record-breaking cricket match
between hosts South Africa and England
in 1939 lasted for more than 40 hours of
playing time, spread over 12 days. On the
12th day, England needed 42 runs to win
but the match ended without a result
because the English team had to stop
playing to catch their ship back home.»

5. Tennis—11 hours, 5 minutes

The longest ever professional tennis
match was played between America's John
Isner and France's Nicolas Mahut at the
Wimbledon Championships in 2010. The
pair played a total of 183 games spread
across three days before Isner won the
decisive fifth set 70–68.

---

*"It was a long trip," Kanakuri said at the finish.
"Along the way I got married, had six children,
and ten grandchildren."

**Kasparov went on to beat Karpov in the finals
of the following four World Championships.

***The referee Gabor Diner had to be replaced
during the match because his neck hurt from
watching the ball go back and forth. Ehrlich
triumphed in the end after Paneth finally lost
patience, hit the ball wildly above his opponent's
head, and ran screaming from the court.

»To find out about an (almost) unbeatable cricket
team, see page 360.

Going for Gold

Five unusual sporting events that were once part of the Olympics

1. Croquet

Last featured: 1900.

The game of croquet involves hitting balls through a series of hoops with a long stick called a mallet. It is significant in sports history because it was the first Olympic sport in which women were allowed to compete.*

2. High jump for horses

Last featured: 1900.

The first and only Olympic high jump for horses ended in a tie, between France's Dominique Gardères on his horse Canela and Italy's Gian Giorgio Trissino on Oreste, who both cleared 6.07 feet (1.85 m).

3. Swimming obstacle course

Last featured: 1900.

During the race, competitors had to swim 656 feet (200 m) along the River Seine in Paris. They also had to climb over a row of boats and a long wooden pole.**

4. Plunge for distance

Last featured: 1904.

Plunging for distance was a popular diving event in the 19th and early part of the 20th centuries. From a standing start, competitors had to dive into the water and glide as far as possible in 60 seconds without using any other parts of their bodies to push themselves forward. American William Dickey, the winner in 1904, managed 62 feet 6 inches (19 m 5 cm).

5. Tug-of-war

Last featured: 1920.

Two teams of eight people held opposite ends of a long rope and attempted to pull the opposing team 6 feet (1.8 m) toward them. Each tug-of-war lasted five minutes, and if no team had pulled the other the full distance, the team who'd pulled their rivals the farthest in their direction was declared the winner.

A tug-of-war team

*However, croquet was not included in any future Olympics, perhaps because only one spectator bought a ticket to watch it at the 1900 games.

**The winner was Australian Fred Lane, who also won gold in the 200 meter freestyle race without obstacles.

Fool's Game

Four of history's greatest hoaxes, tricks, and pranks

1. The Berners Street hoax—1810

One of the most ambitious practical jokes of all time began at 54 Berners Street in London, England, at 5 a.m. on November 27, 1810, when a chimney sweep arrived who hadn't been called for. He was soon joined by 11 other chimney sweeps, then by chefs, butchers, gardeners, doctors, and wig-makers; famous people such as the governor of the Bank of England, the archbishop of Canterbury, and the Lord Mayor of London, plus multiple deliveries of food and furniture, including six pianos. The constant stream of visitors continued for hours, causing a large crowd of curious people to gather outside. The day's chaos had been carefully planned by Theodore Hook, in order to win a bet with a friend that he could make any house he chose the most talked-about place in London.*

2. Tiara of Saitaphernes—1896

The world-famous Louvre museum in Paris, France, paid 200,000 francs to buy what it thought was a 1,600-year-old gold tiara. But some experts thought that the Tiara of Saitaphernes didn't look very old at all. The Louvre ignored their criticisms. The truth was only revealed when the story reached a goldsmith in Ukraine, who came forward to say that he'd been asked to make the tiara in 1894—by the two brothers who then sold the two-year-old tiara to the Louvre.**

3. Cottingley Fairies—1917

Two young cousins, 16-year-old Elsie Wright and nine-year-old Frances Griffiths, who lived in Cottingley, England, took a series of photographs that appeared to show real-life fairies in the garden. The photographs fooled lots of people, including Elsie's own mother and Sir Arthur Conan Doyle, the creator of Sherlock Holmes, who used them to illustrate an article about fairies he wrote for a popular magazine. They took three more photographs in 1920, but decades later, in the 1980s, Elsie and Frances admitted they had faked the photographs using cardboard cutouts of fairies copied from a children's book.

4. Spaghetti Harvest hoax—1957

Where does spaghetti come from? If you've already read the list on page 272, you'll know it's a type of pasta, made from flour, water, and sometimes eggs. But according to a fake BBC news report shown on TV in the UK on April Fool's Day, spaghetti actually grows on trees. The hoax report even included a film of trees covered in long strands of spaghetti being "harvested" by Swiss spaghetti farmers.***

Right: This photo was taken by Frances Griffiths. It shows Elsie Wright, who appears to be being offered a bunch of flowers by a fairy.

---

*Hook had set up his hoax by writing thousands of letters in the name of Mrs. Tottenham, who lived at Number 54, asking for dozens of deliveries and surprise visitors to all arrive at the same time. Hook spent the day in the house opposite Number 54, watching the chaos unfold.

**The Louvre still owns the tiara and in 1954 put it on public display in a "Salon of Fakes," along with eight forged copies of the *Mona Lisa*.

***Even though the made-up news report was shown on TV on April 1, or April Fool's Day, a day traditionally reserved for hoaxes and tricks, many viewers believed it and called the BBC the next day to ask how they could grow their own spaghetti at home. The BBC kept the joke going by replying that they should plant a small piece of spaghetti in a can of tomato sauce and "hope for the best."

Treasure Hunt

Eight amazing lost treasures that no one can find

1. The Copper Scroll treasure

Missing since: around 70 CE.

In the 1940s and 1950s, a series of ancient writings on papyrus, parchment, and bronze were discovered in caves in the Judean Desert in the Middle East. One of them, known as the Copper Scroll, talks about the location of a huge hoard of hidden treasure. Some historians think the treasure is just a legend, while others think it is real—and still hidden.*

2. The Knights Templar treasure

Missing since: 1307.

The Knights Templar was a religious order founded in 1119 that became very powerful and wealthy. King Philip IV of France was worried about their growing power, so he arrested the most important knights in 1307 and broke into their treasury, hoping to take all the gold, jewels, and other valuables stored inside. However, it was empty. Treasure hunters have been trying to track down the Templars' missing gold ever since.

3. Incas' golden city

Missing since: around 1600.

Many old stories tell of an ancient lost city called Paititi, which, according to some, is where the ancient Inca people hid many golden treasures when their homelands in South America were invaded by Europeans. If the lost city does exist, it may be concealed within the jungles of Peru.

4. Shakespeare's lost play

Missing since: 1603.

The great English playwright William Shakespeare seems to have written a play called *Love's Labor's Won*, as records show it was published in 1598 and was still being sold in 1603. However, some people think this might have been an alternative title for one of his other plays, such as *The Taming of the Shrew*, which is still regularly performed today.

*If you'd like to join a 2,000-year-old treasure hunt, you can start looking for clues in the Copper Scroll itself, which is on display at the Jordan Museum in Amman.

5. The Florentine Diamond

Missing since: 1918.

The Florentine Diamond dates back to around the 14th–15th century** and is said to be the largest gem of its type in the world. At the start of the 20th century, it was owned by the Hapsburgs, the royal family of the Austro-Hungarian Empire. After the end of the First World War in 1918, Charles I of Austria took the famous diamond to Switzerland—where it is said to have been stolen by someone close to the royal family and smuggled to South America. The Florentine Diamond may have been cut up into smaller diamonds and sold in the 1920s, but no one knows for sure.

6. Mallory and Irvine's camera

Missing since: 1924.

British explorers George Mallory and Andrew Irvine disappeared in June 1924 while trying to climb Mount Everest. They both died in the attempt, but what remains a mystery is whether they reached the summit first. If they had, they would have beaten Edmund Hillary and Tenzing Norgay (who are currently credited with the achievement) by almost 30 years. In 1999, Mallory's body was discovered without the photograph of his wife, Ruth, that he had planned to leave at the summit. There was also no sign of the camera that Mallory and Irvine took to photograph themselves at the top. If the missing camera is ever found, it could reveal the truth about their doomed expedition.

7. Peking Man

Missing since: 1941.

In 1941, valuable fossils of an early human known as the Peking Man mysteriously disappeared and have never been found. They were originally discovered in China, and some experts think they were lost at sea while being transported to the United States. Others think that they are still in China, buried under a parking lot.

8. The FIFA World Cup

Missing since: 1983.

Between 1930 and 1970, the winners of the soccer World Cup were presented with a gold cup called the Jules Rimet Trophy. Then Brazil won the tournament for a record third time and so were allowed to keep the cup for good. However, in 1983 disaster struck when it was stolen. Despite a huge police search across the whole of Brazil, the famous Jules Rimet Trophy has never been recovered.***

**According to one story, a French nobleman named Charles the Bold was carrying the Florentine Diamond when he was knocked off his horse during the Battle of Morat in Switzerland in 1476. A soldier picked up the diamond but later sold it for a small amount of money because he mistakenly thought it was made of glass.

***The Jules Rimet Trophy was also stolen in England in 1966 shortly before the start of that year's tournament. Luckily, it was later found underneath a hedge by a collie dog named Pickles, who became a national hero.

Chapter 7

Inventions

A list of things you'll encounter in this chapter:

The world's first fireworks

Sticks that tell the time

A flying garbage truck

A poop-powered bus

The world's number 1 tire manufacturer*

An undercover pigeon

Wigs for dogs

A miniature motorcycle

Floating trains

Amphibious bicycles

A mechanical monk

Seatless unicycles

A giant conveyor belt

Self-driving shopping carts

Shoe umbrellas

Violin-playing robots

*Hint: Their tires are surprisingly small . . .

Eureka!

Ten inventions that changed the world and how they did it

1. Wheel Making it easier to move objects and people—before 3500 BCE.

2. Compass Helping humans navigate—around 110 BCE.

3. Gunpowder Changing the nature of war—around 850 CE.

4. Printing press Mass-producing books, newspapers, and posters, which spread knowledge—around 1439.

5. Steam engine Powering the first industrial machines on farms and in factories. They were later used to power trains—1765.

6. Telegraph Making long-distance communication possible*—1837.

7. Internal combustion engine Powering cars and other vehicles—1876.

8. Electric light Illuminating homes, roads, and cities, allowing people to work at night and making places safer—1879.

9. Computer Performing calculations beyond the power of any human—1937.

10. World Wide Web Connecting humanity to a world of information, and each other—1989.

Easy Does It

Six simple machines

A machine doesn't have to be big, complicated, or have lots of moving parts. In fact, any object that is used to apply a force or control movement to perform a task can be called a machine. Here are six of the simplest that you can spot being used around you every day.

1. Inclined planes are used for ramps and slides.

2. Wedges are used for knives, axes, and scissors.*

3. Levers are used for seesaws and wheelbarrows.

4. Wheels and axles are used for cars and bicycles.

5. Screws are used for light bulbs, jar lids, corkscrews, and faucet handles.

6. Pulleys are used for window blinds, garage doors, and flagpoles.

*The telegraph allowed users to communicate over long distances by transmitting a series of electrical signals through a wire, which a machine then wrote onto a piece of paper. Its American inventor, Samuel Morse, also developed Morse code—the system of dots and dashes used for these messages.

*Many people think that the 15th-century Italian inventor (and all-around genius) Leonardo da Vinci invented scissors. In fact, they were in use centuries before Leonardo was born. The ancient Romans definitely used them, while some historians think the very first scissors were invented in the Middle East between 3,000 and 4,000 years ago.

Child's Play

Eight brilliant things created by young inventors

1. Popsicles—Frank Epperson, age 11

One cold night in 1905, Epperson accidentally left a cup that was filled with sugary soda powder, water, and a stirring stick outside. When he woke up, a refreshing frozen treat—the very first Popsicle—was waiting on his porch.

2. Swimming flippers—Benjamin Franklin, age 11

As a boy growing up in Boston in the 1700s, Benjamin Franklin wasn't a very strong swimmer. To increase his speed, he took two wooden paddles and strapped them to his hands, using them like flippers to push himself through the water. Today, swimmers and divers wear flippers just like Franklin's on their feet.*

3. Crayon holders—Cassidy Goldstein, age 12

Drawing with crayons is fun, but it can also be frustrating when the crayons become too small to hold or break into pieces. Cassidy Goldstein created her own solution to this problem: a plastic tube that would protect and hold the crayon in place, making it easier to draw with. After winning a patent** for her idea in 2002, Goldstein's Crayon Holders are now sold around the world.

4. Braille—Louis Braille, age 15

Before 1824, people who were visually impaired read by feeling their way over the raised outline of letters printed in special books. It was a slow process to read each word, letter by letter. Louis Braille, who had been blind himself since the age of three, created a new alphabet of raised dots, which was much quicker and easier for people with visual impairments to read. Braille based his alphabet on a code that the French army used to communicate at nighttime, and he named it "Braille."

5. Earmuffs—Chester Greenwood, age 15

Out ice skating one day in 1873, Greenwood was fed up with freezing cold ears. So he made a simple wire frame and, with his grandmother's help, sewed bits of beaver skin to it to keep his ears warm. Initially called Greenwood's Champion Ear Protectors, they were a big hit with soldiers in World War I.

6. Christmas lights—Albert Sadacca, age 15

In the days before electricity, Christmas trees could be dangerous because they were often decorated with candles, which could light the trees on fire. In 1917, Sadacca invented a string of small lightbulbs, which were much safer, and have been used to decorate trees ever since.

---

*Benjamin Franklin went on to invent many other things, such as the lightning rod, which conducts lightning strikes away from tall buildings. He was also one of the people to sign the Declaration of Independence in 1776.

**A patent is an official license from the government guaranteeing that, for a set period, only its holder can make or sell an invention.

7. Trampoline—George Nissen, age 16

Nissen, a keen gymnast, came up with the idea for the trampoline in 1930 after watching trapeze artists dropping into safety nets at the circus. He wanted to create a net that would bounce the person back up again, so he built his own version from a steel frame and canvas sheet in his parents' garage. Eventually he perfected his invention by adding springs, and trampolining became an Olympic sport.

8. FreshPaper—Kavita Shukla, age 17

FreshPaper looks like a normal square of white paper but is made with a special mix of herbs and spices. If you place a sheet next to fruit or vegetables, it helps them stay fresh for up to four times longer. Its inventor Kavita Shukla was inspired by a healthy spice-based drink made by her grandmother in India. She then researched the antibacterial properties of different herbs and spices as a school science project before winning a patent for her brilliant waste-saving idea in 2002.***

Frank Epperson

***Approximately 25 percent of the world's food goes bad before it can be eaten. Eco-friendly products such as FreshPaper will help stop so much of it from going to waste.

Accidental Genius

Five things invented by people who were trying to make something totally different*

1. Fireworks—invented around 800 CE

According to legend, the first fireworks were invented by a Chinese chemist. The chemist mixed a powder called potassium nitrate with sulfur and charcoal in the hope it would give him eternal life. Instead, the mixture caught fire and exploded. This exploding powder—later known as gunpowder—was packed into bamboo tubes and lit, setting off the world's first fireworks.

2. Silly Putty—invented in 1943

Scottish inventor and chemist James Wright was working on an engineering project to make a hard rubber when, to his surprise, he found that one of the mixtures he'd created could bounce. The company Wright was working for couldn't see a use for this curious material** and businessman Peter Hodgson bought the rights from them at a cost of $147, which is the equivalent of around $6,747 in today's money. Hodgson changed the name from "Nutty Putty" to "Silly Putty" and launched it as a children's toy.

3. Slinky—invented in 1943

Richard James, an American naval engineer, was developing a spring to keep sensitive equipment stable on ships. One day, he accidentally knocked some springs off a shelf, and to his amazement they continued to tumble end over end across the floor in an elegant and satisfying way. It gave him the idea for the Slinky, which is now a famous toy.***

---

*Play-Doh, although not created by accident, is an example of finding a new job for an old invention. It was first invented in 1933 as a putty used to clean soot from open fireplaces or off wallpaper. But in the 1950s, people stopped using fireplaces as much and the putty wasn't needed. So the putty was repurposed, and Play-Doh was born!

**Silly Putty is an unusual type of substance known as a "liquid solid" because in certain situations it behaves like a solid and in others, like a liquid. Pull it apart and it stretches. Throw it to the ground from a height and it shatters. Yet if you hit it with a hammer, it keeps its shape. Silly Putty has serious uses too: NASA astronauts took it with them on the Apollo 8 space mission to hold their tools in place in zero gravity.

***James's wife, Betty, thought of the name Slinky to describe the way the toy springs move. When they were first put on sale in 1945, all 400 were snapped up in 90 minutes. More than 250 million Slinky toys have now been sold.

4. Microwave oven—invented in 1945

American engineer Percy LeBaron Spencer was building a radar machine, which is used to detect the location of aircraft, when he accidentally discovered the cooking power of invisible waves called microwaves. He was standing next to a working radar machine, which uses microwaves, when he suddenly noticed that the machine had somehow melted the candy bar in his pocket. It gave him the idea for the first microwave cooking oven, which he called the Radarange.

5. Scotchgard—invented in 1953

American chemist Patsy Sherman was working in the laboratory trying to develop a new type of rubber for airplanes when one of her assistants accidentally dropped a beaker full of liquid onto her shoes. To her surprise, the liquid didn't stain her shoes, and when she tried to clean it off, the cleaning products just beaded up and slid off! This happy accident led to the invention of Scotchgard, an invisible spray that makes fabric resistant to water, oil, and other things that might stain it.

Turning Back the Clock

Nine machines built to tell
the time

1. Stick or bone—8,000+ years ago

How it works: One of the first ways that prehistoric humans learned to tell the time was by placing an upright stick or bone in the ground, and then following its shadow as the Sun moved across the sky throughout the day.

2. Sundial—around 1500 BCE

How it works: Sundials use shadows in the same way as the sticks and bones. The difference is that on a sundial the shadow is cast by a raised angular plate onto a second flat plate or dial. The dial has markings on it, to indicate the time of day. The oldest known sundial is from Egypt.

3. Candle clock—520 CE

How it works: A candle or set of candles were made to a standard size so that it took approximately the same amount of time for each wax shaft to burn to the bottom. Regular markings on the side of, or alongside, the candle were used to measure units of time as the wax burned down.

4. Weighted clock—1283

How it works: The downward force of the weight inside this clock turns a system of gears regulated by an ingenious mechanism called an escapement. The moving gears then turn a wheel with a pointer attached, which indicates the passing of time on a dial.

5. Hourglass—before 1338

How it works: Hourglasses contain grains of sand that steadily fall from one glass chamber through a narrow opening to a chamber below. When all the sand has reached the bottom, you can start again by turning the hourglass upside down.

6. Spring clock—about 1450

How it works: Whereas weighted clocks were powered by the force of gravity as it pulls downwards on a weight, spring clocks were powered by the elastic tension created when you pull apart the coils of a metal spring. One major benefit of clocks powered by metal springs is that they could be made smaller and more portable, paving the way for the later invention of the pocket watch and wristwatch.

7. Pendulum clock—1656

How it works: One disadvantage of spring clocks is that as the internal spring unwinds the clock becomes less accurate. So the Dutch physicist Christiaan Huygens invented a new type of clock that was powered by the more consistent swinging motion of a pendulum.

8. Quartz clock—1927

How it works: Over time, a swinging pendulum is slowed by the force of gravity. So engineers needed to find a new and more reliable method of regulating clocks. In the 1920s they discovered that if you pass an electric current through the mineral quartz, it vibrates in a very consistently regular way. Quartz clocks, which are powered by electric batteries and regulated by a crystal of quartz, only lose time by one second every ten years.

9. Atomic clock—1955

How it works: Not long after the invention of quartz clocks, scientists started to develop an even more accurate way of keeping time. Atomic clocks are regulated by the very consistent frequency of energy released by atoms of the element cesium. The most accurate modern atomic clocks lose just one second of time every 300 million years.

All Around the World

The fastest times people have traveled around the world using different machines

By airplane—1 day, 7 hours, 27 minutes, and 49 seconds in 1995

By hot-air balloon—11 days, 4 hours, and 20 minutes in 2016

By motorcycle—19 days, 4 hours in 2015*

By car—19 days, 10 hours, and 10 minutes in 2000

By sailboat—40 days, 23 hours, and 30 minutes in 2017**

By submarine—60 days and 21 hours in 1960

By powerboat—60 days, 23 hours, and 49 minutes in 2008

By bicycle—78 days, 14 hours, and 40 minutes in 2017

By tandem bicycle—263 days, 8 hours, and 7 minutes*** in 2020

*It is not possible to travel all around the world on land alone. So people circumnavigating the globe in cars, motorcycles, and other land vehicles have to travel by boat or airplane at some points of their journey in order to cross the sea.

**The first expedition to circumnavigate the globe was led by the Portuguese explorer Ferdinand Magellan in 1519. However, sailing all the way around the world was a risky business in the 16th century. Magellan died halfway through the three-year voyage and of the 260 crew members who set sail with him, only 18 returned.

***A tandem is a bicycle that's designed for two or more riders sitting one behind the other. The longest recorded tandem bicycle is 135 feet 10.7 inches (41.4 m) long with seats for 20 riders. It has yet to circumnavigate the world.

Daredevils

The longest distances jumped using different vehicles

In order to jump, vehicles drive over a ramp that helps them shoot upward and travel through the air before they land.

Pickup truck—379 ft 5 in (115.64 m)* in 2016

Motorcycle—351 ft (106.98 m) in 2008

Snowmobile—301 ft (91.7 m) in 2010

Car—269 ft (81.99 m)** in 2009

Monster truck—237 ft 7 in (72.42 m) in 2013

All-terrain vehicle (ATV)—176 ft 11 in (53.92 m) in 2013

Limousine—103 ft (31.39 m) in 2002

Tractor trailer—83 ft 7 in (25.48 m) in 2014

Skateboard—79 ft (24 m) in 2004

Garbage truck—77 ft 4 in (23.57 m) in 2004

BMX bike—50 ft 6 in (15.39 m) in 2005

Unicycle—9 ft 8 in (2.95 m) in 2006

*That's longer than 20 ice-cream trucks parked end to end!

**The longest jump by a remote-controlled car is 131 feet 9 inches (40.21 m), while the longest jump by a car driving backward is 89 feet 3.25 inches (27.2 m).

Monster Machines

Eight of the biggest machines ever built

1. Large Hadron Collider
Length/diameter: 28,196 ft (8,594 m)

Built: In 2008 to study particles that are smaller than atoms.

Where: Geneva, Switzerland.

The Large Hadron Collider's job is to accelerate tiny particles around a vast loop deep underground at speeds of up to 984 million feet per second (300 million m/s). Why? So scientists can see what happens when they smash into each other.

2. Overburden Conveyor Bridge F60
Length: 1,647 ft (502 m)

Built: In 1969 to remove waste material.

Where: Lusatian coalfields, Germany.

The F60 is a giant conveyor belt that weighs 14,900 tons (13,500 tonnes) and is the longest vehicle ever made. It's used to transport waste material, known as "overburden," after it has been dug up from the ground.*

3. FAST telescope
Length/diameter: 1,640 ft (500 m)

Built: In 2016 to study space.

Where: Guizhou Province, China.

Radio telescopes are designed to pick up radio waves from outer space and FAST is the largest and most sensitive in the world. The name stands for Five-hundred-meter Aperture Spherical Telescope.**

4. The Prelude
Length: 1,601 ft (488 m)

Built: In 2017 to drill and store natural gas.

Where: Off the coast of Western Australia.

Because it floats on the sea and can move, you could argue that this colossal drilling and storage facility for natural gas is the world's biggest ship. It would take longer than 5 minutes to walk from one end of the Prelude to the other.

5. Bagger 293
Length: 738 ft (225 m)

Built: In 1995 to mine coal.

Where: Hambach, Germany.

When the huge wheel at the front rotates, a series of 18 buckets scoops up piles of coal and then drops them on a conveyor belt to be transported away from the mine. Bagger 293 is both the heaviest and largest land vehicle on Earth.

6. NASA crawler-transporter
Length: 131 ft (40 m)

Built: In 1965 to move space rockets.

Where: Kennedy Space Center, Florida.

NASA has two crawler-transporters. Each weighs around 3,300 tons (3,000 tonnes) and can carry a load equivalent to the weight of 777 airplanes.

Right: FAST telescope

*The Overburden Conveyor Bridge is sometimes known as the Reclining Eiffel Tower because it looks a bit like the famous Paris monument lying on its side.

**FAST's giant receiving dish has roughly the same surface area as 30 soccer fields.

7. P&H L-2350 Wheel Loader

Length: 67 ft (20 m)

Built: In 2012 to move earth.

Where: Texas.

The biggest earth mover ever built, its monster tires are 13 feet (4 m) tall, while the bucket at the front holds the same volume of material as five dump trucks.

8. Big Bertha

Diameter: 57.5 ft (17.5 m)

Built: In 2013 to dig tunnels.

Where: Under the city of Seattle.

The giant drills that are used to dig big tunnels» are called boring machines.*** Big Bertha is the widest drill ever built—it's taller than a five-story building—and weighs 6,700 tons (6,078 tonnes).

» To learn about some of the world's deepest and longest tunnels, see page 265.

***Although, they're actually quite interesting!

Micro Machines

Ten of the smallest machines ever made

1. Smallest abacus—
0.00000000000004 in (0.000001 nm*)

A team of scientists built a counting machine using ten molecules of the element carbon that can be moved along a tiny groove on a copper surface like the beads of an abacus.

2. Smallest engine—0.000000004 in (0.1 nm)

Made from a single calcium ion (which is an atom with an electrical charge, and in this case a positive charge), the world's smallest engine converts heat from laser beams into physical movement, which has been used to turn a tiny wheel. It's around 10 billion times smaller than a car engine.

3. Smallest "car"—0.00000016 in (4 nm)

Mostly built from carbon atoms, this molecular "car" is so small you would need a powerful microscope to see it. Created by scientists as an experiment, it's slightly wider than a strand of human DNA.

4. Smallest robot—0.0000047 in (120 nm)

Tiny machines called nanorobots can be sent inside the human body to repair damaged cells and perform other medical tasks.**

5. Smallest watch—0.13 in (3.4 mm)

Despite only being 0.13 inches (3.4 mm) wide, 0.05 inches (1.4 mm) thick, and weighing less than a gram, the smallest mechanical watch has 98 individual parts.

6. Smallest fidget spinner—0.2 in (5.1 mm)

The world's smallest metal fidget spinner could easily sit (and spin) on the tip of a sewing needle.

7. Smallest electric drill—0.26 in (6.7 mm)

This scaled-down electric drill is powered by a small 3-volt battery. Its rotating metal head, or drill bit, can make 0.02-inch- (0.5-mm-) wide holes in foam and soft wood.

8. Smallest telephone—1.87 in (47.5 mm)

The smallest telephone that you can still use to make a phone call is 1.87 inches (47.5 mm) tall, 0.3 inches (10 mm) wide, and 0.8 inches (21 mm) thick.

9. Smallest motorcycle—3.1 in (80 mm)

Tom Wiberg from Sweden built the smallest motorcycle to be ridden by a human. The seat is 2.6 inches (65 mm) off the ground.***

10. Smallest unicycle—11 in (280 mm)

The smallest rideable unicycle is roughly the height of a school ruler. Its wheel has a diameter of just 0.49 inches (12.7 mm).

---

*This stands for nanometer, which is one millionth of a millimeter.

**Doctors control the nanorobots from outside the body using magnets.

***To prove it worked, Wiberg rode his miniature motorcycle, which he named Smalltoe, for a distance of 32.8 feet (10 m). It has a top speed of 1.24 miles per hour (2 km/h).

Smalltoe

Pedal Power

Eleven extraordinary machines powered by pedals*

1. **Boneshaker**—invented in 1868

2. **Monowheel**—invented in 1869

3. **Penny-farthing****—invented in 1869

4. **Quadracycle**—invented in 1885

5. **Snowbike**—invented in 1892

6. **Prone bicycle**—invented in 1897

7. **Tandem**—invented in 1898

8. **Amphibious bicycle**—invented in 1932

9. **Handcycle**—invented in 1987

10. **Pedal-powered plane**—invented in 1988***

11. **Bike bus**—invented in 2002

*There are estimated to be more than two billion bicycles around the world today, with approximately a quarter of them being used by people in China. In the Netherlands, around a third of all journeys are made by bicycle.

**The penny-farthing got its name because the contrasting sizes of its wheels looked like two British coins: the large penny and much smaller farthing.

***On April 23, 1988, the pedal-powered aircraft Daedalus flew over the Mediterranean Sea between the Greek islands of Crete and Santorini. Daedalus flew a distance of 72 miles (115 km) in 3 hours and 54 minutes.

Balancing Act

Nine types of unicycle and what they do

A unicycle has a single wheel with two pedals and a seat directly above, but no handlebars. Because it's hard to balance on a unicycle, acrobats and clowns sometimes use them in performances (acrobats know how to stay on and clowns know how to fall off!).

1. Giraffe unicycles Very tall unicycles with extended seats that need a long chain to reach down to the wheel.*

2. Freestyle unicycles These have smaller wheels and high-pressure tires, and are designed for stunts and tricks.

3. MUnis As the mountain bike of the unicycle world, these are built to cope with hills and off-road terrain.

4. Touring unicycles Larger wheels and comfy seats make these bikes suited for distances of 5 miles (8 km) or more.**

5. Trials unicycles Their fat, knobbly tyres are designed for jumping over obstacles, such as stairs or picnic benches.

6. Kangaroo unicycles Both pedals are fixed at the same height. As you pedal, your left and right feet push at the same time and your body bounces up and down like a kangaroo.

7. Freewheeling unicycles Built to coast along roads at faster speeds, this type of unicycle is one of the few to have brakes.

8. Self-balancing unicycles These electric unicycles have 3-inch- (8-cm-) thick tires to make them easier to balance. Features include front and rear headlights, music speakers, and a maximum speed of 38 miles per hour (61 km/h), which is very fast for a unicycle!

9. Seatless unicycles Also known as the "Ultimate Wheel," this unicycle doesn't have a frame or seat. It's just a wheel with a pedal fixed to either side. Proceed with caution!

Right: The Chinese Yinchuan Acrobatic Troupe performing on giraffe unicycles

*The tallest unicycle on record measured almost 30 feet (9 m) tall and was ridden by Wesley Williams, the "One Wheel Wonder." (Try saying that quickly while riding a unicycle!)

**In 2007, Sam Wakeling from the UK unicycled for a record-breaking 105.5 miles (169.9 km) without his feet touching the ground.

Track Records

Ten of the world's fastest trains

1. **Shanghai maglev,* China**—270 mph (430 km/h)

2. **Fuxing Hao CR400AF/BF, China**—250 mph (400 km/h)

3. **Harmony CRH 380A, China**—240 mph (380 km/h)

4. **AGV Italo, Italy**—224 mph (360 km/h)

5. **Siemens Velaro E/AVS 103, Spain**—217 mph (350 km/h)

6. **Deutsche Bahn ICE, Germany**—200 mph (330 km/h)

7. **Korail KTX, South Korea**—200 mph (330 km/h)

8. **Shinkansen H5 and E5, Japan**—198 mph (320 km/h)

9. **SNCF TGV, France**—198 mph (320 km/h)

10. **Talgo 350, Spain**—198 mph (320 km/h)

---

*"Maglev" is an abbreviation of "magnetic levitation" because, unlike most trains, a maglev has no wheels. Instead, it floats on a magnetic field between the train and the track. The Shanghai maglev can go from standing still to its top speed in 4 minutes.

Fast Track

Ten of the oldest rapid transit systems in the world

Hustle and Bustle

Ten of the busiest rapid transit systems and how many passengers they carry in a year

1. **London Underground, England**—1863*
2. **Budapest Metro, Hungary**—1896
3. **Glasgow Subway, Scotland**—1896
4. **Chicago "L," United States**—1897**
5. **Paris Métro, France**—1900
6. **MBTA Subway, Boston, United States**—1901
7. **Berlin U-Bahn, Germany**—1902
8. **Athens Metro, Greece**—1904
9. **New York City Subway, United States**—1904
10. **SEPTA, Philadelphia, United States**—1907

1. **Beijing Subway, China**—3.95 billion*
2. **Shanghai Metro, China**—3.88 billion
3. **Guangzhou Metro, China**—3.3 billion
4. **Seoul Subway, South Korea**—2.92 billion
5. **Tokyo Metro, Japan**—2.77 billion»
6. **Moscow Metro, Russia**—2.56 billion
7. **Shenzhen Metro, China**—2.02 billion
8. **Mass Transit Railway, Hong Kong**—1.8 billion
9. **New York City Subway, United States**—1.7 billion
10. **Mexico City Metro, Mexico**—1.66 billion

*Despite its name, most of the London Underground is above ground. When its first underground railway line opened in 1863, the trains were powered by steam.

**The "L" is short for "elevated" because, for large parts of the network, the trains run on raised tracks high above the streets of Chicago.

*The Beijing Subway is both the longest and busiest metro system in the world. Its highest recorded number of passenger trips in a single day is 13.75 million.

» To find out how all these people fit in the trains, see page 257.

Big Birds

Nine of the largest planes ever built

1. Stratolaunch*—384-ft (117-m) wingspan

This unique airplane has two bodies, called fuselages, and holds the record for the longest ever wingspan. If you parked it sideways on a soccer field, its wings would extend through the goals by 25 feet (8 m) on either side.

2. Hughes H-4 Hercules—320-ft (97.5-m) wingspan

Known as the "Spruce Goose,"** this giant flying boat was the largest wooden airplane ever built. It only flew once, in 1947, for 26 seconds.

3. Antonov An-225 Mriya—290-ft (88.4-m) wingspan

Only one of these gigantic planes has ever been built—in 1988. It is still in service today, transporting important cargo—such as medicines for the Covid-19 pandemic—around the world.

4. Boeing 747—224-ft (68.4-m) wingspan

At 250 feet (76 m), the Boeing 747 is the world's longest airliner and can fly more than 9,000 miles (14,400 km) between takeoff and landing. Special versions have been used to carry NASA space shuttles and as Air Force One, the official airplane of the US President.

5. Lockheed C-5 Galaxy—223-ft (67.9-m) wingspan

The nose of this military transport plane flips up to allow vehicles and other cargo to drive inside. It is big enough to transport helicopters—and other planes!

*The Stratolaunch is designed to carry rockets high up into the sky, then release them so they can launch from Earth's stratosphere into space.

**Newspaper reporters nicknamed the wooden plane the "Spruce Goose" after the spruce tree, even though it was made almost entirely from birch.

6. Airbus Beluga XL—198-ft (60.3-m) wingspan

Designed to carry huge items of cargo around the world, the gigantic hold, or main body, of the Beluga XL is 207 feet (63 m) long, 26 feet (8 m) wide, and the biggest of its kind in the world. It's shaped like a beluga whale, and also sports painted eyes and a smiling mouth.

7. McDonnell Douglas KC-10 Extender—165-ft (50.4-m) wingspan

The world's largest aircraft tanker can carry 52,250 gallons (197,788 liters) of fuel. By trailing a long hose behind it, the KC-10 Extender is able to refuel fighter jets and other planes in midair.

8. Dornier Do X—157-ft (47.8-m) wingspan

This flying boat was powered by 12 engines and took 4 years to build. At the time of its first flight in 1929 it was the world's largest aircraft. However, due to its great cost, it was eventually abandoned.

9. Korabl Maket—123-ft (37.6-m) wingspan

Known as the "Caspian Sea Monster," the Korabl Maket was an experimental seaplane developed by the Soviet Union that could only fly between 16 and 33 feet (5 and 10 m) above ground or over water.

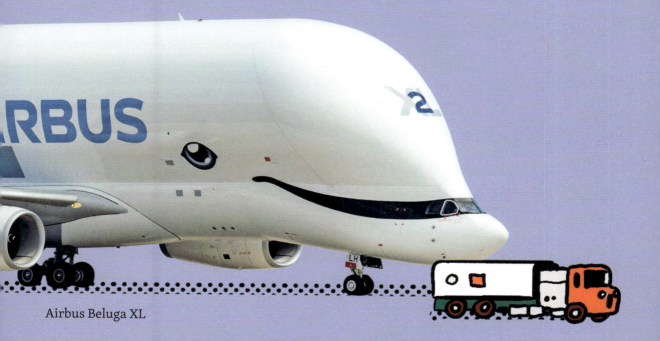

Airbus Beluga XL

In the Driver's Seat

Cars in numbers

1.4 billion The estimated number of cars in the world.*

19 million The price in dollars of the world's most expensive new car in 2019, the Bugatti La Voiture Noire. Only one was ever built.

3,039,122 The number of miles (4,890,993 km) traveled by Irving Gordon in his 1966 Volvo P1800S, the longest total distance driven by a single car.

290,000 The cost in dollars of one of the world's most expensive speeding tickets.**

30,000 The number of individual parts found in the average car.

1885 The year that German engineer Karl Benz built the first car. Benz went on to help found the Daimler-Benz company, which launched the Mercedes-Benz car line in 1926.

304.77 The top speed in miles per hour (490 km/h) of the world's fastest road car, the Bugatti Chiron Super Sport 300+.

231 The longest distance in miles (271 km) driven by a car tipped up on its side and balancing on two wheels. The record-breaking stunt was pulled off by Italian Michele Pilia in 2009.

26 The number of wheels on the world's longest limousine.

Hot Wheels

The ten most popular cars in history

1. **Toyota Corolla (1966–present)**— 43 million+ sold

2. **Ford F-Series truck (1948–present)**— 40 million+ sold

3. **Volkswagen Golf (1974–present)**— 30 million+ sold

4. **Volkswagen Beetle* (1938–2003)**— 23 million+ sold

5. **Lada 1200 (1970–1988)**— 19 million+ sold

6. **Ford Escort (1967–present)**— 18 million+ sold

7. **Honda Civic (1972–present)**— 18 million+ sold

8. **Honda Accord (1976–present)**— 17 million+ sold

9. **Ford Model T** (1908–1927)**— 15 million+ sold

10. **Volkswagen Passat (1973–present)**— 15 million+ sold

---

*No wonder it's tricky finding a parking space!

**The ticket was issued to a driver in Switzerland, where the size of a speeding fine is partly calculated based on how wealthy the driver is.

*With the first model sold in 1938 and the last 65 years later in 2003, the Volkswagen Beetle was in production for longer than any other car.

**The Ford Model T was the first car to be mass produced on an assembly line. This was more efficient because it allowed large teams of factory workers to build lots of cars at the same time. By 1921, 57 percent of all cars made anywhere in the world were Model Ts.

Under the Hood

Twenty unusual fuels that have been used to power cars

Most modern cars are powered by either gas, diesel, or electricity. But some more experimental models have been built to run off surprising sources of energy.

1. Air
2. Alcohol
3. Algae (simple aquatic plants)
4. Ammonia
5. Coal
6. Coffee*
7. Compressed air
8. Cooking oil
9. Human poop**
10. Hydrogen
11. Jet fuel
12. Natural gas
13. Nitrogen gas
14. Sawdust
15. Seawater
16. Solar power***
17. Soybeans
18. Steam
19. Water
20. Wood

*As an experiment, a Volkswagen Scirocco was adapted to drive on a 209-mile (336-km) journey powered only by ground coffee beans. The "Car-puccino," as it was known, traveled 1 mile (1.6 km) for every 56 espressos worth of coffee in its tank and reached speeds of up to 60 miles per hour (100 km/h).

**In 2015, a bus in the UK became the first vehicle to run entirely on human waste (i.e., poop). Named the "Bio-Bus," it had seats for 40 passengers and looked, sounded, and even smelled like any other bus.

***The Lightyear One is an electric car powered by 1,000 solar panels. It has a range of 450 miles (725 km), with more miles per day possible at sunnier times of the year.

Trade Secrets

Fourteen sneaky gadgets that real-life spies have used

1. An exploding briefcase.

2. An umbrella tipped with poison.

3. A compass disguised as a mechanical pencil,* which spies used to read maps and find their way in enemy territory.

4. A camera hidden inside a button.**

5. A microphone disguised as an olive.

6. A machine that looked like a stone and could detect vibrations made by an enemy agent up to 1,000 feet (300 m) away.

7. An undercover pigeon with a miniature camera strapped to its chest.

8. A solar-powered listening device that looked like a tree stump.

9. A gold cigarette case concealing a gun that could fire poison-tipped bullets.

10. A radio transmitter hidden inside the heel of a shoe.***

11. A robot fish that collected water samples without being noticed.

12. A stick of red lipstick that could fire a 0.2-inch (4.5-mm) bullet.

13. A pen that wrote with disappearing ink.

14. A miniature toolkit that came in a smooth oval case. If a spy was caught by the enemy, they could hide it up their bottom.

*Secret compasses and maps were also hidden inside special spy versions of the board game Monopoly during World War II. You can recognize top-secret Monopoly boards by the small red dot added to the "Free Parking" space.

**Spy cameras have also been disguised as ties, matchboxes, and, perhaps cleverest of all, hidden inside a new photocopying machine before it was delivered to a foreign country's embassy. So whenever staff at the embassy used the machine to photocopy a secret document, the spy camera took a picture at the same time.

***Spies have also hidden secret radio transmitters inside hollowed-out dog poop, which, fortunately for the radio operators, was fake.

Playtime

Toys in numbers

91 billion The amount of money in dollars that people around the world spend on toys each year.

700 million The number of tiny rubber wheels made by LEGO each year, which means the Danish toy company is the world's No. 1 tire manufacturer.

500 million+ The number of copies of Tetris that have been sold, making it the most popular paid-for computer game of all time.

6.25 million The price in dollars of L'Oiseleur (which is French for "the bird trainer"), the world's most expensive doll.*

168 The total number of dots on a standard set of dominoes.

74 The distance in miles (120 km) of the world's longest model railway line, which ran between Fort William and Inverness in Scotland.**

40 The number of stories in the tallest recorded Jenga tower, which players build, layer by layer, by balancing wooden blocks on top of each other.

3.47 The time in seconds it took Yusheng Du to solve a Rubik's Cube, setting a new world record.***

Jenga

---

*L'Oiseleur is a 4-foot- (1.2-m-) tall mechanical doll that can move on its own and play the flute thanks to a complex system of internal cogs and gears. The doll has more than 2,300 different parts, needs no batteries or motors, and took more than 15,000 working hours to build.

**The toy train that traveled the length of the record-breaking model railway had a top speed of 3 miles per hour (5 km/h) and took 9 days to complete its journey.

***The largest number of Rubik's Cubes solved in one hour while wearing a blindfold is 59, by Graham Siggins from the United States. Solving a Rubik's Cube while blindfolded is just as tricky as it sounds, as you have to memorize the exact position of all 54 colored squares on the cube before putting on your blindfold and getting started.

At Your Convenience

Forty things you can buy from vending machines*

1. Bananas
2. Batteries
3. Bicycle parts
4. Books
5. Bread
6. Burritos
7. Candles
8. Canned carrots
9. Caviar
10. Cheese
11. Costumes
12. Cupcakes
13. Diapers
14. Eggs
15. Fishing bait
16. Flip-flops
17. Flowers
18. French fries
19. Gold bars
20. Guitar strings
21. Hair extensions
22. Hamburgers
23. Hot dogs
24. Laptops
25. LEGO
26. Lettuce
27. Lucky Charms
28. Mashed potatoes
29. Milk
30. Pecan pie
31. Pizza
32. Popcorn
33. Rice
34. Shoes
35. Ties
36. Toilet paper
37. T-shirts
38. Umbrellas
39. Wigs
40. Wigs for dogs

*The first vending machine is thought to have been designed in the 1st century CE by the Greek engineer Hero of Alexandria. The machine gave out cups of holy water in temples. When a silver coin was placed in a slot at the top of Hero's machine, the weight of the coin would activate a lever that then poured a specific amount of water into a container.

Glorious Technicolor

The four colors of ink used in a color printer*

1. Cyan (blue)

2. Magenta (purple/red)

3. Yellow

4. Black

The images in this book have all been printed using the four colors in the list. This image shows how the colors are printed in dots which, when combined, make an image.

*By mixing just these four colored inks together in different combinations, printers can reproduce on paper almost 70 percent of the million or so colors visible to the human eye.

Hole Numbers

Ten machines that make holes

1. Boring machine
Hole width: 3.3–57.5 ft (1–17.5 m)
Used for: Digging large tunnels.

2. Auger drill
Hole width: 1.5–18 in (3.8–45.7 cm)
Used for: Digging vertical holes in the ground, such as wells.

3. Cookie cutter
Hole width: 2–4 in (5–10 cm)
Used for: Cutting round holes in dough to make cookies.

4. Masonry drill
Hole width: 0.12–1.6 in (3–40 mm)
Used for: Making holes in bricks and other building materials.

5. Hole punch
Hole width: 0.24–0.31 in (6–8 mm)
Used for: Creating holes in a piece of paper
so it can be stored in a three-ring binder.

6. Surgical drill
Hole width: 0.02–0.2 in (0.5–5 mm)
Used for: Medical operations,
including dental fillings.

7. Sewing machine
Hole width: 0.02–0.09 in
(0.5–2.3 mm)
Used for: Fastening together pieces of fabric to make clothing and other cloth products.*

8. Electron beam drill
Hole width: 0.002–0.25 in (0.05–6 mm)
Used for: Making mechanical watches and other machine parts.**

9. Laser drill
Hole width: 0.002–0.04 in (0.05–1 mm)
Used for: Making electronic circuit boards and drilling through rocks to search for oil.

10. EDM micro drill
Hole width: 0.0002–0.0004 in (0.005–0.01 mm)
Used for: Making tiny holes for fuel to flow through in car and jet engines.***

*Before the invention of the sewing machine in 1790, it would take around 10 hours to make a dress by hand. Using one of the first sewing machines, the same job could be done in 60 minutes.

**An electron beam drill can make up to 2,000 holes a second.

***EDM stands for Electrical Discharge Machining because EDM drills use electrical sparks to create tiny holes in metals.

Be Prepared

The thirty-three tools in a pocket Swiss Army Knife

A Swiss Army Knife is an ingenious folding pocketknife that contains dozens of handy tools. The first model was made for Swiss soldiers in 1891. Today, there are more than a hundred different versions sold around the world. Swiss Army Knives have even been used by astronauts on the Moon. The following tools are all part of a Swiss Army Knife called the SwissChamp.

1. 58-mm blade For cutting and slicing.

2. 36-mm blade For small, delicate tasks.

3. Corkscrew For removing corks from the necks of bottles but also handy for unpicking knots.

4. Can opener For piercing and then cutting open a tin can.

5. 3-mm screwdriver (located at the tip of the can opener) For loosening or tightening small screws.

6. Bottle opener For hooking underneath a metal bottle cap to lift and then remove the cap.

7. 6-mm screwdriver For loosening or tightening larger screws.

8. Wire stripper (located on the side of the bottle opener) For stripping the rubber casing from electrical wires.

9. Reamer, punch, and sewing eye For sewing pieces of heavy fabric together. It was originally designed so that soldiers could repair their tents.

10. Key ring For attaching the knife to a belt hook, bag, or set of keys.

11. Tweezers For picking up objects too small for fingers, and for removing wooden splinters.

12. Toothpick For removing bits of food stuck between your teeth.

13. Scissors For cutting. The blades automatically reopen after each cut thanks to a spring between the handles.

14. Multi-purpose hook For holding heavy things. It can hold up to 200 pounds (90 kg), which is heavier than the average adult human.

15. Wood saw For cutting through tough materials with its jagged blade.

16. Fish scaler For removing the scales from fish, but also perfect for carving pumpkins.

17. Hook disgorger For removing the hook from a fish's mouth after it's been reeled in.

18. Ruler (centimeters) For measuring.

19. Ruler (inches) (found on the reverse of the centimeter ruler) Also for measuring!

20. Nail file For smoothing the edge of your fingernails.

21. Metal file For filing down the edges of pieces of metal.

22. Nail cleaner For digging out the dirt beneath your fingernails.

23. Metal saw For cutting through metal.

24. 2.5-mm screwdriver For loosening and tightening tiny screws; ideal for the screws in the hinges of glasses.

25. Wood chisel For carving wood.

26. Pliers For gripping, twisting, and pulling.

27. Wire cutter (located on the inside edge of the pliers) For slicing through wires.

28. Wire crimping tool (located in the middle of the pliers' handles) For connecting different wires.

29. Phillips screwdriver For loosening and tightening Phillips screws.

30. Magnifying glass For enlarging objects to eight times their normal size.

31. Ballpoint pen For writing at any angle. The ink is pressurized, which means you can even write while upside down. So it's perfect for astronauts to use in space.

32. Removable straight pin For digging out splinters or pressing the small reset buttons on cell phones and other devices.

33. Mini 1.5-mm screwdriver (the gray end twists inside the corkscrew so it can be stored away) For loosening and tightening the tiniest screws.

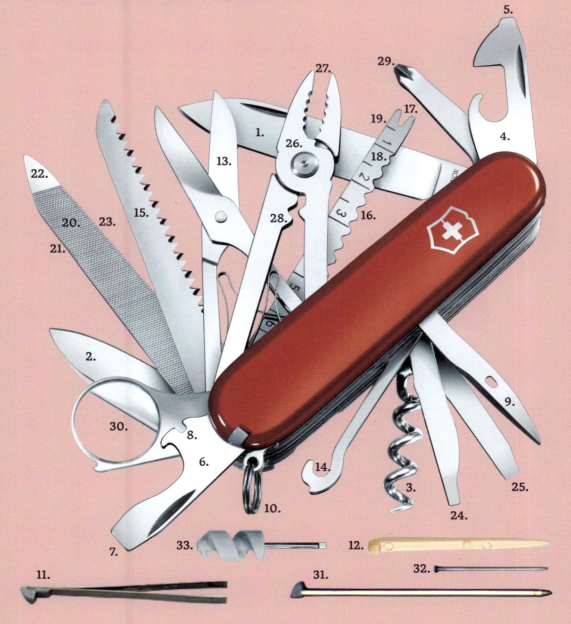

Siege Engines

Six medieval machines designed to attack a castle

In the Middle Ages (500–1500 CE), invading armies could completely surround a castle so no one could get in or out. This was called a siege. Some sieges lasted weeks, months, or even years.* Armies built an array of extraordinary machines to attack castles from outside the walls. Here are a few of them:

1. Siege towers rolled up alongside a castle so the invading soldiers could climb over the top of the castle walls.

2. Trebuchets launched large missiles, including massive stones and buckets of burning oil, at or into the castle.**

3. Ballistas fired arrows as well as other deadly missiles that would have been too heavy for any human to shoot from a handheld bow.

4. Catapults threw rocks and other small objects to break down the castle walls.

5. Battering rams built from tree trunks smashed open the castle gates. Soldiers used their weight and strength to push them forward. The rams were often suspended from wooden roofs that also served to protect the soldiers beneath as they charged forward.

6. Springalds could fire three deadly metal arrows called bolts as far as 525 feet (160 m) in a single shot.

*The longest recorded siege in history was of the city of Candia (which is now called Heraklion) on the Mediterranean island of Crete. It was attacked by armies of the Ottoman Empire in 1648. The defending army held out for 21 years and 149 days before finally surrendering. Candia was a port city, so was able to receive supplies from ally boats.

**The largest trebuchet ever built was called the Warwolf. It could hurl 306-pound (140-kg) rocks a distance of 656 feet (200 m). It took more than 50 craftsmen at least 3 months to build.

Trebuchet

Mechanical Marvels

Six ancient robots

Centuries before the discovery of electricity and the invention of circuit boards and computer chips, inventors built amazing mechanical models designed to move like humans and animals.

1. The floating orchestra

When: 1200s

How it moved: Ismail al-Jazari, a great Arabian engineer, artist, and inventor, created this floating mechanical orchestra.* It included a harp player, flute player, and two drummers, who played music while a crew of mechanical oarsmen seemingly rowed them around in a boat. However, the musicians, oarsmen, and boat actually moved thanks to a complex internal system of levers and pegs.

2. The robot knight

When: 1495

How it moved: According to sketches made by its designer—the great Italian artist and inventor Leonardo da Vinci—the robot knight could stand, sit down, turn its head, cross its arms, and even lift up the metal visor on its helmet.» Although no complete drawings of the knight exist today, there is evidence that Leonardo built a prototype in 1495 to demonstrate to guests at a party.**

3. The mechanical monk

When: 1560s

How it moved: This 15-inch- (38-cm-) tall robot monk, which was built by a clockmaker and inventor named Juanelo Turriano, could walk in a square pattern while moving its eyes, lips, and head as if it was saying a prayer. Its mechanical feet moved up and down as it walked, but it was actually propelled by three wheels hidden beneath the monk's robe.***

4. The digesting duck

When: 1739

How it moved: Designed by French inventor Jacques de Vaucanson, this mechanical duck could beat its wings and splash around in a pool of water. Even more impressively, it would eat grain from a human's hand, appear to digest it, and then push a poop-like pellet out of its bottom onto a silver plate.

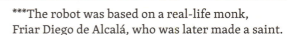

---

*Al-Jazari's other inventions included robotic peacocks, water-powered clocks, and a mechanical handwashing machine that automatically offered people soap and a towel, then used a water-flushing mechanism almost identical to that of a modern toilet.

» For more about Leonardo and other people who were ahead of their time, see pages 374–375.

**In 2002, a NASA scientist named Mark Rosheim built a new robot knight based on Leonardo's sketches that worked in exactly the way that the 15th-century designs predicted.

***The robot was based on a real-life monk, Friar Diego de Alcalá, who was later made a saint.

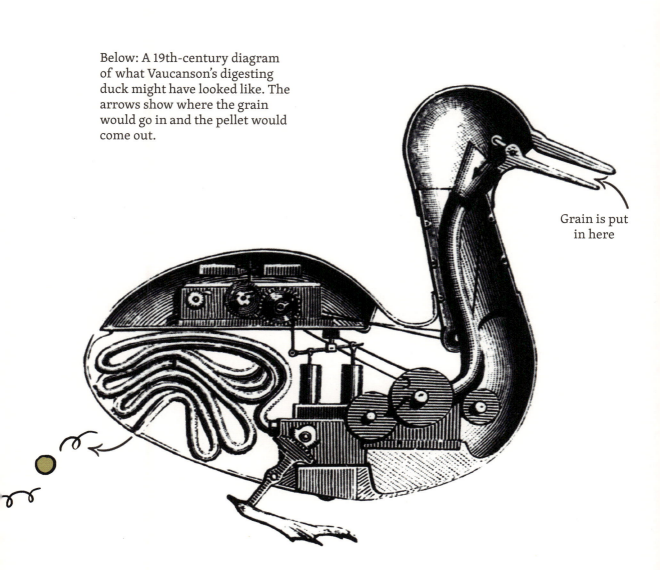

Below: A 19th-century diagram of what Vaucanson's digesting duck might have looked like. The arrows show where the grain would go in and the pellet would come out.

Grain is put in here

5. The three automatons

When: 1768

How it moved: These three 2-foot- (60-cm-) tall robotic dolls, designed by Swiss inventor Pierre Jaquet-Droz, each performed a task while sitting at a desk. The Draughtsman used a pen to draw four pictures, including a portrait of King Louis XV of France. The Writer wrote pre-programmed letters on a sheet of paper using a tiny quill. The Musician played five tunes on an organ, taking a mechanical bow between each song.

6. The Silver Swan

When: 1773

How it moved: Powered by clockwork motors, the Silver Swan was designed to glide across an artificial stream before bending forward to catch and gobble up a mechanical fish moving through the "water" beneath. Originally built by a watchmaker named James Cox and his apprentice John Joseph Merlin, the swan is now on display at the Bowes Museum in the UK—and it still works!

Human Versus Machine

Seven human jobs that are now done by machines

1. Ice-cutter—a common job until the 1930s

To keep food cold before the invention of electric refrigerators, people would place blocks of ice in special "ice boxes" in their kitchens or cellars. But where did the ice come from? Harvesting it from frozen lakes and rivers was the dangerous job of ice-cutters, who would cut it into giant blocks with hand- or horse-drawn saws, ready to be delivered to customers.

Replaced by: Refrigerators.

2. Lamplighter—a common job until the 1930s

Before the invention of light bulbs, gas-powered streetlamps were used to illuminate cities such as London, New York, Moscow, and Tokyo. Each streetlamp had to be lit by hand by a lamplighter and then put out again in the morning.

Replaced by: Electric streetlamps.

3. Knocker-upper—a common job until the 1940s

In the 19th and early 20th centuries, before alarm clocks had been invented, how did people wake up early? In Britain and Ireland, the answer was to employ a knocker-upper. They would come to your house at the time you had requested and knock on your bedroom window, often with a long wooden pole.*

Replaced by: Alarm clocks.

4. Bowling alley pinsetter—a common job until the 1950s

When your ball knocks over the pins at the end of the lane at a modern tenpin bowling alley, a machine drops down to clear them. It then replaces them with a fresh set, neatly arranged in a triangular formation. Before 1936, when the first mechanical pinsetter was invented, a human being had to both clear and reset the pins.**

Replaced by: Mechanical pinsetters.

---

*Knocker-uppers also used pea-shooters to tap on their customers' windows. The tap made by a pole or a pea-shooter was loud enough to wake up the person inside but quiet enough not to wake their neighbors. Some people would write the time they wanted to be woken up on pieces of slate on the sides of their houses that were called "wake-up slates" or "knocky-up boards." It's thought that the last knocker-upper in the UK retired in 1973.

**It could be a painful job if you didn't keep your eye on the ball.

5. Switchboard operator—a common job before the 1970s

In the first half of the 20th century, many telephone calls were connected by human telephone operators sitting in front of large switchboards. They had to place a specific plug into a socket by hand to put the call through.

Replaced by: Computer-operated switchboards.

6. Elevator operator—a common job before the 1980s

The first elevators couldn't automatically stop at the floor where you wanted to get off. Instead, a human elevator operator would judge when to pull a lever to stop it at (hopefully) the correct height, then manually open and close the elevator's doors to let the passengers in and out.

Replaced by: Elevator buttons and automatic doors.

7. Film projectionist—a common job until the 2010s

In the 20th century, showing a movie at the movie theater required the skills of a projectionist, who would physically load and replace several rolls of 35-millimeter movie film during a screening. As well as being quite heavy, each roll of film had to be expertly loaded so there were no on-screen jolts between rolls.

Replaced by: Digital projectors.

A knocker-upper at work

Rules for Robots

Isaac Asimov's three laws of robotics

In 1941, the American science-fiction writer Isaac Asimov wrote a short story that included the author's "three laws of robotics." Asimov's laws were intended to be three simple instructions that would be programmed into every robot to keep them—and the human beings who created them—safe.*

1. A robot may not injure a human being or, through not acting, allow a human being to come to harm.

2. A robot must obey any orders given to it by human beings, except where such orders would conflict with the first law.

3. A robot must protect its own existence as long as such protection does not conflict with the first or second law.

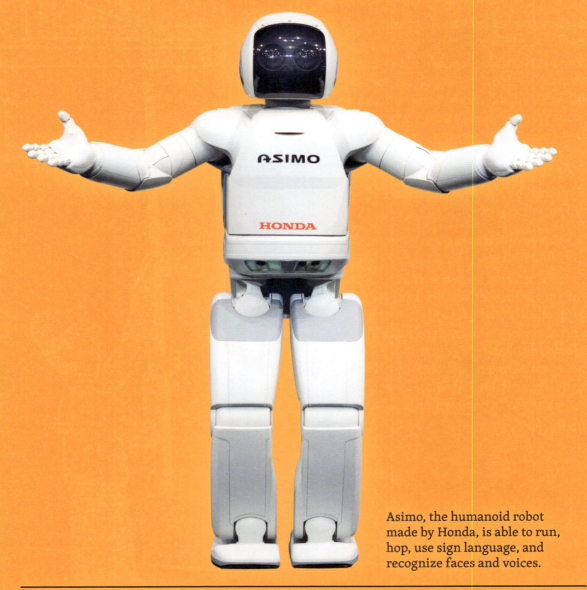

Asimo, the humanoid robot made by Honda, is able to run, hop, use sign language, and recognize faces and voices.

*Many of Asimov's stories explored the thinking and ideas behind these laws and how living alongside intelligent robots could pose interesting problems for future human societies.

Rise of the Machines

Twenty clever things that robots and artificial intelligence can do

Artificial intelligence, or AI, is the ability of a robot or computer to think and behave like a human. The following list gives examples of ways in which robots have successfully performed a complex task, learned a new skill, or solved a problem independently.

1. Drive cars.

2. Write newspaper reports.

3. Beat the best human players at chess, poker, Go, and other strategy games.

4. Do household chores.*

5. Translate between different languages.

6. Invent a secret code.

7. Lip-read.

8. Create valuable art.**

9. Recognize human emotions by watching people's expressions and body language.

10. Fly a drone or airplane.

11. Create new cooking recipes.

12. Write poetry.

13. Predict the weather.

14. Perform medical operations.

15. Compose music.

16. Play the violin.

17. Write computer programs for other computers.

18. Learn from mistakes.

19. Recognize faces.

20. Read minds.***

* "Intelligent" vacuum cleaners, for example, are able to use their internal sensors to move around a house on their own and spot the areas of the floor that need cleaning.

**In 2018, the art auction house Christie's made its first ever sale of a work of art created by artificial intelligence. "Inspired" by historical portraits made by human painters, the computer's work was called Portrait of Edmond Belamy. It sold for $432,500—more than 40 times the expected sale price.

***Computers are being taught to interpret electrical signals inside the human brain and convert those signals into speech. The aim of the research is to help people who are currently unable to speak by allowing them to communicate what they are thinking.

01010000 01000011*

Eight of the most important computers in history

1. Babbage's Difference Engine—1800s

Designed by the English engineer and inventor Charles Babbage, the Difference Engine was a mechanical calculator that used a system of cogs, gears, and levers to solve mathematical equations.**

2. Colossus—1944

The first electronic computer was built in Britain and used to break enemy codes during World War II. As its name suggests, it was colossal and weighed 5.5 tons (5 tonnes), which is the same as a large truck.

3. ENIAC—1946

ENIAC, which stands for Electronic Numerical Integrator and Computer, was the first "universal computer," which means it could perform different tasks depending on how it was programmed. The United States government used it for military research.

4. Small-Scale Experimental Machine—1948

The groundbreaking feature of the Small-Scale Experimental Machine, or Manchester Baby as it was known, was that it was the first computer able to run a program that had been stored in its internal memory.

5. DEC PDP-8—1965

Up until the 1960s, computers were enormously expensive, took up a vast amount of space, and often required a team of operators to take care of them. The DEC PDP-8 was the most successful of a new generation of "mini" computers that were much smaller*** and more affordable.

6. IBM PC—1981

"PC" stands for "personal computer," and the IBM PC was the machine that started a revolution in home computers that would actually fit on a desk. The IBM PC came with its own keyboard but no monitor: you had to plug it into a TV.

7. Apple Macintosh—1984

There were several pioneering features of this desktop computer that made Apple the well-known company it is now, including the fact that it was the first mass-produced computer to come with a mouse.

8. Deep Blue—1996

This powerful one-off computer made by IBM played a game of chess against the world's best chess player, Russia's Garry Kasparov—and lost. Its designers then made some improvements, and an updated version, called Deeper Blue, won the rematch, demonstrating just how far computers had come since the days of Babbage's Difference Engine.

---

*The title of this list says "PC" in the binary code that computers use to store information.

**The Difference Engine was never constructed in Babbage's lifetime, but in 1991 the Science Museum in London built a model following Babbage's original designs. It worked perfectly.

***That said, the DEC PDP-8 was still the size of a refrigerator.

Connected World

The Internet in numbers

4.7 billion The number of Internet users on Earth, which is approximately 60 percent of the global population.

3.96 billion The number of active users on social media.

3 million The number of emails sent every second.

86,000 The number of Google search queries made every second.

9,000 The number of tweets sent every second.

1989 The year the British scientist Tim Berners-Lee invented the World Wide Web, the network of interlinked websites on which the Internet is based.*

1971 The year the first email was sent.**

1,000 The number of photos uploaded to Instagram every second.

144 The average number of minutes Internet users spend on social media each day.

99 The percentage of people in Iceland who have access to the Internet, the highest of any country.

48 The percentage of Internet traffic that comes from human beings.***

10 The percentage of the world's electricity used by the Internet.

6.7 The number of hours the average Internet user spends online each day.

6 The number of new websites created each second.

*The Internet's very first website went live in 1991 and was designed to give scientists around the world "universal access to a large universe of documents." Berners-Lee's pioneering website has been kept in its original form and you can visit it today at info.cern.ch.

**The first email was sent by US computer programmer Ray Tomlinson, who also started the convention of inserting an @ symbol in between the sender's name and the name of their computer. According to Tomlinson, his email was just a test message that he sent to himself and it read: "something like QWERTYUIOP."

***The other 52 percent comes from computer programs known as bots that visit websites and perform other tasks automatically.

Second Sight

Six illuminating inventions
that make the invisible visible

1. Microscope

Invented in: 1590

How it works: It uses a lens or series of lenses to make tiny objects visible. The most powerful electron microscopes* can see objects that are one ten-millionth of a millimeter across, which is narrower than a hydrogen atom.

2. Telescope

Invented in: 1608

How it works: By gathering and focusing light via curved mirrors and lenses, a telescope enables astronomers to see the light given off by faraway objects, including distant stars.

3. X-ray machine

Invented in: 1895

How it works: An X-ray machine directs rays of light that humans can't see through an object, such as a human body. The X-rays** pass easily through some materials (such as skin and muscle) but are blocked by others (such as bone). The rays that get through hit a piece of photographic film, which captures a black-and-white picture of the inside of the object. X-rays have many uses, including detecting broken bones, checking what is inside passengers' bags at airport security, and in art history showing how and when different layers of paint have been applied to a painting.

4. Ultrasound scanner

Invented in: 1956

How it works: The scanner produces high-frequency sound waves that can be sent through objects such as the human body to create a moving picture of what's inside. Ultrasound scanners are often used to monitor babies while they're still inside their mothers' wombs.*** Ultrasound waves are also used to repair damaged muscles and ligaments and to clean delicate objects such as lenses and jewelry.

5. Fiber-optic endoscope

Invented in: 1957

How it works: A flexible tube with a tiny camera at the end is passed into a human or animal's body through a small cut. This allows a surgeon or vet to see inside the body while performing an operation.

6. MRI scanner

Invented in: 1977

How it works: Using a combination of magnets and radio waves, an MRI scanner builds up a very detailed picture of the body's insides. Created by a computer, the MRI scan looks like a photograph of a sliced section of the body. MRI scans are also used to analyze chemicals, the inside of plants, and to check how much water and fat are present in foods.

Right: This portrait of a jumping spider was taken using a camera lens that is similar to one in a microscope. The spider has been magnified to around 40 times its real size.

---

*An electron microscope uses beams of electrons instead of light to see very small objects.

**The German engineer who discovered these mysterious rays, Wilhelm Röntgen, called them X-radiation, or X-rays for short, because at the time he had no idea what they were.

***Ultrasound waves echo off different body tissues—such as muscle and bone—in different ways, creating a pattern of echoes which the scanner then turns into a picture.

Coming Soon?

Sixteen inventions already in development that could shape the future

1. Floating farms that grow vegetables on the sea and are powered by solar energy.

2. A global network of helium balloons that will help everyone in the world access the Internet.

3. Smartwatches for athletes that are powered by human sweat.

4. Building bricks for houses that can store energy like a battery.

5. The Hyperloop, a high-speed transport system that could move people through a tunnel on a cushion of air at speeds of up to 760 miles per hour (1,220 km/h).

6. Robot guide dogs for people with visual impairments.

7. Materials called aerogels that can't conduct heat and so would make the perfect insulation to keep homes and other buildings warm.

8. Tiny robots called xenobots made from living, self-healing animal cells that are small enough to fit inside the human body and deliver medicine. They have also been released into the ocean to clean up the tiny bits of plastic that pollute it.

9. A self-driving shopping cart that leads you through the supermarket, guiding you to the items on your shopping list.

10. Epidermal VR that allows you to feel virtual reality experiences on your skin as well as see and hear them.

11. A T-shirt that monitors your heartbeat.

12. Jetpacks that can fly people at speeds of up to 110 miles per hour (177 km/h) and a maximum height of 18,000 feet (6,000 m).

13. Food labels that alert you when the food inside is about to go bad.

14. A machine that puts out forest fires using sound. The machine shoots sound waves at the fire, creating a barrier between the flames and the oxygen in the air. This starves the fire of the oxygen it needs to keep burning.

15. A hot-air balloon that takes ordinary people up into space.

16. Smart underpants that measure how much your buttock and leg muscles are moving, then tell you if you need to do more exercise.*

---

*Imagine being bossed around by your own underpants!

Bizarre Inventions

**Eight unusual products
that were actually made**

1. A motorized ice-cream cone
that automatically rotates your
ice cream, saving you the effort
of turning the cone around to lick
the ice cream on the other side.

2. An extendable chin rest for when you're
standing up on a crowded bus or train.

3. A goldfish-bowl walker for those
moments when you want to take
your pet fish for a stroll.

4. Shoe umbrellas to keep your toes
dry (though strangely not the rest
of your feet).

5. A rock that you can connect to
your computer with a USB but
that otherwise does nothing.*

6. A cell phone that doubles
as an electric beard trimmer.

7. A walking sleeping bag that has a hole
in the bottom so you can shuffle around
while still being zipped up inside it.**

8. The Useless Machine, which is a square
box with a single switch on the top. If you
flip the switch, a small motorized arm pops
out to flip it back. That's it.

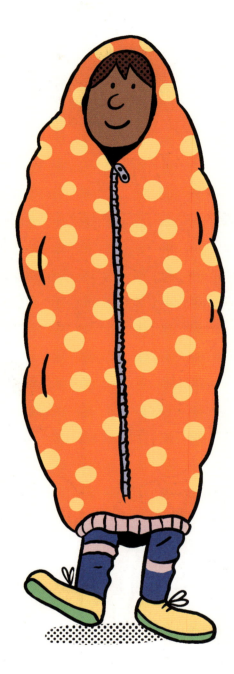

*An earlier model called the Pet Rock, which
came without a USB connector but with a
detailed 32-page instruction manual, sold
for $4 in the 1970s. Pet rocks were so popular
they made their creator, American businessman
Gary Dahl, a millionaire.

**Perfect for those times when you're both late
for school and want to stay in bed!

Chapter 8

Game Changers

A list of things (and people) you'll encounter in this chapter:

A chess grand master

The Sun King

A tightrope walk involving an omelette

Hundreds of games of hopscotch

A warrior heroine

The loudest burp

A baby emperor

The second person to walk on the Moon

A "Human Swan"

Calamity John

A snail with a famous name

The longest-ever concert*

A cheetah called Chiquita

*It's still going!

Whiz Kids

Thirteen remarkable feats achieved by children

1. At age 4, Budhia Singh from India ran a marathon (2006).

2. At age 7, Saugat Bista from Nepal directed a feature-length movie—*Love You Baba*—that was released in movie theaters (2014).

3. At age 8, Wolfgang Amadeus Mozart from Austria composed an orchestral symphony (1764).

4. At age 11, Brian Zimmerman was elected mayor of the town of Crabb, Texas (1983).*

5. At age 12, Stevie Wonder from Michigan sang a number-one hit single, called "Fingertips (Part 2)" (1963).**

6. At age 12, Vicki Van Meter from Pennsylvania flew an airplane across the Atlantic Ocean (1993).

7. At age 12, Sergey Karjakin from Ukraine became a chess grand master (2002).

8. At age 13, Jordan Romero from California climbed Mount Everest (2010).

9. At age 14, Nadia Comăneci from Romania won three Olympic gold medals for gymnastics (1976).***

10. At age 15, Kelvin Doe, a self-taught young engineer from Sierra Leone, built and launched his own community radio station (2011).

11. At age 16, Blaise Pascal from France invented his own theory of geometry, called Pascal's theorem (1639).

12. At age 16, Martina Hingis from Switzerland won the Australian Open, one of tennis's four major world titles (1995).

13. At age 16, Laura Dekker from the Netherlands sailed around the world on her own (2011).

---

*Zimmerman's successful campaign message to the voters was: "The mayor isn't there to sit and worry about keeping his job. He's there to do what's best for the people."

**When he was born, Wonder was named Stevland Hardaway Judkins. He started recording and performing music professionally from the age of 11, as "Little Stevie Wonder." He grew up to be one of the world's most popular musicians.

***Competing in the 1976 Olympic Games in Montreal, Comăneci was also the first gymnast in Olympic history to be awarded a perfect 10. Her faultless performance in an event called the uneven bars was so unexpected that the electronic scoreboards in the stadium weren't able to show her score. The highest score they had been designed to display was 9.99, so Comăneci's perfect 10 appeared on the scoreboard as 1.00. She won gold medals in the uneven bars, the balance beam, and for the best all-around performance.

Stevie Wonder
aged about 11

Brothers and Sisters

Ten sets of famous siblings,
and when they made their mark

1. Trung Trac and Trung Nhi—
1st century CE

Claim to fame: The Trung sisters learned martial arts as children and grew up to become military leaders in Vietnam. They led local resistance to the ruling Chinese Han dynasty and became symbols of Vietnamese independence. They are still celebrated as national heroes today.

2. Charlotte, Emily, and Anne Brontë—19th century

Claim to fame: Each of the three English sisters was a brilliant writer and novelist. The trio's famous novels include *Jane Eyre* (by Charlotte), *Wuthering Heights* (by Emily), and *The Tenant of Wildfell Hall* (by Anne).

3. Sarah Moore and Angelina Emily Grimké—19th century

Claim to fame: The Grimké sisters from South Carolina gave powerful public speeches in support of women's rights and the abolition (ending) of slavery. Their stand against injustice was made even more remarkable by the fact that their father was a judge who strongly disagreed with their views.

4. Jacob and Wilhelm Grimm—
19th century

Claim to fame: Their classic collection of traditional stories and songs—*Grimms' Fairy Tales**—is read by and to children all around the world. Curiously, the German brothers' first names are little known today and the pair are nearly always referred to as the "Brothers Grimm."

5. Ira and George Gershwin—
20th century

Claim to fame: The American Gershwin brothers were both talented musicians. George wrote popular musicals and songs for piano and for orchestra, while Ira wrote the lyrics to go with George's music, as well as musical compositions of his own.

*There are more than 200 stories in *Grimms' Fairy Tales*, including the tales of Rapunzel, Hansel and Gretel, and Tom Thumb.

6. Chico, Harpo, Groucho, Gummo, and Zeppo Marx—20th century

Claim to fame: The Marx Brothers were a successful American family comedy act. They started as live comedy performers before making a series of hit movies in Hollywood in the 1930s.

7. Wilbur and Orville Wright—20th century

Claim to fame: The Wright brothers were engineering enthusiasts who owned a bicycle shop. In 1903 they built and flew the first powered airplane, Flyer 1, at Kitty Hawk in North Carolina. The Wright brothers' pioneering flight lasted just 12 seconds."

8. Wazir, Hanif, Mushtaq, and Sadiq Mohammad—20th–21st centuries

Claim to fame: The Mohammad siblings come from what may be the greatest cricket-playing family of all time. No fewer than four brothers represented their home country of Pakistan, while a fifth, Raees, came very close to being selected.**

9. Kolo and Yaya Touré—20th–21st centuries

Claim to fame: Born in the Ivory Coast in West Africa, the Touré brothers both represented their country at the soccer World Cup and have won multiple trophies while playing for some of the world's best club teams, including Monaco and Barcelona (Yaya) and Liverpool and Arsenal (Kolo). They played together for three years at Manchester City Football Club.

10. Venus and Serena Williams—20th–21st centuries

Claim to fame: The record-breaking American sisters are two of the greatest tennis players of all time. At different times, Venus and her younger sister Serena have both been ranked as the number-one women's player in the world. Between them, they have won 30 major singles trophies.

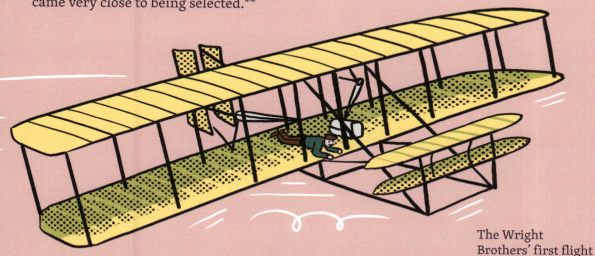

The Wright Brothers' first flight

"Even though its first flight didn't last long, Flyer 1 has since been to great heights—even outer space! To find out more, see page 48.

**Cricket is a bat-and-ball game played by two teams of 11. The teams take turns to pitch and bat and points are scored by completing "runs" between two posts.

King or Queen for the Day

Ten of the shortest-reigning monarchs

1. Louis XIX of France—20 minutes, in 1830*

2. The baby daughter of Emperor Xiaoming of the Chinese state of Northern Wei— a few hours, in 528 CE**

3. Emperor Mo of Jin, China—a few hours, in 1234

4. Min Shin Saw of Burma (now Myanmar)— less than a day, in 1167

5. Vira Bahu I of Polonnaruwa, Sri Lanka— less than a day, in 1196

6. Michael I of Trebizond—1 day, in 1341***

7. Napoleon II of France—2 days, in 1814

8. Khalid bin Barghash of Zanzibar—2 days, in 1896

9. Lady Jane Grey of England—9 days, in 1553

10. Eleanor of Navarre, Spain— about two weeks, in 1479

The baby daughter of Emperor Xiaoming

*During the French Revolution of 1830, Louis' father, Charles X, was forced to abdicate, or give up, the throne. This meant his son Louis technically became king of France for less than half an hour before he too signed an official document confirming his own abdication. France's next king was Charles X's cousin Louis Philippe I.

**Xiaoming became emperor of the ancient Chinese state of Northern Wei when he was still a boy. Because he was so young, his mother, Empress Dowager Hu, ruled in his place. However, when Xiaoming grew up, there was conflict between the emperor and his mother. Rumor has it that she poisoned her son, then put Xiaoming's baby daughter on the throne, pretending she was a boy. The baby was only emperor for a matter of hours before being replaced with Xiaoming's cousin Yuan Zhao. And because Yuan Zhao was only three years old, Empress Dowager Hu was able to maintain her grip on the throne—just as she had wanted all along.

***Michael I of Trebizond, a kingdom that once formed part of the Byzantine Empire, was removed as king and thrown in prison by his political enemies on his first day on the job. However, Michael became king again in 1344 and reigned for five years before being removed once more. After losing the throne of Trebizond for a second time, he became a monk.

Game of Thrones

Ten of the longest-reigning monarchs

1. Louis XIV of France*—72 years, 110 days (between 1643 and 1715)

2. Bhumibol Adulyadej of Thailand— 70 years, 126 days (between 1946 and 2016)

3. Johann II of Liechtenstein— 70 years, 91 days (between 1858 and 1929)

4. Elizabeth II of the UK— 69 years and counting (her reign began in 1952 and continues today)

5. K'inich Janaab' Pakal I of Palenque**— 68 years, 33 days (between 615 and 683 CE)

6. Franz Joseph I of Austria— 67 years, 355 days (between 1848 and 1916)

7. Constantine VIII of the Byzantine Empire***— 66 years, 226 days (between 962 and 1028 CE)

8. Basil II of the Byzantine Empire— 65 years, 237 days (between 960 and 1025 CE)

9. Ferdinand III of Sicily— 65 years, 90 days (between 1759 and 1825)

10. Victoria I of the UK— 63 years, 216 days (between 1837 and 1901)

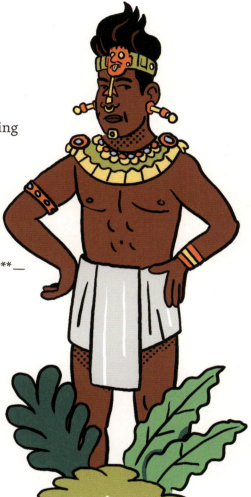

K'inich Janaab' Pakal I

---

*Louis began his reign at the age of four. He later became known as the Sun King because he thought that all of France should revolve around him like the planets revolve around the Sun. He owned 413 beds and more than 1,000 wigs.

**Palenque was a city-state founded by the Mayan civilization in modern-day Mexico.

***For most of his reign, Constantine was the co-ruler of the Byzantine Empire with his brother Basil, who appears at number eight on this list. The Byzantine Empire covered much of modern-day Turkey and Greece.

The Real Deal?

Five famous figures who may not have existed

1. Homer—ancient Greece

The Greek poet Homer causes lots of arguments among historians. They can't agree when he lived—at the time of the Trojan War* in the 12th or 13th century BCE, or 500 years later. And they're almost certain that the same person didn't write the two famous poems he's credited with creating: the *Odyssey* and the *Iliad*. In fact, he may not have existed at all.

2. Mulan—4th-century China

Disney's warrior heroine is based on a character who appears in a real Chinese folk song from the 5th or 6th century.** The song celebrates Mulan's fight of about ten years as the leader of a real-life northern Chinese clan against an invading army. All the details in the poem describe a real time and place, but Mulan's name does not appear in a text about important women from the clan. So whether she was a real historical figure remains a mystery.

3. King Arthur—5th–6th-century Britain

The stories that tell of King Arthur, ruler of an ancient British kingdom where noble knights sat at a round table in a castle at Camelot, have been retold by different writers for centuries. But is there any truth to the legend? There are accounts of a Roman general named Lucius Artorius Castus who fought battles against invaders in the 2nd century. But because these reports were written centuries later, it's hard to know how accurate they are.

4. Pope Joan—9th-century Italy

According to a famous old story, a woman named Joan disguised herself as a man so successfully that she was eventually elected Pope and became the leader of the Roman Catholic Church. Two historians later wrote that this actually happened, and the legend of Pope Joan was believed across Europe for centuries despite the lack of solid evidence.

5. Robin Hood—13th–14th-century England

Lots of people have heard the story of Robin Hood, a well-meaning outlaw who, with his band of merry men, lived in Sherwood Forest in England. Did they really rob from the rich to give to the poor? Well, there are lots of historical documents that refer to a "Rabunhod," but this may just be a nickname for a robber.

*In fact, historians can't even agree whether there was a Trojan War.

**In the song about her, Mulan was a warrior who went to war in place of her father, dressing in his clothes to disguise herself as a man and join the army. The ballads suggest she was offered a position by the emperor that really existed—one that would have meant she must have been trained in martial arts.

Right: A silk painting of warrior heroine Mulan, shown armed with weapons to prepare for battle.

木蘭

Role Swap

Eight women who blurred gender boundaries

Throughout history and up to the present day, women have often been treated unfairly purely because of their gender. Each woman in the list decided, for her own particular reasons, to bend gender boundaries, by adopting a male name, voice, or clothing.

1. Hatshepsut—about 1507–1458 BCE

Queen Hatshepsut reigned over ancient Egypt for 15 years, and she is often shown on statues as having a male body and wearing a false beard. Although Hatshepsut's subjects knew that she was a woman, historians think she adopted a masculine appearance to demonstrate that she had the same power and authority as male pharaohs.

2. Saint Marina—400s CE

In the Middle East, a young girl named Marina disguised herself as a boy. This allowed her to stay with her father when he became a monk and joined a monastery, which did not allow women inside. When Marina grew up, she became a monk herself, using the name Marinus.*

3. Joan of Arc—about 1412–1431

This famous heroine in French history fought in the Hundred Years' War while dressed as a man. Although she died at the age of 19, Joan of Arc is still remembered today for her courageous efforts to lead the French army and defend her country.

4. Charlotte Brontë—1816–1855

This brilliant English writer published her early works, including *Jane Eyre*, under the pen name Currer Bell. At the time, female authors were not as well respected as male authors, so in order to be taken seriously, she decided to use a different name. Charlotte's sisters Emily and Anne used the same tactic and published poems as Ellis Bell and Acton Bell. In time, all three would be recognized as great writers and use their own names.**

5. Cathay Williams—about 1842–1893

Born into slavery in Missouri, Williams was captured by the Union Army (the army of the North) during the Civil War. She became "contraband," the term used to describe Black captives whom the Union refused to return to slavery in the South and who often worked in support roles for the army. After the war, she disguised herself as a man and used the made-up name William Cathay in order to serve in the US Regular Army, which she did between 1866 and 1868. Williams then joined an emerging all-Black regiment that would later become part of the Buffalo Soldiers, a famous African-American regiment.

---

*Years later, "Marinus" was falsely accused of being the father of someone's child. Instead of revealing the truth, she kept her secret and looked after the child herself—even though this meant she would be thrown out of the monastery. Marina's real identity stayed a secret until her death—and she was later made a saint for her kind-hearted behavior.

**Another great "male" writer who was actually a woman was George Eliot. Eliot, whose real name was Mary Ann Evans, didn't want the fact she was a woman to affect what readers thought of her books. She penned seven novels as George Eliot, and one of them, *Middlemarch*, is widely considered to be one of the greatest novels ever written.

6. Rena Kanokogi—1935–2009

In 1959, Rena Kanokogi disguised herself as a man to enter a judo tournament in New York City. She won the event but was forced to return her medal when officials found out that she was a woman. Kanokogi would not be beaten, though: she later traveled to Japan to train at the famous Kodokan Institute, making her the first woman to train alongside men. She then founded the first-ever female judo world championship.

7. Bobbi Gibb—1942–present

In 1966, Bobbi Gibb became the first woman to complete the Boston Marathon after she disguised herself as a man at the starting line by wearing a hooded sweatshirt and her brother's Bermuda shorts. At the time, women's running races were limited to a maximum distance of 1.5 miles (2.4 km). Gibb's performance led to a change in the rules so women could run in marathons too.***

8. Norah Vincent—1968–present

The journalist Norah Vincent disguised herself as a man for 18 months so that she could go undercover and investigate how women and men are treated differently. Using the name Ned Vincent, she wore masculine clothes, took voice lessons to lower her voice, and in 2006 published a book about her experiences called *Self-Made Man: My Year Disguised as a Man.*

Rena Kanokogi

***Gibb finished the 26.2-mile (42.2-km) race in 3 hours, 21 minutes, and 40 seconds, placing her ahead of two-thirds of the male competitors.

Incredible Journeys

Twelve people who went on epic adventures

1. Jean Béliveau—47,200 mi (76,000 km)

Setting off from Montreal, Canada, in 2000, Béliveau spent 11 years walking through 64 different countries to promote peace and end violence toward children.*

2. Peace Pilgrim—an estimated 43,500 mi (70,000 km)

To make a personal protest against the Korean War, Pilgrim (born Mildred Norman) started to walk back and forth across the United States. Taking her first step for peace in 1953, she kept walking until her death in 1981.

3. John Francis—39,000 mi (62,800 km)

Nicknamed the "Planetwalker," Francis is a champion of the environment. Between 1972 and 1995 he spent 23 years going on very long walks, including across the United States and the length of South America. True to his environmental beliefs, during this time Francis didn't use motorized transport on land and always sailed over stretches of water.**

4. Rick Hansen—24,900 mi (40,100 km)

Hansen, who was paralyzed from the waist down following a car accident in 1973, holds the record for the longest journey by wheelchair. The Canadian crossed four continents and 34 countries on a two-year adventure between March 1985 and May 1987.

5. George Meegan—19,000 mi (30,600 km)

Meegan holds the record for the longest unbroken walk (without having to take a boat or airplane to travel to a different continent) after walking the length of South and North America. Wanting to be the first recorded person to complete this challenging journey, Meegan set off in 1977 from the southern tip of Argentina and walked north until he reached Alaska. He arrived in 1983.

6. David Kunst—14,500 mi (23,300 km)

Kunst is the first person to have been officially recorded walking around the world.*** Kunst set off in 1970 from his home state of Minnesota with $1,000 and a mule called Willie Makeit ("will he make it?") that carried his camping supplies. It took him just over four years to walk all the way around.

*On the way, Béliveau wore out 49 pairs of shoes and met four winners of the Nobel Peace Prize, including the South African political leader Nelson Mandela. Like all the intrepid adventurers on this list, Béliveau took an airplane or boat to travel between different continents.

**As Francis walked the planet for 17 years, he did not speak. Instead, he listened, drew pictures, recorded his thoughts in a journal, and played the banjo.

***Some people think that Konstantin Rengarten from Russia was the first person to walk around the world, between 1894 and 1898. Rengarten's route is said to have included Siberia, Mongolia, Japan, the United States, France, and Germany. But, because there is no way to independently confirm the full details, it's impossible to know for sure whether he really did walk all the way.

7. Prem Kumar—10,500 mi (16,900 km)

Leaving his home in Ahmedabad, India, on October 2, 1982—the 113th anniversary of Indian political leader and pacifist Mahatma Gandhi's birth—Kumar walked through 14 countries to promote global peace and understanding.

8. Bob Hanley—9,000 mi (14,500 km)

At the age of 61, Hanley was told by his doctor to rest more because he was suffering from a serious medical condition and might soon have to use a wheelchair. Hanley's response was to walk all the way around Australia with his two dogs, Cindy and Tammy, while pushing a wheelbarrow. Hanley wore out 20 pairs of shoes and 50 pairs of socks along the way.

9. Plennie L. Wingo—8,000 mi (12,900 km)

Between April 1931 and October 1932, this intrepid American walked from Santa Monica, California, across the United States before catching a boat to Germany and then walking to Istanbul, Turkey. What made Wingo's journey even more remarkable was the fact he traveled the entire route walking backward.

10. Kenichi Horie—4,660 mi (7,500 km)

It took Horie an unusually long time—around three and a half months—to sail across the Pacific Ocean between Hawaii and Japan. However, the Japanese sailor had good reason to take things slowly: he was traveling in a pedal-powered boat.

11. Sacha Dench—4,350 mi (7,000 km)

Known as the "Human Swan," Dench is an Australian-born conservationist who in 2016 joined a flock of Bewick's swans as they migrated from the north of Russia to the UK. Dench flew alongside the swans on a paramotor, which is a paragliding sail with a chair suspended beneath and a giant motorized fan to push it through the air.

12. Robert Swan—1,600 mi (2,575 km)

In 1989, Swan became the first person to walk to both ends of the Earth when he led an eight-person team to the North Pole. Three years earlier, Swan had walked to the South Pole with a three-person team, following the route of his fellow British adventurer Robert Falcon Scott.

Sacha Dench

Runners-Up

Eleven people who came second

1. The Egyptian pharaoh Khafre built the second-tallest pyramid (about 2530 BCE).

2. English seaman Sir Francis Drake was the second person to sail around the world on a single expedition (between 1577 and 1580).

3. British tennis player Charlotte Cooper was the second woman to win an Olympic gold medal (July 11, 1900).

4. British explorer Robert Falcon Scott led the second team of adventurers to reach the South Pole (January 17, 1912).*

5. American aviator Amelia Earhart was the second person to fly solo across the Atlantic Ocean (May 22, 1932).

6. American Jesse Owens was the second track-and-field athlete to win four gold medals at one Olympic Games (in Berlin in August 1936).

7. Australian John Landy was the second person to run a mile in under 4 minutes (June 21, 1954).

8. Swiss mountaineers Ernst Schmied and Jürg Marmet were the second team of climbers to reach the summit of Mount Everest (May 23, 1956).

9. American scientist Linus Pauling was the second person to win two Nobel Prizes (for Chemistry in 1954 and Peace in 1962).**

10. American astronaut Buzz Aldrin was the second person to walk on the Moon (July 20, 1969).***

11. Russian cosmonaut Svetlana Savitskaya was the second woman to go into space (August 19, 1982).

Robert Falcon Scott

*Scott and his team had been racing a rival Antarctic expedition led by the Norwegian explorer Roald Amundsen. When they finally reached the South Pole, Scott's team found a tent with a Norwegian flag flying at the top: Amundsen had beaten them to it by 34 days.

**The first person ever to win two Nobel Prizes was the Polish scientist Marie Curie, who won prizes in both Physics (1903) and Chemistry (1911).

***American astronaut Neil Armstrong was the first human to walk on the Moon. Here's what Aldrin had to say about following in Armstrong's more famous footsteps: "As the senior crew member, it was appropriate for him to be the first. But after years and years of being asked to speak to a group of people and then be introduced as the second man on the Moon, it does get a little frustrating."

Unlucky Charms

Six of the world's unluckiest people

1. Ann Hodges from Alabama is the only reported person in history to have been struck by a meteorite.

2. Pierre Desarmes was living in the Caribbean country of Haiti in January 2010 when a terrible earthquake struck. With the help of friends in Chile, Desarmes was able to fly himself and his family to safety and a new home near the Chilean capital of Santiago—where an even bigger earthquake struck less than a month later.

3. Costis Mitsotakis was the only resident of a small village in Spain called Sodeto who didn't win a share of a €740 million ($965 million) lottery prize in 2011. Mitsotakis was the only person out of 250 villagers not to contribute to buying the winning ticket.

4. Describing himself as "Britain's unluckiest man" and "Calamity John," John Lyne estimates that he's had at least 15 major accidents in his lifetime. These include falling down a manhole, falling off a horse and cart, and being struck by lightning.*

5. Violet Jessop, a nurse and stewardess on ocean liners, had terribly bad luck with ships. She was on board both the RMS *Titanic* and HMHS *Britannic* when they famously sank in the early 1900s. She was also on board the RMS *Olympic* when it crashed into another ship while at sea.**

6. Melanie Martinez from Louisiana has been called the "unluckiest woman in America" after five of her houses were destroyed by hurricanes. In 2012, Martinez's luck seemed to have changed after a reality TV show paid for her latest home to get a $20,000 makeover. A few months later, it was destroyed by a hurricane.

---

*However, Lyne's unluckiest moment of all happened after he'd fallen out of a tree and broken his arm. The next day, Lyne was on his way back to the hospital for a follow-up appointment when the bus he was traveling in crashed—breaking the same arm in a different place.

**Amazingly, Jessop survived all of these catastrophes and continued to work on ships. She became known as "Miss Unsinkable."

The Invincibles

Phenomenal winning streaks achieved in sports

132 years unbeaten—the New York Yacht Club: sailing

The America's Cup is the oldest international trophy in sports. It was first won in 1851 by the New York Yacht Club, who defeated a British Royal Yacht Squadron off the south coast of England. They went on to defend their title for more than a century, before finally losing to an Australian team in 1983.

26 years unbeaten—USA: golf

Except in cases of war and disaster, the Ryder Cup has taken place every two years since 1927. Originally, a team made up of the best golfers from Great Britain took on the best from the US. Since 1979, it has been Europe versus the US. But for a long time it didn't matter who turned up to play the Americans. Between 1959 and 1983, they were unbeatable, winning the Ryder Cup 13 times in a row, remaining champions until they lost in 1985.

15 years unbeaten—West Indies: cricket

The West Indies cricket team (nicknamed the "Windies") from the Caribbean began an amazing winning streak when they defeated England 1–0 in the summer Test series of 1980. The streak lasted through 29 series, played against six different countries, before the Windies finally lost a Test series, 2–1 to Australia, in 1995.

10 years unbeaten—Edwin Moses: athletics

The athlete with the longest-ever winning streak is the phenomenal Edwin Moses, an American 400-meter hurdler who won 122 races in a row (including 109 finals) between August 1977 and June 1987.*

10 years unbeaten—Esther Vergeer: wheelchair tennis

The remarkable Dutch wheelchair tennis player Esther Vergeer retired from the sport in 2013 after winning 470 matches in a row over ten years. During that time, Vergeer won 120 tournaments.

5 years unbeaten—Jahangir Khan: squash

Pakistan's Jahangir Khan is arguably the greatest squash player of all time, and for a long while, it seemed that he was invincible. In 1981, at age 17, he won the World Open (now called the World Championship). Over the next five years, Khan won an estimated 555 matches in a row, a winning streak that finally ended in the 1986 World Open final, when he lost to Australia's Ross Norman.

5 years unbeaten—University of Connecticut: basketball

The women's basketball team at the University of Connecticut have a history of mammoth winning streaks. They went two years and 90 games without defeat between 2008 and 2010 and then topped that achievement by going a full five years and 126 games without losing between 2014 and 2019.

---

*Other athletes to have achieved impressive winning streaks include Jamaican sprinter Usain Bolt (45 races) and American 200-meter and 400-meter runner Michael Johnson (58 races).

2 years, 11 months unbeaten—
Futabayama: sumo wrestling

Sumo wrestlers compete in contests called "bouts," which are a test of strength, skill, and strategy. Between January 1936 and January 1939, the mighty Futabayama went 69 bouts without losing once. He is now widely considered the greatest sumo wrestler of all time.**

10 months unbeaten—
Martina Navratilova: tennis

Between February 20 and December 6 1984, the great Czech-American champion Navratilova won 74 matches in a row, the longest winning streak for a singles player in professional tennis. On the way, Navratilova won the French Open, Wimbledon, and US Open titles.

1 season unbeaten—
Miami Dolphins: football

It was only the third season that the Miami Dolphins had been in the National Football League, but 1972 became the only "perfect season" in the history of the sport. The Dolphins won all 17 games they played, including the Super Bowl.

1 season unbeaten—
Preston North End: soccer

In September 1888, in the first soccer league season in the world, Preston North End became the sport's original "Invincibles." The small-town English team went unbeaten for the entire season and a total of 27 matches. In doing so, they became the first team to win a league championship and FA Cup "double." Other soccer teams have accomplished this feat since, but Preston North End was the first.

Esther Vergeer

**After his retirement, Futabayama revealed that as a boy he had been accidentally blinded in one eye, a disadvantage that made his record-breaking career all the more extraordinary.

Faster, Higher, Stronger

Amazing physical feats in numbers

2,900 The height in feet (884 m) climbed by the US's Alex Honnold in 2017 as he became the first and only person to climb the smooth and almost-vertical face of a rock formation known as El Capitan in Yosemite National Park in California on his own and without any climbing ropes. This is called free solo climbing.

900 The number of degrees the American Tony Hawk spun around in midair on a skateboard—that's two and a half complete turns—in 1999 to become the first skateboarder ever to pull off this trick (called the 900).

843.6 The speed in miles per hour (1,357.6 km/h) reached by Austrian Felix Baumgartner while completing the world's highest skydiving jump in 2012. Baumgartner leapt from a hot-air balloon floating 24 miles (39 km) above the Earth.*

643 The number of people in the world's largest human pyramid, in 1981. The pyramid, which was built by people standing on each other's shoulders, had nine levels and was completed when Josep-Joan Martínez Lozano reached the top, 43.79 feet (13.34 m) in the air.

183.9 The speed in miles per hour (296 km/h) pedaled by America's Denise Mueller-Korenek in 2018 to become the fastest human being on a bicycle.

160 The height in feet (49 m) above the Niagara Falls gorge at which France's Charles Blondin balanced on a 396-meter-long tightrope. In 1859 he became the first person to cross the thunderous waterfalls in this way.**

119 The time in minutes it took Eliud Kipchoge from Kenya to run a marathon in 2019 to become the only human to have run the distance in under two hours. Kipchoge's official time was 1 hour, 59 minutes, and 40 seconds.

100 The time in minutes that it took Thomas Geierspichler from Austria to complete a marathon in a wheelchair in 2008, setting a world record time of 1 hour, 40 minutes, and 7 seconds.

---

*It took Baumgartner 9 minutes and 3 seconds to reach the ground. At his top speed he was traveling faster than the speed of sound, which is 1,115 feet per second (340 m/s) at sea level.

**Blondin later crossed Niagara Falls on a tightrope in various other ways, including while pushing a wheelbarrow and walking on a pair of stilts. Once he even sat down in the middle to make an omelette.

77 The time in minutes that Paolo Ballesteros from the Philippines managed not to blink during a TV challenge in 2019.

28 The number of Olympic medals won by American swimmer Michael Phelps between 2004 and 2016, the most by any male athlete.

18.46 The length in feet (5.62 m) of the longest hair ever recorded on a human. The record holder is Xie Qiuping from China. When her hair was officially measured in 2004, it hadn't been cut for 31 years."

18 The number of Olympic medals won by Soviet gymnast Larisa Latynina between 1956 and 1964, the most by any female athlete.

11 The largest number of balls juggled at the same time, by the UK's Alex Barron in 2012.

10 The time in hours that American Mark Jordan juggled a soccer ball with his feet without it touching the ground, in 2018.

9.58 The time in seconds that it took Jamaica's Usain Bolt to run 100 meters at the World Athletics Championships in Berlin in 2009, setting a record that has yet to be beaten.

8.5 The height in inches (21.59 cm) of the limbo bar under which Shemika Campbell of the United States danced in 2010, to set a new world record.

8.04 The height in feet (2.45 m) jumped by Cuban athlete Javier Sotomayor in 1993, setting a high jump world record that has remained unbroken for 27 years.

8 The time in hours it is thought to have taken Pemba Dorje Sherpa from Nepal to climb Mount Everest in 2004, the fastest ever ascent of the world's highest mountain.

Xie Qiuping

» To find out how long human hair can grow in a year, see page 203.

Record Breaker

Thirty world records set by Ashrita Furman

Ashrita Furman is a health food shop manager from New York City. He has dedicated his life to setting and breaking world records, and so far he has set over 700. This list features 30 of more than 200 that he still holds today.*

1. Most lit candles on a birthday cake—72,585

2. Most consecutive forward rolls—8,341

3. Most eggs balancing on their ends at the same time—888**

4. Most games of hopscotch in 24 hours—434

5. Most balloons inflated by the nose in 1 hour—380

6. Heaviest shoes walked in—323 lbs (146.5 kg)

7. Farthest distance walked balancing a lawn mower on the chin—234 ft, 6.96 in (71.5 m)

8. Most pencils snapped in 1 minute—102

9. Most grapes caught in the mouth in 1 minute—86

10. Fastest 10-kilometer race while wearing a sack—82 minutes

11. Most pint glasses balanced on the chin—81

12. Fastest time to jump up all 1,899 steps of the CN Tower in Ontario, Canada» on a pogo stick—57 minutes, 51 seconds

13. Most grapes sliced in the air with a sword while balancing on an exercise ball—55

14. Tallest object balanced on the nose***—52 ft, 3.84 in (15.95 m)

15. Most marshmallows caught in the mouth after being fired by a homemade catapult in 1 minute—47

16. Farthest distance to spit a table tennis ball—42.1 ft (12.83 m)

17. Most ping-pong balls caught with chopsticks in 1 minute—32

18. Fastest time to burst 100 balloons with the feet—29.7 seconds

19. Longest table tennis rally playing with an egg—28 shots

20. Most baseballs held in a baseball glove at the same time—26

---

*Furman also holds the world record for holding the most world records.

**It took 12 hours to get all 888 eggs balancing on their ends at the same time.

***It was a very, very long pole.

»The CN Tower stands at 1,815 feet (553 m) tall and is the tallest building in Canada. To find out about the tallest building in the *world*, see pages 262–263.

21. Most stuffed animals caught blindfolded in 1 minute—25

22. Fastest mile walked with shovels strapped to the feet—24 minutes, 0.25 seconds

23. Fastest mile on a pogo stick while dribbling a basketball—23 minutes, 2.91 seconds

24. Fastest time to push an orange a distance of 1 mile using the nose—22 minutes, 41 seconds

25. Farthest distance to blow a coin—16 ft, 2.76 in (4.95 m)

26. Most hats thrown onto a hatstand in 1 minute—16

27. Fastest mile hula-hooping while balancing a milk bottle on the head—13 minutes, 37.35 seconds

28. Fastest mile walking on stilts—12 minutes, 23 seconds

29. Fastest time to blow up ten balloons underwater—2 minutes, 52.01 seconds

30. Farthest distance unicycling underwater—1.3 mi (2.1 km)

Ashrita Furman performing feat number seven

Great All-Arounders

Eleven people who were great at more than one sport

1. Lottie Dod—tennis, archery, golf, field hockey

Born: England, 1871

Charlotte "Lottie" Dod is still the youngest woman ever to win the Wimbledon Tennis Championship, at just 15, in 1887. She won the title five times, then won the British Ladies Amateur Golf Championship in 1904, played field hockey for England, and won a silver medal in archery at the 1908 Olympic Games.

2. Jim Thorpe—track and field, basketball, baseball, football, lacrosse, ballroom dancing

Born: United States, 1888

At the 1912 Olympic Games in Stockholm, Sweden, Thorpe won both the pentathlon, which includes five separate athletic events, and the decathlon, which includes ten, becoming the first Native American to win an Olympic gold medal. Described at the time as "the world's greatest athlete," Thorpe later played both football and baseball professionally for more than 15 seasons. He was also a fine ballroom dancer, winning the US inter-collegiate championships.

3. Duke Kahanamoku*— swimming, surfing

Born: Hawaii, 1890

Known as "the Father of Surfing" and the "Big Kahuna," Duke Kahanamoku was born in Hawaii before it became part of the United States. He won three Olympic gold medals as a swimmer between 1912 and 1924 and introduced the Hawaiian sport of surfing to the world as he traveled between swimming competitions.

4. Iftikhar Ali Khan Pataudi— cricket, field hockey

Born: India, 1910

As well as being the only player in the history of cricket to represent both India and England, Pataudi was also a member of the Indian field hockey team that won the gold medal at the Olympic Games in Amsterdam, Netherlands, in 1928.

5. Babe Didrikson—track and field, golf

Born: United States, 1911

In the 1930s, Didrikson was a world-class athlete, winning medals in the hurdles, javelin, and high jump at the 1932 Olympics in Los Angeles, where she set four world records in a single afternoon. In the 1940s, she then became the greatest female golfer of her era, winning ten major championships.**

---

*The full name of "the Father of Surfing" was Duke Paoa Kahinu Mokoe Hulikohola Kahanamoku.

**In 1932, Didrikson entered the US women's track-and-field championships. She was the one and only member of her team, while rival teams included 12 or more athletes. Didrikson entered eight events, and despite having to rush from one contest to immediately start another, she won five of them. In the process, she gained enough points to single-handedly win the team competition too.

6. Constantin Herold—basketball, volleyball, handball, track and field

Born: Romania, 1912

Constantin Herold took the idea of "all-arounder" to a new level, competing for the national team in basketball, volleyball, handball, and track and field, but also excelling in alpine skiing, water polo, fencing, rugby, and shooting. Just think of the size of his sports bag!

7. Vsevolod Bobrov—soccer, ice hockey

Born: Soviet Union, 1922

As a young boy, Bobrov was a talented skater. After fighting in the Second World War he began playing soccer for the Soviet Army. He played for the national team in the 1952 Summer Olympics, and four years later led the Soviet Union to the gold medal in ice hockey at the Winter Olympics.

8. Jim Brown—football, lacrosse

Born: United States, 1936

As a young man, Brown excelled at lots of sports including track and field and basketball. He was truly exceptional at two: football, where he set new records playing in the key position of running back, and lacrosse. Brown is considered an all-time great player in both sports.

9. Jackie Stewart—car racing, skeet shooting

Born: Scotland, 1939

The "Flying Scot" won the first of three Formula One Drivers' World Championships in 1969, but nine years earlier he competed to represent Britain at a completely different sport: skeet shooting.

10. Jenny Williams—lacrosse, soccer, cricket, Australian rules football

Born: Australia, 1957

As a lacrosse player for Australia, Williams won the world championship and captained the national team, but she also played for her state, South Australia, in soccer, cricket, and Australian rules football.

11. Primož Roglič—road cycling, ski jumping

Born: Slovenia, 1989

In 2019, Primož Roglič became the highest-ranked road cyclist in the world, winning the famous Vuelta a España. However, he was originally a junior world champion ski jumper who competed internationally in the sport until 2011.

The many skills of Lottie Dod

Keep It Down

Ten of the loudest sounds made by humans

Sound is measured in decibels. The quietest sound that can be heard by the human ear is 0 decibels. A whisper is 30 decibels, a normal conversation is 60 decibels, and a jet engine at takeoff is about 140 decibels.

1. **Loudest sneeze, 176 decibels**—Yi Yang, China*

2. **Loudest scream, 129 decibels**—Jill Drake, UK

3. **Loudest whistle, 125 decibels**—Marco Ferrera, United States, and Luca Zocchi, Italy (joint record holders)

4. **Loudest shout, 121.7 decibels**—Annalisa Wray, UK**

5. **Loudest click of the tongue, 114.2 decibels**—Kunal Jain, Canada

6. **Loudest clap, 113 decibels**—Alastair Galpin, New Zealand

7. **Loudest burp, 109.9 decibels**—Paul Hunn, UK

8. **Loudest snap of the fingers, 108 decibels**—Bob Hatch, United States

9. **Loudest snoring, 93 decibels**—Kåre Walkert, Sweden

10. **Loudest crack of the knuckles, 83.2 decibels**—Miguel Ángel Molano, Spain

---

*Yang's sneeze was louder than a shotgun being fired, which creates a sound of approximately 160 decibels.

**Wray shouted the word "quiet."

Paul Hunn and his great burp.

Rebel Spirit

Seven people whose act of protest changed the world

1. Martin Luther, in 1517

The act of protest: A German priest named Martin Luther pinned a document listing his criticisms of the Roman Catholic Church, along with his personal religious beliefs, to the door of a church in Wittenberg, Germany.

What happened next: Luther's controversial document, known as "The Ninety-five Theses," was quickly reprinted, translated, and read throughout Europe. It helped to start a religious revolution by creating a split within the Catholic Church. This led to the formation of a new branch of Christianity called Protestantism.

2. Emily Davison, in 1913

The act of protest: Davison was a leading member of the British suffragette movement, which campaigned for women to be allowed to vote in elections. During a famous horse race called the Epsom Derby, Davison walked out onto the racecourse carrying two purple-white-and-green flags promoting the suffragettes' cause and died after being knocked over by a horse.

What happened next: Davison's death drew global attention to the suffragette movement. After repeated campaigning, women won the right to vote in the UK in 1918.

3. Mahatma Gandhi, in 1930

The protest: Mahatma Gandhi was a great Indian political leader and pacifist (a person who doesn't believe in violence). Between 1858 and 1947, India was ruled by Britain, and during this period, it was illegal for Indians to collect or sell their own salt. Salt was a very valuable substance that had lots of different uses. To raise awareness of this injustice, Gandhi decided to deliberately disobey the law by staging a peaceful protest and set out on a 24-day journey to collect salt from the coast. Many Indian people joined him on his march.

What happened next: Gandhi and more than 60,000 other Indians who followed his example were imprisoned for disobeying the government. However, the Salt March became one of Gandhi's most famous acts of nonviolent protest and helped to bring global attention to India's struggle for independence. India became an independent country in 1947.

4. Rosa Parks, in 1955

The protest: Although African Americans in the United States officially gained freedom from slavery in 1865, they were still often subject to different rules from white Americans, such as having to sit in Black-only sections of public buses. On December 1, 1955, in the city of Montgomery, Alabama, a bus driver asked civil rights activist Rosa Parks to give up her seat to a white person because the white section of the bus was already full. Parks refused and was arrested.*

What happened next: Parks's protest led to African Americans refusing to ride any public buses in Montgomery to show their support—and after a long legal campaign that had begun before Parks's arrest, the law was changed. Hers was one of many individual acts of resistance that inspired the rapid growth of the American civil rights movement,** which campaigned against segregation and racial inequality. Today, people in America and around the world are still fighting for racial equality.

Rosa Parks (center)

List continued over the page

*Following Parks's courageous act of protest, she said: "Stand for something or you will fall for anything. Today's mighty oak is yesterday's nut that held its ground."

**One of the most famous and influential leaders of the American civil rights movement was an African American minister named Martin Luther King Jr. When he was born in Atlanta, Georgia, Martin Luther King Jr. was originally named Michael. But his father changed both his own and his son's names to Martin Luther after the free-thinking 16th-century German priest who is featured in the first entry of this list.

5. Marsha P. Johnson, in 1969

The protest: In New York City, a bar called the Stonewall Inn was raided by the police. The bar was popular with members of the LGBTQ+ community (which includes lesbian, gay, bisexual, transgender, and queer people), who were often unfairly treated by others, including by the police, because of their sexuality and gender expression. This time, however, the bar's patrons refused to be bullied and started a protest at the bar that lasted several days. Drag queen*** Marsha P. Johnson was a leading figure in what became known as the "Stonewall Riots."

What happened next: The riots inspired a wider movement of LGBTQ+ liberation in the United States and elsewhere. Within six months, numerous activist groups and newspapers were set up in New York City, promoting rights for gay and lesbian people. The first gay pride marches took place a year later. Unjust laws that discriminated against LGBTQ+ people slowly began to change and people from the community were able to be more open about their lives. Today, LGBTQ+ pride events are held each year around the world and the campaign for the equal treatment of people of all genders and sexualities continues.

6. Wamsutta (Frank B.) James, in 1970

The protest: James was a leader of the indigenous Wampanoag people of Massachusetts. He wanted to bring the country's attention to the unjust treatment that indigenous peoples had suffered at the hands of white Europeans who came to colonize North America. So, on the 350th anniversary of the 1620 landing of the *Mayflower*, the ship that brought a group of settlers to Massachusetts, James gave a powerful speech. He declared that instead of being the national celebration of Thanksgiving, the anniversary of the *Mayflower's* landing should become a national day of mourning to highlight the injustice and suffering of indigenous peoples.

What happened next: James founded the United American Indians of New England, a group that campaigns for the rights of indigenous peoples and continues to mark James's annual National Day of Mourning in Massachusetts to this day.

7. Malala Yousafzai, in 2012

The protest: When Malala was growing up in Pakistan, parts of the country were ruled by an extreme group called the Taliban who wanted to close all girls' schools. Yousafzai defied them, writing a blog to say that all children should be educated, including girls, while continuing to go to school herself.

What happened next: On October 9, 2012, Malala was shot by a Taliban gunman while on her way home from school. She survived and continued to protest against the Taliban and their policies. The next year she was invited to give a speech to world politicians at the United Nations and in 2014 became the youngest person ever to win the Nobel Peace Prize.

***A drag queen is someone who dresses or performs in a feminine way, often in an exaggerated manner.

Marsha P. Johnson

Seeing the Future

Nine people who imagined things years before they actually happened

1. Leonardo da Vinci, 1452–1519— helicopters, hang gliders, cars, submarines, and parachutes

Leonardo da Vinci was an Italian painter, sculptor, architect, and engineer. One of the many brilliant things he is famous for (along with painting the *Mona Lisa*) is drawing the first known sketches of several ingenious vehicles, which other people then invented and built hundreds of years later.*

2. Cyrano de Bergerac, 1619–1655— space rockets

The French writer Cyrano de Bergerac wrote about a machine that launches with the help of fireworks tied underneath it, and flies to the Moon. This was more than 300 years before the first real spaceships blasted off.»

3. Margaret Cavendish, 1623–1673— submarines

In the same year as the Great Fire of London, English author and philosopher Margaret Cavendish wrote a book called *The Description of a New World, Called the Blazing-World*, in which the heroine travels home in a submarine towed by "fish-men."

4. Jane Webb Loudon, 1807–1858— human-like robots and oxygen masks

The science-fiction writer Jane Webb Loudon wrote in 1827 about the 2100s, when women wore pants,** human surgeons and lawyers were replaced by mechanical robots, and people took supplies of oxygen on their travels so they could breathe in outer space.

5. Edward Bellamy, 1850–1898— radio, movies, and television

In 1888, the American novelist wrote a book called *Looking Backward*, which was set in the year 2000 and successfully predicted modern technologies including radio and TV. It became one of the bestselling books of the 19th century and led to people setting up "Bellamy Clubs" to discuss how the author's ideas would influence society.

6. Nikola Tesla, 1856–1943—smartphones

Inventor Nikola Tesla*** helped to create the electricity supply system we use today, but almost 100 years ago, in 1926, he imagined a communications device, which might sound familiar. Tesla's machine would be small enough to fit in a pocket and would allow users to speak to people on the other side of the world as if they were in the same room, complete with a moving image of their face. Was he the first human to imagine a smartphone?

---

*Many of the notes that appear alongside Leonardo's sketches in his notebooks are written in mirror script, a style of reverse handwriting that can only be read by holding the pages up to a mirror.

» Since the first spaceships launched in the 1940s and 1950s, space technology has been getting bigger and better. To find out about some of the most powerful rockets, see pages 34-35.

**Although women had been wearing pants for centuries in some cultures, such as ancient China and ancient Greece, Jane Webb Loudon was born in London, UK, at a time when almost all women wore skirts. Pants didn't become popular for women in England until the 20th century.

***Tesla was also an early environmentalist. He worried that humans were using up the Earth's resources and wanted people to use non-fossil, renewable fuels instead. So it seemed fitting for the Tesla electric car to be named after him.

7. H. G. Wells, 1866–1946—tanks, audiobooks, lasers, and atomic bombs

H. G. Wells was a science-fiction writer who predicted lots of inventions that became reality, such as tanks, although he called them "land ironclads." Just before the First World War, in 1913, Wells even imagined how an atomic bomb would work and the terrible damage that would be caused by its radiation.

8. Robert A. Heinlein, 1907–1988—Internet and microwaved food

In 1938, this science-fiction writer predicted a searchable information network a lot like the modern Internet. Ten years later, he imagined frozen food that would only require "high-frequency heating" to be ready to eat. His idea sounds similar to a modern-day frozen dinner.

9. Octavia E. Butler, 1947–2006—global warming

Butler was a science-fiction writer who wrote about future human societies. One of Butler's books is set in an imagined world of droughts and rising seawater caused by global warming.

Friends of the Earth

Eight people with a mission to protect our planet

1. Rachel Carson, 1907–1964— marine biologist and conservationist

As well as being a leading expert on the world's oceans, Carson was an influential author. Her book *Silent Spring*, published in 1962, helped to inspire the modern environmental movement in the United States. It also led to a nationwide ban of harmful chemicals used in farming that had been polluting the countryside.

2. David Attenborough, 1926–present— naturalist and broadcaster

Attenborough's nature documentaries have made hundreds of millions of people around the world more aware of the Earth's natural wonders. He has also highlighted humanity's negative impact on the environment and the urgent need to find solutions to issues such as global warming.»

3. Dr. Jane Goodall, 1934–present— zoologist

In 1960, Goodall traveled to Tanzania in Africa to live alongside and study human beings' closest living relatives: chimpanzees. Goodall's pioneering discoveries transformed the world's understanding of chimpanzees and other primates, and she has since become an inspiring campaigner for wildlife conservation and animal welfare.

4. Wangari Maathai, 1940–present— conservationist

Known as the "Woman of Trees," Maathai founded an environmental organization called the Green Belt Movement in Kenya in 1977. Maathai's initiative has led to the planting of more than 50 million trees, and in 2004 she became the first environmentalist to win the Nobel Peace Prize.

5. Hammer Simwinga, 1964–present— anti-poaching* environmentalist

Simwinga has won global awards for his work reducing the illegal hunting of elephants and rhinoceroses in his home country of Zambia. Simwinga's success came from setting up community projects—such as fish-farming and beekeeping—so that more than 30,000 local people could earn a living without the need to hunt elephants and rhinos to sell their meat and horns.

6. Von Hernandez, 1967–present— environmental campaigner

When trash is burned instead of being recycled, it releases clouds of harmful gases into the atmosphere. Hernandez, a former teacher, successfully campaigned so that in 1999 his home country of the Philippines became the first in the world to make it illegal to burn trash. Since then, Hernandez has led campaigns to raise awareness of other environmental issues such as deforestation, pollution, and climate change.

» David Attenborough is such a celebrity that he's even had an insect named after him! To find out what kind of insect it is, see page 384. (Look out for Greta there too!)

*Poaching is when an animal is illegally hunted or captured. Animals are often poached for valuable substances; for example, elephants are poached for their ivory tusks.

7. Mya-Rose Craig, 2002–present—ornithologist and conservationist

Known as "Birdgirl," Craig is a young British-Bangladeshi ornithologist and conservationist. Her passion for birds led her to write a newspaper column called "Birding Tales" at age 12, and she has made TV appearances and speeches in support of environmental causes while still in high school. One of Craig's ideas is Black2Nature, which runs nature camps for children of color.

8. Greta Thunberg, 2003–present—environmental activist

At the age of 15, Thunberg started campaigning for the environment by missing school on Fridays and protesting outside the Swedish parliament. The story of Thunberg's protests was reported around the world, inspiring thousands of other children to join similar "school strikes" and environmental rallies. Thunberg has since made speeches to world leaders urging them to do more to protect the planet.

Greta Thunberg gives a speech in Lausanne, Switzerland.

Lifesavers

Fourteen women who advanced the cause of medicine

1. Metrodora, around 100–600 CE

Metrodora was a doctor in ancient Greece. She is credited with writing *On the Diseases and Cures of Women*, an influential ancient text that covered many areas of medicine. The book is over 63 chapters long and includes Metrodora's original theories and research. She is widely considered the first female medical writer.

2. Saint Hildegard, 1098–1179

Hildegard was the abbess, or leading nun, in a monastery in Bingen, in what is now Germany. She was celebrated across Europe for her achievements as a writer, composer, and religious philosopher. Among Hildegard's writings were important studies of natural medicines and cures, which were partly based on her own experience working in the monastery's herb garden.

3. Mary Seacole, 1805–1881

Born on the Caribbean island of Jamaica, Seacole was known as a compassionate and courageous nurse. Seacole demonstrated these qualities while caring for sick and wounded British soldiers during the Crimean War in Russia, where she became known as "Mother Seacole."*

4. Florence Nightingale, 1820–1910

As a young nurse, Nightingale was put in charge of caring for soldiers who were injured in Turkey during the Crimean War. The insights she gained there led her to set up the world's first scientifically-based nursing school, in London, UK, in 1860. To recognize Nightingale's many pioneering achievements, International Nurses' Day is now celebrated each year on May 12th, which was her birthday.

5. Dr. Elizabeth Blackwell, 1821–1910

Born in England, Blackwell became the first female doctor in the United States and the first woman to be entered on the official register of doctors in Britain. Her achievements included helping to found the New York Infirmary for Women and Children, and writing a book whose title summed up her life's mission: *Pioneer Work in Opening the Medical Profession to Women*.

6. Marie Curie, 1867–1934

In 1903, Curie became the first woman to win a Nobel Prize, after she and her husband, Pierre, discovered two new radioactive elements—polonium and radium—which led to huge advances in medicine. The Polish-born French scientist also developed a mobile X-ray machine that enabled more than a million wounded soldiers to be treated on the battlefield during the First World War.**

7. Dr. Virginia Apgar, 1909–1974

Apgar was the American doctor who created the "Apgar score" in 1952. The test assesses whether newborn babies need urgent medical attention and is still in use today.

---

*Seacole was so brave she even rode on horseback onto the battlefield, sometimes under fire, to nurse wounded soldiers.

**These mobile X-ray units were known as "Little Curies."

8. Kofoworola Abeni Pratt, 1915–1992

Born in Nigeria, Pratt trained as a nurse in the UK and was the first qualified nurse of color to work for the UK National Health Service. She later returned to Nigeria, becoming the country's chief nursing officer, and in 1973 was awarded the Florence Nightingale Medal, nursing's highest international honor.

9. Gertrude Elion, 1918–1999

Elion was a brilliant American biochemist who shared the Nobel Prize in Medicine in 1988. Through her research, Elion changed the way that drugs were developed. Instead of using the traditional trial-and-error method, she used a logical, scientific approach. Elion helped to invent treatments for many widespread diseases, including leukemia, malaria, gout, and AIDS, saving hundreds of thousands of lives around the world.

10. Dr. Jane Cooke Wright, 1919–2013

Working and teaching in hospitals and universities in New York City, Wright played a leading role in the study of cancer. Her research contributed to the development of chemotherapy, a treatment for cancer that has since saved millions of lives.

11. Rosalind Franklin, 1920–1958

Franklin's greatest achievement was using X-ray photographs to reveal the structure of DNA, the genetic code that helps all living things to grow and reproduce. It was a breakthrough that led to enormous medical advances. She would almost certainly have won a share of the Nobel Prize awarded to Francis Crick, James Watson, and Maurice Wilkins in 1962 for their studies of DNA, had she not tragically died from cancer at the age of 37.

12. June Almeida, 1930–2007

Scottish-born Almeida was a pioneer in taking detailed images of viruses, and in 1964 she discovered the first human coronavirus. Almeida's research laid the groundwork for modern scientists' understanding of SARS-CoV-2, which is the virus that caused the COVID-19 pandemic.

13. Tu Youyou, 1930–present

Malaria is a disease that can give humans a dangerous and potentially deadly fever. It is caused by parasites spread by insects such as mosquitoes. By studying traditional Chinese medicine—including ancient texts written thousands of years ago—Tu Youyou identified a natural substance called artemisinin that combats the parasite. It has since been used in drugs that have prevented millions of deaths. Tu Youyou's discovery earned her the Nobel Prize in Medicine in 2015.

14. Dr. Patricia Goldman-Rakic, 1937–2003

Goldman-Rakic was one of the world's greatest brain scientists. Her research focused on how the brain's frontal lobes, or sections, are related to memory. Her findings greatly improved our understanding of medical conditions that affect the brain, such as dementia, Alzheimer's disease, Parkinson's, and schizophrenia.

Making It Big

Creators of incredibly large
or long works of art

The longest piece of music
By: John Cage

How long: 639 years

Cage composed "As Slow as Possible" for the piano with the intention that his piece is played . . . as . . . slow . . . as . . . possible. The longest performance so far attempted is a version that has been adapted to be played on the organ. It began on September 5, 2001, in St. Burchardi church, Halberstadt, Germany, and is scheduled to finish in 2640.*

The longest play
By: Deepika Chourasia

How long: 30 hours, 33 minutes

Chourasia's play is an epic celebration of the history and culture of India. She performed it solo in New Delhi, India's capital city, between 2:52 pm on August 15, 2020, and 9:25 pm the next day. She took just seven, five-minute breaks during the entire performance.

The longest story
By: Marcel Proust

How long: 1,267,069 words

A story longer than 40,000 words is sometimes called a novel. *In Search of Lost Time* by the great French writer Marcel Proust is widely considered the longest novel ever written. It took Proust 13 years to write and was published between 1913 and 1927 in seven volumes.

The longest poem
By: Unknown Kyrgyz poets

How long: 500,000 lines

Manas is an immensely long poem created by the Kyrgyz people of central Asia. It has been performed, memorized, and passed down from generation to generation for centuries. One version has more than half a million lines.

The biggest hand-painted portrait
By: Hung Chi-Sung

How big: about 546 ft by 240 ft (167 m by 73 m)

In 2001, two famous statues of the Buddha were destroyed in Bamiyan, Afghanistan. This inspired artist Hung Chi-Sung to start painting a giant portrait of the Indian spiritual leader on the ground the following year. Covering an area larger than 60 singles tennis courts, the portrait took him 17 years to finish.

The biggest sculpture
By: Unknown Chinese sculptors

How big: 715 ft (218 m) high by 656 ft (200 m) wide

The world's largest stone sculpture is a statue of the Chinese God of Longevity.** It was carved by a team of sculptors into the northwest face of Guimeng mountain, China, in 2004.

---

*This record-breaking performance began with a silent pause that lasted until February 5, 2003. The first chord was then played until July 5, 2005. Sandbags are placed on the pedals of the specially built organ to keep the same notes playing for years at a time.

**Longevity means long life.

Making It Small

Creators of incredibly small
or short works of art

The shortest piece of music

By: Sly Stone

How short: 0 seconds

In 1971 the American funk band Sly and
the Family Stone listed a song on their
new album called "There's a Riot Goin' On"
which lasted for 0 seconds. When asked
to explain why he had created this
non-existent song, the band's peace-loving
leader Sly Stone said: "I did it because I felt
there should be no riots."

The shortest play

By: Samuel Beckett

How short: 35 seconds

Breath, by the famous Irish playwright
Samuel Beckett, features no words or
actors. The play opens on a stage that is
covered in trash. The audience then hears
the recorded sound of a baby's first cry
followed by the sound of deep breathing.
The play ends with a second baby's cry.
It was first performed in 1969.

The shortest story

By: Unknown writer

How short: 6 words

One of the world's shortest stories has no
title, but reads "For sale: baby shoes, never
worn."—showing that in just six words
it is still possible to create an intriguing
plot. Many people think it was written
by the great American author Ernest
Hemingway. However, like the unworn
shoes themselves, the origin of the story
remains a mystery.

The shortest poem

By: Aram Saroyan, poet

How short: 1 letter

In the 1960s Aram Saroyan wrote a poem
that consisted of an adapted letter "m"
(see above) that has four downward lines
instead of the usual three.

The smallest hand-painted portrait

By: Wayne Malkin

How small: 0.09 in by 0.09 in (2.3 mm
by 2.3 mm)

The world's smallest portrait painted by
hand is of the Australian comic character
Dame Edna Everage. Malkin painted it in
2019 on the wooden end of matchstick
using a single bamboo fiber as a brush.

The smallest hand-made sculpture

By: Willard Wigan

How small: 78 microns (0.08 mm) high
by 53 microns (0.05 mm) wide*

This minute sculpture was made in 2017
and is of a human embryo made from
a strand of carpet fiber, placed inside
a hollowed-out strand of Wigan's hair.

Dame Edna Everage's portrait
on the end of a matchstick.

*There are 25,400 microns in an inch (2.5 cm).

Colorful Characters

Nine colors named after people
(and small animated henchmen)

1. Titian red This red-orange color, often used to describe people's hair, is named after the great Italian artist of the 1500s, who painted lots of people with red hair in his pictures.

2. Minion Yellow In 2015, the bright yellow animated characters known as the Minions were given their very own color, Minion Yellow.

3. Hooker's green The 19th-century British scientific illustrator William Hooker created this warm, gentle green for his drawings, so he could perfectly match the shade of green found in leaves.

4. Alice blue Alice Roosevelt Longworth, the daughter of the 26th US president, Theodore Roosevelt, was known for wearing dresses of this icy pale blue color.

5. Wallis blue In 1937, Wallis Simpson married Edward, Duke of Windsor, the former British king who had abdicated the throne to be with her. Her wedding gown was a light, grayish blue that was reportedly designed to match her eyes. The company that made the dress, Mainbocher, called the color Wallis blue.

6. International Klein Blue French artist Yves Klein invented a deep, dark blue color, then registered the formula for his new color with the government. It was known as IKB for short.*

7. Baker-Miller pink An American scientist called Alexander G. Schauss designed this soothing pink color. He had been conducting studies into the effect different colors had on mood and behavior and hoped his new pink would make people who looked at it less worried and frustrated. It's named after two members of staff at a Naval prison where Schauss completed one of his experiments: the naval commander (Baker) and warden (Miller).

*At one point in Klein's career, known as his "Blue Period," he only exhibited paintings and other works of art that were blue. To celebrate one of these exhibitions, Klein released 1,001 blue balloons into the skies above Paris.

8. Perkin's mauve A bright purple, this mauve color was invented in 1856 by an 18-year-old UK chemistry student named William Henry Perkin.**

9. Vandyke brown Anthony van Dyck was a 17th-century painter from Belgium best known for his portraits of kings, queens, and members of their courts. Van Dyck often used a deep, warm brown color in his paintings, and the color was later named after him.***

An Yves Klein exhibition

**Perkin patented his new color and it became so fashionable that a magazine complained that the whole of England was suffering from a case of the "mauve measles."

***In order to get the perfect shade of brown, van Dyck often added real dirt in with the paint!

Celebrity Creatures

Fourteen famous people who have animals named after them

1. The dragonfly *Acisoma attenboroughi* was named after the naturalist and broadcaster David Attenborough.

2. The moth *Adaina atahualpa* was named after the Inca emperor Atahualpa.

3. The fish *Aesopichthys erinaceus* was named after the ancient Greek storyteller Aesop.

4. The spider *Aptostichus barackobamai* was named after former US president Barack Obama.

5. The prehistoric pterosaur *Arthurdactylus conandoylei* was named after the creator of Sherlock Holmes, Sir Arthur Conan Doyle.

6. The wasp *Aleiodes shakirae* was named after the singer Shakira.

7. The bird *Confuciusornis sanctus* was named after the ancient Chinese philosopher Confucius.

8. The snail *Craspedotropis gretathunbergae* was named after the environmental activist Greta Thunberg.*

9. The spider *Desis bobmarleyi* was named after the musician Bob Marley.

10. The dinosaur *Jenghizkhan* was named after the ancient Mongol leader Ghengis Khan.

11. The bacterium *Legionella shakespearei* was named after the playwright William Shakespeare.**

12. The pterosaur *Maaradactylus spielbergi* was named after the film director Steven Spielberg, whose movies include the dinosaur action-adventure *Jurassic Park*.

13. The moth *Neopalpa donaldtrumpi* was named after former US president Donald Trump.***

14. The nudibranch *Mandelia mirocornata* (which is a type of sea slug) was named after the South African politician Nelson Mandela.

---

*The snail is named after Thunberg because it is affected by problems caused by climate change.

**The bacterium was first identified in Stratford-upon-Avon, the place in England where William Shakespeare was born.

***This moth's name comes from the scales on its head, which are said to look like Donald Trump's distinctive hairstyle.

Deep Thoughts

Twelve wise sayings of Laozi

Little is known today about the life of Laozi,* a Chinese writer and philosopher who is thought to have flourished in the 6th century BCE. However, he is traditionally regarded as the founder of Taoism, a Chinese system of thought based on living humbly, in harmony with the universe.

1. "A journey of 1,000 miles begins with a single step."

2. "He who boasts has no merit."

3. "Leave all things to take their natural course."

4. "Failure is the foundation of success and the means by which it is achieved."

5. "Extreme straightness is as bad as crookedness."

6. "He who overcomes others is strong but he who overcomes himself is mightier still."

7. "The softest things in the world override the hardest."

8. "He who is content always has enough."

9. "Avoid putting yourself before others and you can become a leader among men."

10. "Nature does not hurry yet everything is accomplished."

11. "Be content with what you have; rejoice in the way things are. When you realize there is nothing lacking, the whole world belongs to you."

12. "Return injury with kindness."

Laozi

---

*Laozi means "Old Master" in Chinese.

Wise Words

Twelve pieces of advice from Albert Einstein

The German-born physicist Albert Einstein was one of history's greatest thinkers. Here are some of the things he said when he wasn't working on mind-boggling new theories about the speed of light.

1. "Logic will get you from A to B. Imagination will get you everywhere."

2. "Only a life lived for others is a life worthwhile."

3. "The most valuable thing a teacher can impart to children is not knowledge and understanding per se but a *longing* for knowledge and understanding."

4. "People are like bicycles. They can keep their balance only as long as they keep moving."

5. "A happy man is too satisfied with the present to think too much about the future."

6. "Politics is more difficult than physics."

7. "The most beautiful thing we can experience is the mysterious. It is the source of all true art and science."

8. "If A is success in life then A = x + y + z. Work is x, play is y, and z is keeping your mouth shut."

9. "Peace cannot be kept by force. It can only be achieved by understanding."

10. "The value of achievement lies in the achieving."

11. "We have to do the best we are capable of. That is our sacred human responsibility."

12. "The important thing is not to stop questioning."

Albert Einstein

Josephine Baker with her
pet cheetah, Chiquita

Still Here

Five people who could have (or did!) read their own obituaries

An obituary is a report that appears in a newspaper or other publication shortly after someone has died. As well as reporting the fact of a person's death, it sometimes contains details about their life and what they achieved during it.*

1. Samuel Taylor Coleridge In 1816, the famous English poet was enjoying a cup of coffee at a hotel when he overheard the people sitting at the next table discussing his recent death, after they had read a mistaken report in the newspaper. Coleridge asked to borrow the newspaper so he could read the article himself . . . and then, to their great surprise, introduced himself.

2. P. T. Barnum At the age of 80, the famous American circus showman became seriously ill. Knowing he wouldn't live for too much longer, Barnum mentioned to a friend that he'd like to know what people would say about him after he died. His friend told this story to the editor of the *Evening Sun* newspaper in New York City, who published Barnum's obituary early so he would get his wish. It appeared under the headline: "Great and Only Barnum. He Wanted To Read His Obituary; Here It Is." Barnum died two weeks later, on April 7, 1891.

3. Josephine Baker The American-born French singer and dancer lived an extraordinary life. Her performances created a sensation in Paris in the 1920s, and she went on to become a spy and member of the secret French Resistance during the Second World War. In 1942, it was widely reported that Baker had died in Morocco in North Africa. She was living there at the time and had been seriously ill, but thankfully her condition had improved. When word got out, newspapers around the world printed new articles announcing that the popular performer was alive after all. Baker continued to dance onstage right up until her death in 1975 at the age of 68.»

4. Ernest Hemingway The famous American author was almost killed in a plane crash in 1954. Several newspapers published reports saying that he'd died in the accident. Hemingway, however, wasn't alarmed by all the false reports of his death—and is said to have collected them together in a scrapbook that he read after breakfast every day while drinking a glass of champagne.

5. Margaret Thatcher The British politician never read her own obituary in a newspaper, but officials of the UK government were contacted by the Canadian prime minister Stephen Harper in 2009, after reports of Thatcher's death started circulating in Canada. The source of the confusion was the Canadian Transport Minister John Baird, who had sent a message simply reading: "Thatcher has died." He was referring to his pet cat, which he'd named after the former British prime minister.

---

*The first obituaries were published in around 59 BCE in ancient Rome. They appeared in newspapers that were made of papyrus and called *Acta diurna*, which means "daily events" in Latin.

» To find out what Baker's last words were, turn to the next page.

Anna Pavlova performs in the ballet *The Dying Swan*, by Camille Saint-Saëns.

Just One More Thing

Fourteen memorable things people are believed to have said just before they died

1. The English physicist Sir Isaac Newton, in 1727: "I don't know what I may seem to the world. But as to myself I seem to have been only like a boy playing on the seashore and diverting myself now and then in finding a smoother pebble or a prettier shell than the ordinary, whilst the great ocean of truth lay all undiscovered before me."

2. Madame de Vercellis, a French noblewoman, in 1728: "Good," she said after apparently passing gas. "A woman who can fart is not dead."

3. English travel writer and poet Mary Wortley Montagu, in 1762: "It has all been most interesting."

4. The American poet Emily Dickinson, in 1886: "I must go in, for the fog is rising."

5. The Irish playwright Oscar Wilde, in 1890: "My wallpaper and I are fighting a duel to the death. One or the other of us has to go."

6. American abolitionist Harriet Tubman, in 1913: "Swing low, sweet chariot." The words are part of a song that expresses a desire to escape slavery. Tubman sang it with her family just before she died.

7. Russian prima ballerina Anna Pavlova, in 1931: "Get my swan costume ready."

8. American blues musician Lead Belly, in 1949: "Doctor, if I put this here guitar down now, I ain't never gonna wake up."

9. Japanese author Yukio Mishima, in 1970: "Human life is limited, but I would like to live forever."

10. French fashion businesswoman Coco Chanel, in 1971: "You see, this is how you die."

11. American-born French entertainer Josephine Baker as she left a party being held in her honor, in 1975: "Oh, you young people act like old men. You have no fun."

12. The Jamaican musician Bob Marley, in 1981: "Money can't buy life."

13. UK film director and artist Derek Jarman, in 1994: "I want the world to be filled with white fluffy duckies."

14. The American comedian Bob Hope, in 2003, to his wife after she'd asked him how he would like to be buried: "Surprise me."

List of Useful Words (a.k.a. Glossary)

abdicate To leave an important position or function, such as being a king or queen.

abdomen The back part of an insect's body, or the belly of a human or other vertebrate.

abolition The act of officially ending or stopping something.

abstract (art) Expressing ideas and emotions by using elements such as colors and lines without attempting to create a realistic picture.

agnostic A person who holds the view that any supreme power (such as God) is unknown and probably impossible to understand.

altitude The height of something above a surface, such as the Earth. The altitude of a mountain on Earth is usually measured from sea level.

ammonites Extinct swimming relatives of squid and octopuses. They had flat coiled shells that are often found as fossils.

amphibian A group of cold-blooded vertebrates. Most spend part of their lives in water and part of their lives on land. They include frogs, toads, and newts.

amplified Made louder.

ancestor A person or organism that lived in the past and from which a living individual or species is descended. For example, your grandmother's grandmother's grandmother is your ancestor.

ancestral Relating to, or inherited from, an ancestor.

anesthetize To make a body part numb, or to make a person or animal unconscious.

anniversary A date that is remembered or celebrated because a special or notable event occurred on that date in a previous year.

antibodies Types of proteins found in the blood and bodily fluids of humans and certain animals that help the body fight disease.

aquatic Living in water.

aqueduct A channel made by people for water to flow through.

archaeologist A type of scientist who studies remains, such as tools, pottery, and jewelry, of past human life.

arteries Blood vessels that take blood from the heart to the rest of the body.

arthropod A type of invertebrate with an outer body that is broken up into segments, jointed legs to allow them to move, and often a skeleton on the outside of their body, known as an exoskeleton. Insects such as beetles, arachnids such as spiders, and crustaceans such as crabs are all types of arthropod.

artificial intelligence The ability of a machine to mimic intelligent human behavior.

assembly line An arrangement of machines, equipment and workers that each do a different job in creating something.

asteroid A rocky object made from clay, rock, and sometimes metal that travels around the Sun. They are smaller than planets and come in lots of different shapes and sizes.

astronaut A person who is specially trained to travel into space.

astronomer A scientist who studies objects in space, including stars, planets, and moons.

atheist A person who does not believe in the existence of any god.

atmosphere The layer of gases that surround a planet.

atom The smallest unit of matter. Matter is the stuff that makes up everything around us, from air and water to the Sun and the Moon. Even you are made from atoms.

auction A sale where people bid (offer money) on items. The winner is the person who bids the most money.

aviator A person who flies airplanes, helicopters, or other flying machines; a pilot.

axle A pin or rod on which a wheel or pair of wheels turn.

bacteria (singular, bacterium) Microscopic single-celled living things. Some bacteria cause diseases, while others aid digestion or help break down dead material in the environment.

ballad A kind of poem or song that tells a story.

ballista An ancient military engine designed to hurl large missiles. It often takes the form of a crossbow.

BCE Before Common Era: used to refer to the years that came before the Common Era (CE), which starts with year 1.

Big Bang A sudden explosion that happened about 13.8 billion years ago. It was the beginning of the universe, which is everything that exists.

billion A very large number that's a thousand million. It has nine zeroes and is written as 1,000,000,000.

binary A number system based only on 0 and 1.

biofuel A type of fuel that comes from living things, such as plants or animal waste.

bioluminescent A living thing that can create its own light from a chemical reaction that happens inside its body. Fireflies, anglerfish, and some squid are bioluminescent creatures.

black hole An area in space that pulls everything around it into it, including light.

blood cells Cells that are found in the blood. They include: red blood cells, which carry oxygen around the body; white blood cells, which help to protect the body from disease; and platelets, which form blood clots to help stop bleeding.

boring machine A machine that uses the twisting or turning movement of a tool to make holes.

botanist A scientist who studies plant life.

braille A system of writing that uses characters made up of raised dots. People can read braille by feeling the patterns with the tips of their fingers.

bubonic plague A disease caused by bacteria and often spread by fleas. It can cause the sufferer to have a fever and swollen lymph nodes.

calligraphy Artistic handwriting or lettering.

camouflage Hidden by blending with surroundings. The coloration of some animals allows them to hide in plain sight.

canine teeth Teeth with a single sharp point used to tear prey. Large canine teeth are called fangs.

capillaries Tiny blood vessels that form a network through tissues in the body. Capillaries exchange nutrients, waste products, and oxygen between the blood and tissues.

carnivore A meat-eater.

CE Common Era: used to refer to the years from year 1 onwards.

cell One of the microscopic living units that your body is made up of. There are many different kinds, including nerve, skin, and blood cells.

ceratopsians Horned dinosaurs, including *Triceratops*.

chemical elements The "building blocks" that everything in the universe is made of. Elements are made of atoms, the smallest units of matter.

chemist A person trained in chemistry—the science of the composition, structure and properties of substances, and the transformations they undergo.

circuit The complete path that an electric current travels along.

circulation The pumping of blood from the heart around the body and back again to the heart.

circumnavigate To go completely around something.

clan A group of people who are similar or who are interested in the same thing.

climate The average weather conditions over a long period of time.

climate change Significant and long-lasting change in the Earth's climate and weather patterns.

clone To make an exact copy of something.

code A system of signals or symbols for communication.

coelacanth Rare type of fish with fleshy fins that is more closely related to four-legged land animals than to most fish. Coelacanths have been around for 350 million years.

cold-blooded Unable to control one's body temperature. Cold-blooded animals rely on their environment to keep them warm or cool.

colony A group of animals of the same species that live together.

comet An object made from ice and dust that travels around the Sun. When it moves closer to the Sun, some of it turns to gas, creating a tail.

connective tissue A type of body tissue made of cells, fibers, and a gel-like substance that connects or supports other tissues and organs in the body. Bone, tendons, and ligaments are all connective tissues.

conservation The protection of animals, plants, and natural resources.

conservationist Someone who works to protect animals, plants, and natural resources, or to prevent the loss or waste of natural resources.

consonant Any letter of the English alphabet that is not a, e, i, o, or u.

conveyor A mechanical piece of equipment used for moving things from one place to another.

coprolites Fossilized poop.

core The middle or center of something, such as a planet or star.

cosmonaut An astronaut in the space program of Russia or the former Soviet Union.

Cretaceous Period A time period that lasted from about 145 to 66 million years ago.

crop A plant that can be grown and harvested for profit or food.

crust The outer layer of a rocky planet, such as Earth. The Earth's crust is divided into seven major and 15 minor moving pieces, known as tectonic plates.

crustaceans A type of animal that has several pairs of legs and a body made up of sections that are covered in a hard outer shell. Crabs, shrimp, lobsters, and pill bugs are examples of crustaceans.

currency Something, such as coins or banknotes, that can be exchanged for goods or services.

dark energy A mysterious force that is causing the universe to grow and expand more quickly than when it was first formed.

dark matter An invisible and unknown substance that makes up about 30 percent of the universe. It doesn't absorb, reflect, or give off light. Scientists know it exists because of the impact it has on objects around it, such as stars.

decay To rot.

decibel Unit used to measure how loud or powerful a sound is.

decompose To rot and break up.

deforestation The act or result of cutting down or burning all the trees in an area.

descendant A person's (or other living thing's) descendants are their children, grandchildren, great-grandchildren, etc., who inherit their DNA.

dinosaurs The group of reptiles that includes famous extinct animals such as *Tyrannosaurus rex*, *Diplodocus*, and *Triceratops*. Unlike other types of reptiles such as crocodiles, dinosaurs held their legs underneath their bodies, not out to the side.

diversity Variety.

DNA Deoxyribonucleic acid: the substance inside every living thing that contains the instructions to make it grow and function.

domesticated Something, such as an animal, that has adapted over time from a wild or natural state to life in close association with, and to the benefit of, humans.

drag queen Someone who performs in a feminine way, often in an exaggerated manner. Many drag queens are entertainers who wear clothes and makeup that are stereotypical of women.

dwarf planet A round object that travels around the Sun and is bigger than a comet or asteroid, but smaller than a planet. The most famous dwarf planet is Pluto.

earthquake A shaking or trembling of the Earth's surface. Earthquakes can be caused by the pieces of Earth's crust pushing past one another.

echolocation A technique, used by animals such as bats and dolphins, to determine the location of an object by using reflected sound waves.

electricity A form of energy that can occur naturally (as in lightning) or be produced by a machine.

element *See* chemical elements

elliptical Oval, or egg-shaped.

embryo A human or animal in the early stages of development before it has been born or hatched.

emperor Someone who rules an empire.

endangered When something, such as an animal, is in danger of dying out completely, so none are left.

energy Usable power.

engineer A person trained to use math and science to develop things that help people.

epic A long poem that tells the story of a hero's adventures.

equator An imaginary line that runs around the middle of a planet, moon, or star.

erosion The wearing away or removal of rock, soil, or sand by natural causes, such as wind or water.

eruption The sudden release of something, often forcefully, after being held back. Hot gases, ash, lava, and rock can all erupt from a volcano.

esophagus The muscular tube that connects your throat to your stomach.

evolution The development of new living things from older ones over time.

evolve To change or develop over a period of time.

excavate To make a hole in the ground, or to dig something out of the ground.

exoplanet A planet that travels around a star other than the Sun.

extinct No longer in existence.

feat An act or achievement that shows courage, strength, or skill.

fingerprints Tiny ridges and patterns on the tips of your fingers. Everyone's fingerprints are unique to them.

formula A plan or method for doing, making, or achieving something.

fossil The remains or traces of an ancient living thing that has been preserved in the ground.

fungus Any one of a group of living things (such as molds, mushrooms, or yeasts) that often look like plants but have no flowers and that live on dead or decaying things.

galaxy A huge collection of stars, gas, and dust. Our galaxy is known as the Milky Way.

gamma ray A type of radiation. Gamma rays have the most energy of any kind of radiation, even more than X-rays, which have more energy than visible light.

gene One of the thousands of different "instructions" in your DNA. Genes control how your body grows and functions, and are passed on from parents to children.

generation All of the people or creatures that are around the same age within a society or family. For example, parents are one generation, children the next generation, and grandchildren the generation after that.

genetic Involving genes and their effects.

geometry A branch of mathematics that deals with the measurement, properties, and relationships of certain points, lines, angles, surfaces, and objects.

glacier A huge, slow-moving river of ice. Glaciers are made from layers of snow that are squeezed over hundreds of years until they become ice.

global warming The recent increase in the world's temperature that is believed to be caused by the increase of certain gases (such as carbon dioxide) in the atmosphere.

glucose A simple kind of sugar. Glucose is transported in the blood and provides energy to cells.

government A group of people who are in charge of a country or state.

grand master A title awarded to expert chess players by the World Chess Federation.

gravity A force that pulls objects toward each other. Earth's gravity pulls everything on it, including people, toward its center. The Sun's gravity pulls Earth, and the other planets, toward it.

great ape A large primate that doesn't have a tail. Great apes are larger and smarter than other apes. Examples are chimpanzees, gorillas, and orangutans.

habitat The place or environment where a plant or animal naturally lives.

hadrosaurs Duck-billed dinosaurs.

heliosphere The area of space that is impacted by the Sun and its solar wind, which is one of the kinds of energy that flows from it.

herbivore A plant-eater.

hibernate To go into a deep, sleeplike state for a long time, usually over winter.

hoax An act intended to trick others.

hormones Chemicals that carry messages and instructions around a living thing's body. Hormones are usually carried in the blood.

hurricane An extremely large, powerful, and destructive storm with strong circular winds that occurs especially in the western part of the Atlantic Ocean.

hydrate To provide or add water to.

ice age A period of time when large sheets of ice, known as glaciers, cover much of the Earth's surface.

ichthyosaurs Extinct predatory reptiles that lived in the sea. Ichthyosaurs looked like sharks or dolphins, but weren't closely related to either of them.

illegal Something that is against the law.

immortal Able to live forever.

immune system All the parts of the body, including cells, tissues, and organs, that are designed to fight infections and diseases.

improbable Unlikely to be true or to happen.

inclined plane A flat surface that is tilted at an angle. Also known as a ramp.

indigenous Relating to the earliest known inhabitants of a place.

infection Invasion of the body by disease-causing microscopic agents such as bacteria and viruses.

inflammation Your body's main reaction when it tries to fight back against disease. It involves redness, swelling, and usually pain.

inherit To receive something from an ancestor, such as genes from your parents. Inherited genes can cause you to have similar features to your parents, such as the shape of your face.

insect A type of invertebrate whose adults have six legs and one or two pairs of wings. Examples are flies, moths, and beetles.

internal combustion engine A type of engine, often used in cars, within which fuel is burned and converted into energy to power the vehicle.

Internet The electronic communications network that connects computer networks around the world.

intestine The tubelike part of the digestive system that food enters after it leaves the stomach.

invertebrate An animal that doesn't have a backbone, such as a worm, jellyfish, insect, spider, or crab.

invincible Impossible to defeat or overcome.

iris The colored part of the eye that surrounds the pupil.

isolate To keep something separate from something else.

joint A place in an animal (including humans) where different bones join together. Most joints allow movement between bones.

Jurassic Period A time period that lasted from 201 to 145 million years ago.

Kuiper belt A huge doughnut-shaped area in the far reaches of our solar system, beyond Neptune. Thousands of icy objects can be found there including the dwarf planet Pluto.

larva (plural, larvae) The young stage of an insect when it looks very different from the adult. For example, a caterpillar is the larva of a moth or butterfly.

lever A rigid bar or plank used to apply a force or pressure.

LGBTQ+ Refers to people who identify as lesbian, gay, bisexual, transgender, queer, or questioning—the + encompasses any other sexual identities or genders that are not represented by the letters.

ligament A band of tough body tissue that joins one bone to another.

light-year The distance light travels in one year. It is used to describe things that are very, very far away. One light-year is about 6 trillion miles.

lyrics The words of a song.

machine A device that increases or replaces human or animal effort to complete physical tasks.

maglev An abbreviation of "magnetic levitation," a method of using magnetic fields to cause an object (such as a train) to float above a solid surface.

mammals A group of warm-blooded vertebrates whose females produce milk to feed their young. Examples include human beings, dogs, and whales.

mantle The mantle is the middle layer of a planet, between its outer layer, known as its crust, and its center, known as its core.

marathon A long-distance running race of 26 miles and 385 yards (42.2 km).

marine Relating to the sea. A marine animal is one that lives in the sea.

martial arts Any one of several forms of fighting and self-defense (such as karate and judo) that are widely practiced as sports.

mass The amount of stuff, known as matter, an object is made up of. A large object, such as Earth, has a greater mass than a small object, such as you.

matter The stuff that makes up everything around us, from air and water, to the Sun and the Moon. Matter usually appears in one of three forms: as a solid, a liquid, or a gas.

mausoleum A large tomb, such as a stone building, where dead bodies can be kept above ground.

mayor An official who is elected to be the head of the government of a city or town.

mechanism A piece of machinery or a system of parts that work together in a machine.

melanin A dark-colored substance (called pigment) that is found in skin and hair. Some people have more melanin than others, which affects their skin tone and hair color.

membrane A thin surface or covering.

microscopic Too small to be seen by the naked eye.

Mesozoic Era A time period that lasted from 252 to 66 million years ago, sometimes known as the age of the dinosaurs. It includes the Triassic, Jurassic, and Cretaceous periods.

meteor The bright streak of light created when a meteoroid comes close enough to Earth to enter its atmosphere, burn up, and vaporize. They're often called shooting stars.

meteorite A small rocky object that comes from space and lands on a planet.

meteoroid A rocky object in space that is smaller than a dwarf planet. It can even be as small as a grain of dust.

metro An underground railway system, often in a city.

microscope An instrument that is made of a lens or a combination of lenses that enlarges a person's view of very small objects.

migration Traveling a long distance, especially a regular to-and-fro movement of animals from one region to another.

Milky Way The name given to the galaxy that we live in.

millipedes Invertebrates that have an elongated body made of lots of segments. Each segment, apart from the head and the next three segments, has two pairs of legs.

mimic To imitate, or copy.

mineralization The natural process in which the remains of a plant or animal preserved inside rock are replaced with minerals. Mineralization is one of the ways fossils are made.

mineralogist A person who studies solid naturally formed objects, known as minerals, that are found on or under Earth's surface. Some common minerals are metals, such as gold and copper, and salt.

molecule A group of two or more atoms joined together that form the smallest identifiable unit into which a chemical element can be divided and still retain the composition and chemical properties of that substance.

molluscs A group of invertebrates that have soft bodies, some of which also have shells. Examples are octopuses, oysters, snails, and squid.

moment magnitude scale A way of measuring how strong an earthquake is. The higher the number on the scale, the more powerful the earthquake is.

monarch A person (such as a king or queen) who rules a kingdom or empire.

monk A member of a religious community of men who usually promise to remain poor, unmarried, and separated from the rest of society.

monument A stone or a building erected in remembrance of a person or event.

moon A natural object that travels around a planet, dwarf planet, or asteroid. Some planets, including Saturn, have many moons. Earth has only one moon.

mosasaurs Extinct giant swimming lizards.

mucus A slimy substance produced in the nose and other places in the body, such as the intestines. Mucus protects cells and allows for the smooth movement of substances within the body.

muscles Bands of tissue in the body of a human or animal that can contract and extend, causing the body to move.

mutualism A relationship between two species of animals in which both species benefit.

mythological Relating to mythology (a type of story that is usually about gods or legendary heroes).

naked eye Human vision without any artificial aids such as telescopes or microscopes.

nanometer A measurement that is one-millionth of a millimeter.

naturalist A person who studies plants and animals as they live in nature.

navigation The process of getting from one place to another accurately.

nebula (plural, nebulae) An enormous, and often very beautiful, cloud of dust and gases found in space that can appear in many shapes and colors. Stars often form in nebulae.

nerves Long, thin, cable-like structures in the body that transmit instructions and messages.

neuron A nerve cell. Neurons are responsible for carrying messages, or signals, around the body.

neutron star The collapsed center, or core, of a massive star. When a huge star is at the end of its life, it explodes and sometimes its center collapses in on itself. This creates a very dense object known as a neutron star.

newton A unit that is used to measure force.

Nobel Prize One of six annual prizes awarded to people for important work in the fields of literature, physics, chemistry, medicine, and economics, and for helping to bring about peace in the world.

nothosaurs Extinct swimming reptiles that may have lived like today's seals, coming ashore to rest and breed.

novelist A person who writes a novel (a long story).

nutrients Substances found in food or the environment that help living things survive and grow.

obituary An article in a newspaper about the life of someone who has recently died.

observable universe The area that contains all of the objects in the universe that are close enough to Earth for light from them to have reached us in the time since the universe began. This light allows us to see them using the naked eye, telescopes, or probes. Scientists believe that the universe is probably larger than we can observe, and it is still growing.

odds The possibility that something will happen—the chance that one thing will happen instead of a different thing.

Olympics A series of international athletic contests held in a different country every four years. There are Summer Games and Winter Games, which alternate every two years.

omnivore An animal that eats both plants and meat.

opossums Small mammals with pouches that are native to the Americas and are distant relatives of kangaroos.

organ A structure in an animal's body (including human bodies) with a particular function—for example, a heart or a kidney.

organism Any living thing. Examples are plants, animals and bacteria.

ornithologist A scientist who studies birds.

outlaw A person who has broken the law and who is hiding or running away to avoid punishment.

pacifist Someone who believes that war and violence are wrong and who refuses to participate in or support a war.

paleontologist A person who studies fossils, and what fossils can tell us about prehistoric life.

papyrus A thick paper material that was often used in ancient times.

paralyzed Unable to move or feel all or part of the body.

parasite An animal that lives on or in a larger animal and feeds on it, for example by sucking blood.

parchment The skin of a sheep or goat prepared for writing on.

particle Any of the basic units of matter and energy, such as a molecule, atom, or electron.

patent An official license from the government guaranteeing that, for a set period, only its holder can make or sell an invention.

PC Personal computer—a small computer designed for use by one person at home or in an office.

Permian Period A time period that lasted from 299 to 252 million years ago, just before dinosaur times.

pharaoh A ruler of ancient Egypt.

phenomenon A fact or event.

philosopher A person who studies ideas about knowledge, truth, and the nature and meaning of life.

phobia An extreme fear of something.

phonemes Individual sound units that make up words. For example some of the phonemes in the English language are: "s" as in "sat" or "th" as in "the."

planet A large spherical object in space that travels around the Sun or another star. It must be big enough for its gravity to clear the area around it of other large objects. Earth is one of eight planets that travel around the Sun; the others are Mercury, Venus, Mars, Jupiter, Saturn, Uranus, and Neptune.

plankton Creatures, often tiny, that live floating in seawater or freshwater and drift with the currents.

plate tectonics The movement of Earth's tectonic plates, which are the large pieces that make up the Earth's crust.

plesiosaurs Extinct reptiles with long necks, tails, and four paddle-like flippers that lived in the sea.

plot A series of events that form the story in a novel or movie.

pollinate To transport pollen grains between flowers of the same species, so that the plants are fertilized and seeds can form.

Pope The head of the Roman Catholic Church.

portrait A painting, drawing, or photograph of a person that usually only includes the person's head and shoulders.

predator An animal that kills and eats other animals.

prehistoric Refers to the time period before written records. This period is different in different places.

prey Any animal that is hunted for food.

probability A measure of how likely something is to happen.

program (noun) A sequence of coded instructions that can be given to a machine, such as a computer.

program (verb) To provide a machine, such as a computer, with coded instructions that tell it how to perform a certain task.

proteins Large molecules in the body that do many important jobs. They are needed to build cells and regulate tissues and organs.

protest To show or express strong disagreement with or disapproval of something.

protist A microscopic organism that is usually made up of a single cell.

pterosaurs Extinct flying reptiles that are related to dinosaurs, including pterodactyls and *Quetzalcoatlus*.

pulley A small wheel with a grooved rim that a rope or chain runs within. This simple machine makes it easier to lift heavy objects.

pupil The black circle at the center of an eye through which light passes to the retina. It changes in size depending on the brightness of the light.

quadruplets Four offspring produced in the same pregnancy.

quarry A type of mine or pit where people dig stone out of the ground.

radar A device or system used for detecting, locating, tracking, and recognizing objects from far away, by sending out radio waves and observing the echoes that return from them.

radiation A type of dangerous and powerful energy that is produced by radioactive substances and nuclear reactions.

rain forest A type of lush forest which usually grows in tropical regions that surround the equator and receives a large amount of rainfall.

rapid transit system A system of railways, usually electric, that is used for transporting people to, from, and around cities.

raptors A group of fast-moving predatory feathered dinosaurs or birds.

recycle To make something new from something old.

reflect To cause something to change direction, for example when light bounces off a mirror rather than going through it or being absorbed by it.

regulate To control and keep things in balance.

reign The period of time during which a king, queen, or emperor is ruler of a country.

reptiles A group of cold-blooded vertebrates. Modern examples include lizards, snakes, turtles, and crocodiles. Most reptiles lay eggs.

retina The layer of tissue at the back of the eye that converts light into signals that are sent to the brain.

robot A machine that can do the work of a person and that works automatically or is controlled by a computer.

rodents The large group of mammals that includes mice, rats, and squirrels. Their front teeth continually grow throughout their lives.

rostrum A snout or similar structure that sticks out from the front of an animal's head.

saint A person who is believed to be very holy because of the way they lived.

saliva The liquid inside your mouth that helps you chew and swallow food.

satellite An object that travels around another larger object. They can be natural, such as the Moon, or human-made, such as the International Space Station.

sauropods The group of giant long-necked, plant-eating dinosaurs that includes *Diplodocus*, *Brachiosaurus*, and *Supersaurus*.

screw A solid cylinder with spiral grooves around its outside. It fits into a hollow cylinder with matching grooves. A screw can be used to fasten two things together.

segregation The practice or policy of keeping people of different races or religions separate from each other.

shrub A woody plant that is smaller than a tree and has several stems that come up from the ground.

sibling Two or more people who share the same parents.

siege A military mission to block goods or people from entering or leaving a city or defended place, with the mission to force the people inside to surrender.

sign language A language that consists of hand gestures and placements, facial expressions, body postures, and finger spelling instead of spoken words.

silica A substance made when the element called silicon combines with the gas oxygen. Silica makes up much of the Earth's surface, known as its crust, and is the main ingredient in glass.

slavery The practice of one person owning another.

solar power Energy captured from sunlight.

solar system A group of objects in space that includes a star or pair of stars and everything that travels around them, such as planets, moons, and comets. Our solar system has just one star, the Sun.

sound waves Vibrations in the air, water, or ground that transmit sound.

Soviet Union A former Eurasian empire that included Armenia, Azerbaijan, Belorussia (now Belarus), Estonia, Georgia, Kazakhstan, Kirgiziya (now Kyrgyzstan), Latvia, Lithuania, Moldavia (now Moldova), Russia, Tajikistan, Turkmenistan, Ukraine, and Uzbekistan in its final years.

space The universe beyond the Earth's atmosphere. Space begins 62 miles above our planet, at a place called the Kármán Line.

species Any one kind of animal or other living thing. Members of the same species can breed with each other to produce young that will continue the species.

stamina Ability to remain active for a long time.

star A huge ball of exploding gases that glows in space. Stars are made mostly of the gases hydrogen and helium. The Sun is the closest star to Earth, but we can see lots of other stars on a clear night.

steam engine An engine that creates power from steam in order to perform mechanical work.

suffragette A woman who campaigns to get voting rights for women.

Sun The closest star to Earth and the center of our solar system.

supernova The incredibly bright and powerful explosion that happens when a massive star comes to the end of its life.

syllable In spoken languages, a unit of language that has a vowel sound, with or without a consonant, and is either a stand-alone word or part of a larger word.

symphony orchestra A large orchestra of wind, string, and percussion instruments that plays complex pieces of music called symphonies.

syntax The way in which linguistic elements (such as words) are put together to form phrases or clauses.

Taliban An ultraconservative political and religious group that emerged in Afghanistan in the mid-1990s.

tame Made friendly and gentle. Animals that have been tamed are no longer wild, dangerous, or frightened of humans.

tardigrades Microscopic animals with stubby legs that are good at surviving extreme conditions.

tectonic plates Large, moving pieces that make up the outer layer of the Earth, known as its crust.

telescope An instrument used for viewing distant objects. A telescope is usually a tube with a series of mirrors or lenses inside that reflect rays of light and create a close-up image of something that is far away, such as the Moon.

tendon A tough cord or band of body tissue that connects a muscle to a bone, or to another body part.

terrestrial Relating to the land. A terrestrial animal is one that lives on the land.

tissue Any part of the body made up of similar cells, such as fatty tissue or nervous tissue. Organs are made of several tissues combined together.

tournament A sports competition or series of contests that involves many players or teams and that usually continues for at least several days.

trace fossil A fossil that preserves traces of an animal's activities, for example fossil footprints.

Triassic Period A time period that lasted from 252 to 201 million years ago.

trillion A huge number that's a million times a million. It has 12 zeroes and is written as: 1,000,000,000,000.

tsunami A huge wave that is caused by the sudden movement of the ocean floor. They can be triggered by earthquakes, landslides, or volcanic eruptions.

umbilical cord The flexible rope-like structure that (along with an organ called the placenta) connects an unborn baby to the inner surface of the mother's womb. Blood vessels inside the umbilical cord supply oxygen and nutrients to the baby.

United Nations An international organization with the objective of maintaining peace between countries.

universe Everything that exists. The universe began with a sudden explosion known as the Big Bang and has been expanding ever since.

urine The watery, usually yellow, substance that you let out from your bladder when you go to the bathroom. Its purpose is to rid the body of excess water and other waste substances.

vertebrate Any animal with a backbone, such as a mammal, reptile, bird, fish, or amphibian.

virus A microscopic parasite that needs a host body to thrive. Once inside a human, animal, or plant, a virus can make lots of copies of itself and cause disease. In humans, viruses cause many health problems such as colds, flu, measles, and Covid-19.

volcano An opening in a planet's or moon's surface that allows molten rock, known as lava, and hot gases to flow or erupt through it.

volume The amount of space that something takes up.

vowel A speech sound made by holding your mouth and throat mostly open. In English, the vowel sounds are represented by the letters a, e, i, o, u and sometimes y.

warm-blooded Able to control one's own body temperature. Warm-blooded animals can keep their bodies warmer than their surroundings.

water vapor Water in gas form. Steam is a type of water vapor.

wedge An object, such as a piece of wood, that is thick at one end but tapers to a thin edge at the other end. An example of a wedge that is used to split things is an axe.

wingspan The distance from the tip of one wing of a bird or airplane to the tip of the other wing.

womb The organ inside a female body that a baby grows inside. The medical term for this organ is a uterus.

World Wide Web The network of information on the Internet. The World Wide Web, or Web for short, gives users access to documents, or websites, that are linked to each other by hyperlinks—electronic connections.

List of Things You Might Want to Look Up (a.k.a. Index)

Sources

This book's research process was multilayered. The author used a wide range of reliable sources for each list, then fact-checkers used additional sources to check each fact is correct. The result is more sources than there is room to share here. What follows is a small sample of the author's sources.

General Sources

www.amnh.org
www.bbc.co.uk
www.britannica.com
www.ft.com
www.guinnessworldrecords.com
www.metoffice.gov.uk
www.nasa.gov
www.nationalgeographic.com
www.newscientist.com
www.newyorker.com
www.nhm.ac.uk
www.nytimes.com
www.ourworldindata.org
www.smithsonianmag.com
www.solarsystem.nasa.gov
www.space.com
www.statista.com

Chapter 1: Space

p.10–11 The Expanding Universe Siegel, Ethan, "The Expanding Universe Might Not Depend on How You Measure It, But When," www.medium.com; Siegel, Ethan, "Ask Ethan: How Do We Know Space Is Expanding?," www.medium.com; Feltman, Rachel, "The Big Bang Got Its Name from a Man Who Thought the Theory Was Total Nonsense," www.popsci.com **p.12–13 What's the Matter?** "What Is the Universe Really Made Of?," www.cms.cern; "Dark Matter and Dark Energy," www.nationalgeographic.com; Hogenboom, Melissa, "What Is Our Universe Made Of?," www.bbc.com **Intergalactic** Kornei, Katherine, "20 Things You Didn't Know About Galaxies," www.discovermagazine.com; "Type of Galaxies Facts," www.nineplanets.org **p.14–15 Galaxy Quest** Mann, Adam, "11 Fascinating Facts About Our Milky Way," www.livescience.com; Taylor Redd, Nola, "Milky Way Galaxy: Facts About Our Galactic Home," www.space.com **The Hole Truth** Gefter, Amanda, "The Strange Fate of a Person Falling into a Black Hole," www.bbc.com; Sutter, Paul, "Take a Fun Trip into a Black Hole: What's It Like Inside?," www.space.com; Siegel, Ethan, "Ask Ethan: What's It Like When You Fall into a Black Hole?," www.forbes.com **p.16–17 Heavens Above** Sessions, Larry, "Top 10 Space Objects to See During the Day," www.earthsky.org **Bird's-Eye View** Sundermier, Ali, "6 Man-Made Structures Visible from Space," www.weforum.org **Space Dust** Harris, William, "How Nebulae Work," www.science.howstuffworks.com; "Types of Nebulae," www.nineplanets.org **p.18–19 Sunny Delight** "The Sun," www.nasa.gov; "Sun Facts," www.theplanets.org **p.20–21 You're A Star/You're A Mega Star** Cain, Fraser, "What Are the Different Types of Stars?," www.universetoday.com; "The Sun—Yellow Dwarf Star," www.solarsystem.nasa.gov **p.22–23 Great Balls of Fire** Brown, Daniel, "What Is the Biggest Star in the Universe?," www.theconversation.com; Millis, John P., "Which Are the Largest Stars in the Universe?," www.thoughtco.

com **Starlight Express** Tate, Karl, "The Nearest Stars to Earth," www.space.com **p.24–25 Planetarium/p.26–27 Light Speed/Spin Cycle** Individual Planet Profiles, www.solarsystem.nasa.gov **Taking the Temperature** "Solar System Temperatures," www.solarsystem.nasa.gov; Individual Planet Profiles, www.solarsystem.nasa.gov **A World of Your Own** Lamb, Robert, "How Do Planets Form?," www.science.howstuffworks.com **p.28–29 What Goes Around** "10 Things About Our Solar System's Most Marvelous Moons," www.solarsystem.nasa.gov; "Moons in Our Solar System," www.solarsystem.nasa.org **Moonstruck** Aderin-Pocock, Maggie, "A Guide to the Eight Phases of the Moon," www.penguin.co.uk **p.30–31 We Will Rock You** "Asteroid or Meteor: What's the Difference?," www.spaceplace.nasa.gov; Line, Brett, "Asteroid Impacts: 10 Biggest Known Hits," www.nationalgeographic.com **Cold As Ice** "10 Things to Know About the Kuiper Belt," www.solarsystem.nasa.gov; "Kuiper Belt Facts," www.theplanets.org **p.32–33 Alien Worlds** "20 Intriguing Exoplanets," www.nasa.gov; "Most Amazing Exoplanets," www.iflscience.com **p.34–35 Blast-Off!** Malik, Tariq, "The World's Tallest Rockets: How They Stack Up," www.space.com; Özgür Nevres, M., "Top 10 Tallest Rockets Ever Launched," www.ourplnt.com **p.36–37 Star Trek** Times calculated using average orbital distances from Earth, www.nasa.gov **High Jump** Lowe, Stuart and North, Chris. *Cosmos: the Infographic Book of Space* (Aurum Press, 2015) **p.38–39 Space Creatures** Tate, Karl, "Cosmic Menagerie: a History of Animals in Space," www.space.com; Forrester, Ellie May, "10 Animals That Have Been to Space," www.discoverwildlife.com **Friends in High Places** O'Callaghan, Jonathan, "What Is Space Junk and Why Is It a Problem?," www.nhm.ac.uk; "UCS Satellite Database," www.ucsusa.org **p.40–41 Celestial Bodies** Springel, Mark, "The Human Body in Space: Distinguishing Fact from Fiction," www.sitn.hms.harvard.edu; Koren, Marina, "What One Year of Space Travel Does to the Human Body," www.theatlantic.com **p.42–43 Life in Space** "A Day in the Life Aboard the International Space Station," www.nasa.gov **p.44–45 Fly Me to the Moon** "The Apollo Missions," www.nasa.gov; Waxman, Olivia B., "Lots of People Have Theories About Neil Armstrong's "One Small Step for Man" Quote. Here's What We Really Know," www.time.com **p.46–47 Leftovers** "The Strange Things Humans Have Left on the Moon," www.rmg.co.uk; Stromberg, Joseph, "The 8 Weirdest Things We've Left on the Moon," www.vox.com; Bartels, Meghan, "The Weirdest Things Apollo Astronauts Left on the Moon," www.space.com **Appliance of Science** "20 Things We Wouldn't Have Without Space Travel," www.jpl.nasa.gov; Kiger, Patrick J., Spoon, Marianne, "Top 10 NASA Inventions," www.science.howstuffworks.com **p.48–49 Space Oddities** Orf, Darren, "10 Weird Things We've Sent to Space," www.popularmechanics.com; "What Are the Contents of the Golden Record?," www.voyager.jpl.nasa.gov; Cavendish, Lee, "Eight of the Strangest Things Sent into Space," www.space.com **p.50–51 Eye in the Sky** "James Webb Space Telescope," www.jwst.nasa.gov; "James Webb Telescope Overview," www.nasa.gov **p.52–53 Strangers in the Night** Boeree, Liv, "The Fermi Paradox: Why Haven't We Found Aliens Yet?," www.vox.com; Field, Louisa, "Five Reasons Why We Haven't Found Aliens Yet," www.sciencefocus.com **Endgame** Beall, Abigail, "A Big Freeze, Rip or Crunch: How Will the Universe End?," www.wired.co.uk; Trosper, Jaime, "Four Ways That Our Universe Might End, According to Science," www.futurism.com;

Cendes, Yvette, "How Will the Universe End?," www.discovermagazine.com **p.54–55 For Future Reference** "The Future," www.nasa.gov; Adams, Dallon, "Prepare for Lift-off! 17 Upcoming Space Missions Worth Getting Excited About," www.digitaltrends.com

Chapter 2: Nature

p.58–59 A Cosmic Year Gupta, Harsh, "Cosmic Calendar: History of the Universe in Just 365 Days," www.scienceabc.com; Sagan, Carl. *The Dragons of Eden: Speculations on the Evolution of Human Intelligence* (Random House, 1977) **p.60–61 Journey to the Center of the Earth** Williams, Matt, "What Are the Earth's Layers?," www.phys.org; Piesing, Mark, "The Deepest Hole We Have Ever Dug," www.bbc.com **p.62–63 The World on a Plate** "Major Plates of the Lithosphere: Earth's Tectonic Plates," www.study.com; King, Hobart M., "Plate Tectonics Map—Plate Boundary Map," www.geology.com **Ground Force** "20 Largest Earthquakes in the World," www.usgs.gov; "The 10 Biggest Earthquakes in History," www.livescience.com **p.64–65 Blowing Their Tops** "The 11 Biggest Volcanic Eruptions in History," www.livescience.com; Pound, Matthew, "Santorini Eruption: New Theory Says "Pyroclastic Flows" Caused Devastating Bronze Age Tsunamis," www.theconversation.com **p.66–67 On Top of the World** McGraw, Kathy, Quinney, Maria, "15 Tallest Mountains in the World from Base to Peak," www.visihow.com; "How Many People Have Climbed Mount Everest?," www.haexpeditions.com **Solid as a Rock** "Three Types of Rock," www.amnh.org; Andrei, Mihai, "The Types of Rock: Igneous, Metamorphic and Sedimentary," www.zmescience.com **Tough Stuff** "The Mohs Hardness Scale and Chart for Select Gems," www.gemsociety.org; "Mohs Hardness Scale," www.geology.com **p.68–69 Planet Rock** Dasgupta, Shreya, "The 15 Most Amazing Landscapes and Rock Formations," www.bbc.co.uk; "Richat Structure," www.earthobservatory.nasa.gov **p.70–71 Rich Pickings** "The Most Valuable Substances in the World by Weight," www.telegraph.co.uk; Nace, Trevor, "12 Most Expensive Gemstones in the World," www.forbes.com **p.72–73 Following a Pattern** Leary, Catie, "How the Golden Ratio Manifests in Nature," www.treehugger.com; "Golden Ratio," www.mathsisfun.com **p.74–75 Big Stink** Parry, James, "Why Does the Hoatzin or "Stink Bird' Stink?," www.discoverwildlife.com; "World's "Smelliest' Cheese Named," www.telegraph.co.uk **p.76–77 Wonderlands** "Seven Natural Wonders," www.sevennaturalwonders.org; "Reef Facts," www.gbrmpa.org.au **p.78–79 Journey to the Top of the Clouds** "7 Facts About Clouds," www.metoffice.gov.uk; Piui, Tibi, "The Types of Clouds: Everything You Need to Know," www.zmescience.com; Pretor-Pinney, Gavin. *The Cloudspotter's Guide* (Sceptre, 2009) **p.80–81 Journey to the Bottom of the Sea** Lloyd, Christopher (Ed.). *Britannica All New Children's Encyclopedia: What We Know and What We Don't* (Britannica Books, 2020) **p.82–83 Surface Features** Mullen, Kimberly, "Information on Earth's Water," www.ngwa.org; "Surface Area of the Earth," www.chartsbin.com **Water World** "Where Is Earth's Water?," www.usgs.gov; "How Much Water Is There On Earth?," www.science.howstuffworks.com **Making a Splash** "Angel Falls," www.britannica.com; "World's Tallest Waterfalls," www.theworldgeography.com **p.84–85 Crystal-Gazing** Fessenden, Marissa, "Snowflakes All Fall in One of 35 Different Shapes," www.smithsonianmag.com **p.86–87 Over the Rainbow** "Rainbow," www.

nationalgeographic.org; "How to See a Full Circle Rainbow," www.earthsky.org **p.88–89 Flashdance** "10 Striking Facts About Lighting," www.metoffice.gov.uk; "Types of Lightning," www.theweatherclub.org.uk **p.90–91 Skyfall** Zielinski, Sarah, "Strange Rain: Why Fish, Frogs and Golf Balls from the Skies," www.smithsonianmag.com; Ortiz, Aimee, Zraick, Karen, "Beware Falling Iguanas, Florida Warns," www.nytimes.com **p.92–93 Breaking the Ice** "How Would Sea Level Change if All Glaciers Melted," www.usgs.gov; Davies, Bethan, "Mapping the World's Glaciers," www.antarcticglaciers.org **Going with the Flow** Williams, Matt, "What Are the Longest Rivers in the World?," www.phys.org; "Longest River," www.guinnessworldrecords.com **p.94–95 Land Ahoy!** "8 of the World's Most-Remote Islands," www.britannica.com; "Easter Island Mystery Solved? New Theory Says Giant Statues Rocked," www.nationalgeographic.com **p.96–97 Trees of Life** Nunez, Christina, "Rainforests, Explained," www.nationalgeographic.co.uk; Bradford, Alina, "Facts About Rainforests," www.livescience.com **Dry Patches** "The World's Largest Deserts," www.geology.com; "What Is a Desert?," www.pubs.usgs.gov **p.98–99 The Only Way Is Up** "Fastest Growing Plant," www.guinnessworldrecords.com; Cary, Zulma, "Top 12 Fastest Growing Plants in the World," www.earthnworld.com **Mushroom Magic** Briggs, Helen, "The Secret Life of Fungi," www.bbc.co.uk; "Largest Living Organism," www.guinnessworldrecords.com **p.100–101 When Plants Attack** "Carnivorous Plants Facts," www.edenproject.com; Ralevski, Alexandra, "Biological Strategies: Leaves Rapidly Snap Shut," www.asknature.org; Strauss, Bob, "Meet 12 Carnivorous Plants That Eat Everything from Insects to Mammals," www.thoughtco.com **p.102–103 Weight of the World** Ritchie, Hannah, "Humans Make Up Just 0.01% of Earth's Life—What's the Rest?," www.ourworldindata.org; Resnick, Brian, Zarracina, Javier, "All Life on Earth, in One Staggering Chart," www.vox.com **That's Life** Watson, Traci, "86 Percent of Earth's Species Still Unknown?," www.nationalgeographic.com; "New Census: We Share Earth with Millions of Unknown Species," www.earthsky.org

Chapter 3: Dinosaur Times

p.106–107 Lost Worlds "The Dino Directory," www.nhm.ac.uk; *Dinosaurs—a Visual Encyclopedia* (DK, 2018) **p.108–109 Before the Dinosaurs** Bagley, Mary, "Permian Period: Climate, Animals & Plants," www.livescience.com; Mitchell Crowe, James, "Before the Dinosaurs," www.cosmosmagazine.com **p.110–111 They're Alive!** Pavid, Katie, "Fossils Provide Evidence of Oldest Animal Life," www.nhm.ac.uk; Davis, Josh, "Shark Evolution: a 450 Million Year Timeline," www.nhm.ac.uk; Brauner, Emily, "These Prehistoric Ocean Animals Are Still Around Today," www.oceanconservancy.org **Gardeners' World** Schultz, Colin, "Long Before Trees Overtook the Land, Earth Was Covered by Giant Mushrooms," www.smithsonianmag.com; "A Guide to Prehistoric Plants," www.edenproject.com **p.112–113 Meat vs Veg** Yong, Ed, "How Many Types of Dinosaurs Were There?," www.nationalgeographic.com; Halstead, Beverly (Ed.). *Modern Geology* (Gordon and Breach Science Publishers, 1991) **p.114–115 Leaf Lovers/ Meat Lovers** Kaplan, Matt, "How Does Your Dinosaur Smell?," www.nature.com; Switek, Brian, "Claws, Jaws, and Spikes: the Science of the Dinosaur Arsenal," www.wired.com; "Tail Whips and Face Bites," www.nationalgeographic.com; Strauss, Bob, "Understanding

Dinosaur Combat," www.thoughtco.com; Black, Riley, "The *Tyrannosaurus Rex*'s Dangerous and Deadly Bite," www.smithsonianmag.com; **p.116–117 Top Predators** Montanari, Shaena, "The Eight Deadliest Dinosaurs," www.forbes.com; *Dinosaurs—a Visual Encyclopedia* (DK, 2018) **p.118–119 In at the Deep End** "The Dino Directory," www.nhm.ac.uk; "Plesiosaur," www.britannica.com; *Dinosaurs—a Visual Encyclopedia* (DK, 2018) **Making a Splash** Greshko, Michael, "Bizarre Spinosaurus Makes History as First Known Swimming Dinosaur," www.nationalgeographic.com **p.120–121 Off the Scale** "Titanosaurs: 8 of the World's Biggest Dinosaurs," www.britannica.com; Geggel, Laura, "What's the World's Largest Dinosaur?," www.livescience.com **Mini-Monsters** Strauss, Bob, "The 19 Smallest Dinosaurs and Prehistoric Animals," www.thoughtco.com **p.122–123 Out of This World** Sykes, Ben, "17 Unusual, Bizarre, and Downright Weird Dinosaurs," www.sciencefocus.com; Strauss, Bob, "The Top 10 Weirdest Dinosaurs," www.thoughtco.com **p.124–125 I Don't Believe It!** "10 Things We Got Wrong About Dinosaurs," www.bbc.co.uk; Hecht, Jeff, "Egg-stealing Dinosaur Was Innocent," www.newscientist.com; Strauss, Bob, "The Biggest Dinosaur Blunders," www.thoughtco.com **p.126–127 Long in the Tooth** "Walking with Dinosaurs," www.bbcearth.com; Ohio University, "Researchers Determine Dinosaur Replaced Teeth as Fast as Sharks," www.phys.org **Bitesize** Bates, K.T., Falkingham, P.L., "Estimating Maximum Bite Performance in *Tyrannosaurus rex* Using Multi-Body Dynamics," www.ncbi.nlm.nih.gov; Anderson, Philip S.L., Westneat, Mark W., "Feeding Mechanics and Bite Force Modelling of the Skull of *Dunkleosteus terrelli*, an Ancient Apex Predator," www.ncbi.nlm.nih.gov; Henderson, Donald M., Nicholls, Robert, "Balance and Strength—Estimating the Maximum Prey-Lifting Potential of the Large Predatory Dinosaur *Carcharodontosaurus saharicus*," www.anatomypubs.onlinelibrary.wiley.com; Strauss, Bob, "The 10 Strongest Bites in the Animal Kingdom," www.thoughtco.com **p.128–129 King of the Tyrant Lizards** "Tyrannosaur," www.britannica.com; Castro, Joseph, *Tyrannosaurus Rex: Facts About T.Rex, King of the Dinosaurs*," www.livescience.com **p.130–131 T. rex and Friends/Never Met a T. rex** "The Dino Directory," www.nhm.ac.uk; *Dinosaurs—a Visual Encyclopedia* (DK, 2018) **Comeback Kid** Osterloff, Emily, "Could Scientists Bring Dinosaurs Back to Life?," www.nhm.ac.uk; Geggel, Laura, "Is it Possible to Clone a Dinosaur?," www.livescience.com; Daley, Jason, "1.7-Million-Year-Old Rhino Tooth Provides Oldest DNA Data Ever Studied," www.smithsonianmag.com **p.132–133 Speed Demons and Slowpokes** Sellers, William Irvin, Manning, Philip Lars, "Estimating Dinosaur Maximum Running Speeds Using Evolutionary Robotics," www.ncbi.nlm.nih.gov; "The Dinosaur Race," www.bbc.co.uk **High-Flyers** "The Dino Directory," www.nhm.ac.uk; *Dinosaurs—a Visual Encyclopedia* (DK, 2018) **p.134–135 Ready for Take-Off** Udurawane, Vasika, "*Quetzalcoatlus*, the Largest Flying Animal of All Time," www.eartharchives.org; Simon, Matt, "The 16-Foot-Tall Reptilian Stork that Delivered Death Instead of Babies," www.wired.com **Taking Flight** "Feather Evolution," www.emilywilloughby.com **p.136–137 Eggstraordinary!** *Dinosaurs—a Visual Encyclopedia* (DK, 2018); "Dinosaur Reproduction," www.enchantedlearning.com **p.138–139 Millions of Years in the Making** *Dinosaurs—a Visual Encyclopedia* (DK, 2018) **p.140–141 Dino Detectives** Osterloff, Emily, "Dinosaur Footprints: How Do They Form

and What Can They Tell Us?," www.nhm.ac.uk; Strauss, Bob, "Step Through Time with Dinosaur Footprints and Trackmarks," www.thoughtco.com **p.142–143 Under the Hammer** Skinner, Curtis, "Dueling Dinosaur Bones Could Set Fossil Auction Record," www.reuters.com; Warwick-Ching, Lucy, "The Dinosaurs Being Snapped Up by the Wealthy," www.ft.com **p.144–145 Can You Dig It?** Benton, Michael. *The Dinosaurs Rediscovered* (Thames & Hudson, 2020); "How Long Did a *T.rex* Live?," www.amnh.org **p.146–147 Fake Fossils** Wenz, John, "9 Fossils and Finds That Were Total Fakes," www.popularmechanics.com; Black, Riley, "Oops! Dinosaur Find Actually Fossilized Wood!," www.smithsonianmag.com; "The Beringer Hoax," www.archive.archaeology.org **p.148–149 Wipeout!** Brusatte, Steve. *The Rise and Fall of the Dinosaurs* (Picador, 2019); Black, Riley, "The Top Ten Weirdest Dinosaur Extinction Ideas," www.smithsonianmag.com; "Why Did the Dinosaurs Die Out?," www.history.com **Deadly Impact** Brusatte, Steve. *The Rise and Fall of the Dinosaurs* (Picador, 2019) **p.150–151 Sole Survivors** Pavid, Katie, "How Dinosaurs Evolved into Birds," www.nhm.ac.uk

Chapter 4: Animals

p.154–155 Short and Sweet Venner, James, "Longevity: a Look at the Shortest and Longest Lives in the Animal Kingdom," www.zooportraits.com; "Top 10 Shortest Living Animals in the World," www.themysteriousworld.com **Old-Timers** "An Age: the Animal Ageing and Longevity Database," www.genomics.senescence.info/species; Bittel, Jason, "Healthy Diet Helps 183-Year-Old Tortoise Feel Young Again," www.nationalgeographic.com **p.156–157 Between Meals** Palmer, Jane, "The Creatures That Can Survive Without Water for Years," www.bbc.co.uk; "10 Animals That Can Live Without Food and Water for Months," www.timesofindia.com **Two of a Kind** Nowak, Claire, "11 Monogamous Animals That Mate for Life," www.rd.com **Extended Families** Langley, Liz, "These Animals Spawn the Most Offspring in One Go," www.nationalgeographic.com; Davies, Ella, "One Animal Has More Babies Than Any Other," www.bbc.co.uk **p.158–159 Do Me a Favor** Bailey, Regina, "Mutualism: Symbiotic Relationships," www.thoughtco.com; "Mutualism Examples: Relationships That Work Together," www.examples.yourdictionary.com **p.160–161 Bird Sanctuary/ Going Underground/Tower of Strength/World Wide Web** Bates, Mary, "5 Animals That Are Awesome Architects," www.nationalgeographic.org; Griggs, Mary Beth, Hernandez, Daisy, "10 Amazing Architects of the Animal Kingdom," www.popularmechanics.com; McNabb, Max, "The Giant Spider Web That Swallowed Up Trees in Texas," www.texashillcountry.com **p.162–163 Noisy Neighbors** Davies, Ella, "The World's Loudest Animals Might Surprise You," www.bbc.co.uk; Hsiao, Patrick, "The 10 Loudest Animals on Earth," www.australiangeographic.com.au **p.164–165 Fantastic Beasts** Gentle, Louise, "Five Comic Book Superpowers That Really Exist in Animals," www.theconversation.com; "Extraordinary Animals with Real Superpowers," www.bbc.co.uk **p.166–167 They've Got It Licked** Langley, Liz, "5 of Nature's Weirdest Tongues," www.blog.nationalgeographic.org; McGarry, Anthony, "7 Fascinating Facts You (Probably) Don't Know About Okapi," www.discoverwildlife.com **True Visionaries** Pavid, Katie, "Amazing Eyes: 17 Vision Champions," www.nhm.ac.uk; DeRemer, Susan, "32 Facts About Animal Eyes," www.discoveryeye.org **p.168–169 It Wasn't Me** Caruso,

Nick and Rabaiottie, Dani. *Does It Fart?: The Definitive Field Guide to Animal Flatulence* (Quercus, 2017) **No Way Out** McFadden, Christopher, "7 Animals to Identify by Their Characteristic Poop," www.interestingengineering.com **Doing Their Business** Guarino, Ben, "9 Quirky Animals with Very Special Ways of Pooping," www.thedodo.com; "29 Fantastic Animal Poop Facts," www.certapet.com **p.170-171 Sweet Dreams** "How Much Do Animals Sleep?," www.faculty.washington.edu; Wong, Sam, "Elephants Sleep for Just 2 Hours a Day—the Least of Any Mammal," www.newscientist.com **Bloodsuckers** "8 Animals That Suck (Blood)," www.britannica.com; Gorvett, Zaria, "Nine Creatures That Drink the Blood of Other Animals," www.bbc.co.uk **p.172-173 Fighting Back** McFadden, Christopher, "11 of the Greatest Defense Mechanisms in Nature," www.interestingengineering.com **Masters of Disguise** "8 Animals That Are Masters of Deception," www.earthtouchnews.com **p.174-175 Animal Smarts** Choi, Charles Q. "10 Animals That Use Tools," www.livescience.com; "Top 10 Smartest Animals," www.animals.howstuffworks.com **Clever Canines** Coren, Stanley. *The Intelligence of Dogs: a Guide to the Thoughts, Emotions, And Inner Lives of Our Canine Companions* (Bantam Books, 1995) **p.176-177 Working Like a Dog** "7 Animals with Jobs," www.britannica.com; "10 Downing Street: Larry, Chief Mouser to the Cabinet Office," www.gov.uk/government/history; "Ferrets Save Millennium Concert," www.news.bbc.co.uk **p.178-179 Speed Merchants** Neilson, B.D. et al. "Racing Speeds of Quarter Horses, Thoroughbreds and Arabians," www.pubmed.ncbi.nlm.nih.gov **Endurance Athletes** Resnick, Brian, "The Animal Kingdom's Top Marathoners," www.popularmechanics.com; Latham-Coyle, Harry, "Eliud Kipchoge Breaks Two-Hour Marathon Barrier in Historic Ineos 1:59 Challenge," www.independent.co.uk **p.180-181 Feats of Strength** Davies, Ella, "The World's Strongest Animal Can Lift Staggering Weights," www.bbc.com; "Top 10 Strongest Animals," www.onekindplanet.org **Liftoff** "Highest Jump by an Insect," www.guinnessworldrecords.com; "Top 10 Highest Jumpers," www.onekindplanet.org **p.182-183 Fly Like the Wind** "Astonishing Flying Speed," www.incrediblebirds.com; DiLonardo, Mary Jo, "10 of the World's Fastest Birds," www.treehugger.com **Follow the Crowd** Bates, Mary, "Strength in Numbers: 5 Amazing Animal Swarms," www.blog.nationalgeographic.org **p.184-185 Globetrotters** Joly, Kyle, et al. "Maximum Total Cumulative Annual Distance Traveled by Different Terrestrial Mammals," www.nature.com; Lorenzo, Irene, "Migration Marathons: 7 Unbelievable Bird Journeys," www.birdlife.org **p.186-187 Bugging Out** Hadhazy, Adam, "20 Startling Facts About Insects," www.livescience.com; "25 Cool Things About Bugs!," www.natgeokids.com **Team Players** Durant, Charlie, et al. "Six Amazing Facts You Need to Know About Ants," www.theconversation.com **p.188-189 Beetlemania!** "List of Beetles," www.britannica com **p.190-191 Creepy Crawlies** *Dinosaurs: a Children's Encyclopedia* (DK Children, 2019) **p.192-193 Jaws/Jaws Junior** *Pocket Eyewitness: Sharks* (DK, 2018) **Deep Blue** "10 Blue Whale Facts," www.natgeokids.com; "Amazing Facts About the Blue Whale," www.onekindplanet.org **p.194-195 Absent Friends** "The IUCN Red List of Threatened Species," www.iucnredlist.org; "WWF Species Directory," www.worldwildlife.org **p.196-197 Celebrity Creatures** Jenner, Greg, "10 Famous People in History and Their Bizarre Pets," www.historyextra.com; "Lord Byron and the Bears Beneath Cambridge," www.cam.ac.uk **p.198-199 Animal Fantasies** Stevens, Sidney, "23 Widespread Myths About Animals," www.treehugger.com

Chapter 5: The Body

p.202-203 This Is Your Life! Aminoff, Michael J. et al. "We Spend About One-Third of Our Life Either Sleeping or Attempting to Do So," www.pubmed.ncbi.nlm.nih.gov; "Calculate Your Lifetime Activities and Sequence," www.productiveclub.com **Human Factory** Iorgulescu, Gabriela, "Saliva Between Normal and Pathological: Important Factors in Determining Systemic and Oral Health," www.ncbi.nlm.nih.gov; "Ask a Biologist: Cell Division," www.askabiologist.asu.edu **Let It Grow** Dean, Laura. *Blood Groups and Red Cell Antigens* (National Centre for Biotechnology Information, 2005); Yaemsiri, S. et al. "Growth Rate of Human Fingernails and Toenails in Healthy American Young Adults," www.pubmed.ncbi.nlm.nih.gov; Loussouarn, Geneviève, et al. "Diversity of Hair Growth Profiles," www.onlinelibrary.wiley.com **p.204-205 Sticky Fingers** "Fingerprint," www.britannica.com **Handy Information/High Five!** "The Incredible Human Hand and Foot," www.bbc.co.uk; "What's the Average Hand Size for Men, Women, and Children?," www.healthline.com; "Hand Facts and Trivia—the Electronic Textbook of Hand Surgery," www.eatonhand.com **Foot Feats** Ficke, Jennifer, Byerly, Doug W., "Anatomy, Bony Pelvis and Lower Limb, Foot Muscles," www.ncbi.nlm.nih.gov; "Advanced Anatomy 2nd. Ed.," www.pressbooks.bccampus.ca **p.206-207 It's Elementary** "What Is the Body Made Of?," www.newscientist.com; Schirber, Michael, "The Chemistry of Life: the Human Body," www.livescience.com; Lotzof, Kerry, "Are We Really Made of Stardust?," www.nhm.ac.uk **A Number Two** Ho, Vincent, "Your Poo Is (Mostly) Alive. Here's What's In It," www.theconversation.com; Dockrill, Peter, "Scientists Have Determined the Exact Composition of Your Poo," www.sciencealert.com **Bodily Fluid** "The Water in You: Water and the Human Body," www.usgs.gov; "How Much of Your Body Is Water?," www.thoughtco.com **Breaking Point** Silver, Natalie, "How Long Can You Live Without Water?," www.healthline.com; Everitt, Lauren, Izundu, Chi Chi, "Who, What, Why: How Long Can Someone Survive Without Food?," www.bbc.co.uk; Swain, Frank, "How Long Can You Go Without Air?," www.bbc.com **Are You a Banana?** Hoyt, Alia, "Do People and Bananas Really Share 50 Percent of the Same DNA?," www.science.howstuffworks.com; Deziel, Chris, "Animals That Share Human DNA Sequences," www.sciencing.com **p.208-209 Express Yourself** Ekman, Paul, "Universals and Cultural Differences in Facial Expressions of Emotions' in Cole, J. (Ed.). *Nebraska Symposium on Motivation* (Lincoln, NB: University of Nebraska Press, 1972). Matsumono, David, Hwang, Hyi Sung, "Reading Facial Expressions of Emotions," www.apa.org **A Familiar Face?** Woods, Catherine, "Debunking the Biggest Genetic Myth of the Human Tongue," www.pbs.org; "Dominant Inheritance," www.knowgenetics.com **p.210-211 Growth Spurts/Early Starters** "Fetal Development Week by Week," www.babycentre.co.uk; "Babies May Start Crying While in the Womb," www.webmd.com; Cadman, Bethany, "What Causes Hiccups in Babies in the Womb?," www.medicalnewstoday.com **p.212-213 Gray Matter** Wells, Diana, "Fun Facts About the Brain You Didn't Know," www.healthline.com; "10 Interesting Facts About the Human Brain," www.sciencefirst.com; "41 Fascinating Facts About Your Amazing Brain," www.askthescientists.com **p.214-215**

Chasing the Dream "Psychoanalytic Interpretations," www.britannica.com; Hyde, McKenzie, "America's Most Common Recurring Dreams," www.amerisleep.com **The Power of Sleep** Nunez, Kirsten, Lamoreux, Karen, "What Is the Purpose of Sleep?," www.healthline.com; "7 Amazing Things That Happen to Your Body While You Sleep," www.health.qld.gov.au **p.216–217 Mind Games** Bach, Michael, "141 Optical Illusions & Visual Phenomena," www.michaelbach.de/ot; "The Illusions Index," www.illusionsindex.org **p.218–219 Fear Factor** O'Keefe Osborn, Corinne, "Common and Unique Fears Explained," www.healthline.com; Curtis, G.C. et al. "Specific Fears and Phobias—Epidemiology and Classification," www.pubmed.ncbi.nlm.nih.gov; Cherry, Kendra, "A to Z: Strange and Common List of Phobias," www.verywellmind.com **Boo!** Weisberger, Mindy, "Scary Science: How Your Body Responds to Fear," www.livescience.com; "What Happens to Your Body When You're Scared?," www.wonderopolis.org; "The Difference Between Regular Sweat and Stress Sweat," www.piedmont.org **p.220–221 Hair-Raising Information/Luscious Locks** "Hair," www.britannica.com; Radford, Tim, "Secrets of Human Hair Unlocked at Natural Museum in London," www.theguardian.com; "Hair Facts," www.sciencekids.co.nz **Sensational!** Bradford, Alina, "The Five (and More) Senses," www.livescience.com; Jarrett, Christian, "Psychology: How Many Senses Do We Have?," www.bbc.com **p.222–223 Color Vision/Eye Caramba!** Moyer, Nancy, "Eye Spy: Worldwide Eye Colour Percentages," www.healthline.com; "Optic Nerve—an Overview," www.sciencedirect.com; DeRemer, Susan, "20 Facts About the Amazing Eye," www.discoveryeye.org **p.224–225 Big Mouth** "Teeth Facts and Figures," www.nhs.uk; Booth, Stephanie, "How to Stop Bad Bacteria in Your Mouth from Migrating to Your Brain," www.healthline.com; "Mouth Microbes: the Helpful and the Harmful," www.newsinhealth.nih.gov **Power Players** Norton, Lily, "What's the Strongest Muscle in the Human Body?," www.livescience.com **p.226–227 Extreme Muscles** Rettner, Rachael, "Meet Your Muscles: 6 Remarkable Human Muscles," www.livescience.com; Ernlund, Lucio, de Almeida Vieira, Lucas, "Hamstring Injuries: Update Article," www.ncbi.nlm.nih.gov **Get a Move On** Scheve, Tom, "How Many Muscles Does It Take to Smile?," www.science.howstuffworks.com; Highfield, Roger, "Sealed with... 146 Muscles," www.telegraph.co.uk; Bryce, Emma, "How Your Muscular System Works," www.ed.ted.com **p.228–229 Pump It Up** "Blood Groups," www.nhs.uk; Christiano, Donna, "What's the Rarest Blood Type?," www.healthline.com **Seeing Red** Bailey, Regina, "12 Interesting Facts About Blood," www.thoughtco.com; "Blood—Biochemistry," www.britannica.com **Going with the Flow/It's in the Blood** Karppanen, H. "Minerals and Blood Pressure," www.pubmed.ncbi.nlm.nih.gov; "The Water in You: Water and the Human Body," www.usgs.gov; Gillespie, Claire, "How Is Urea Made?," www.sciencing.com; Felman, Adam, "How Does Blood Work, and What Problems Occur?," www.medicalnewstoday.com **p.230–231 Big Bones** "What Are the 5 Largest Bones in the Body?," www.study.com; "Longest Bones in the Human Body," www.infoplease.com **Skeleton Crew** Gnanadev, Raja, et al. "An Unusual Finding of the Hyoid Bone," www.ncbi.nlm.nih.gov; Gardner-Thrope, Christopher, "Petrous Part of the Temporal Bone," www.sciencedirect.com; "What Is the Hardest Bone in the Body?," www.study.com **Ouch!** Scheve, Tom, "5 Most Commonly Broken Bones," www.health.

howstuffworks.com; "Wrist Bones," www.mayoclinic.org; Baniukiewicz, Andrew P., "10 Broken Arm Facts: Symptoms, Treatment, and Pain Relief," www.emedicinehealth.com **p.232–233 Tipping the Scales** "What Are the Heaviest Organs in the Human Body?," www.sciencefocus.com **p.234–235 Spare Parts** Taylor, Adam, "Seven Body Organs You Can Live Without," www.theconversation.com; Villazon, Luis, "How Many Organs in the Body Could You Live Without?," www.sciencefocus.com **What's That Stuff?** "10 Gross Body Fluids and Gunk, Explained," www.everydayhealth.com; "Body Waste: Facts," www.sciencetrek.org **p.236–237 Parp!** Rockwood, Kate, "13 Weird Noises Your Body Makes and What They Really Mean," www.health.com; "Farting (Flatulence)," www.nhs.uk; Herndon, Jamie, "Why Do We Hiccup?," www.healthline.com; "What Happens in My Body When I Sneeze?," www.sciencefocus.com **p.238–239 Survival of the Fittest** "Human Characteristics: Walking Upright," www.humanorigins.si.edu; Choi, Charles Q., "How Evolving Traits Helped Humans Survive Unstable World," www.livescience.com **Completely Useless!** "7 Vestigial Features of the Human Body," www.britannica.com; Vulliamy, Elsa, "7 Useless Body Parts We No Longer Need," www.independent.co.uk **p.240–241 Odd Ones Out** Gholipour, Bahar, "10 Little-Known Body Parts," www.livescience.com; Gorvett, Zaria, "How Modern Life Is Transforming the Human Skeleton," www.bbc.com **p.242–243 Going Down** Nestor, James, "Your Body's Amazing Reaction to Water," www.ideas.ted.com; Wilkinson, Alec, "The Deepest Dive," www.newyorker.com; "Perforated Eardrum," www.health.harvard.edu **Going Up** Scheve, Tom, "How Altitude Sickness Works," www.adventure.howstuffworks.com; Berkowitz, Bonnie, Cai, Weiyi, "What It's Like to Climb Mount Everest without Oxygen," www.independent.co.uk **p.244–245 Myth Busted!** Brown, Matt. *Everything You Know About the Human Body Is Wrong* (Batsford Ltd, 2018) **You Are One in Seven Billion** Gray, Richard, "The Seven Ways You Are Totally Unique," www.bbc.com; Ward, Jodie, "How Do We Identify Human Remains?," www.theconversation.com; Krishan, Kewal et al. "Dental Evidence in Forensic Identification," www.ncbi.nlm.nih.gov **p.246–247 It's a Wrap** Lloyd, Christopher. *Absolutely Everything: A History of Earth, Dinosaurs, Rulers, Robots and Other Things Too Numerous to Mention* (What on Earth Books, 2018); "Ancient Egypt—The British Museum," www.ancientegypt.co.uk

Chapter 6: Being Human

p.250–251 What Are the Chances? Baer, Gregory. *Life: The Odds (And How to Improve Them)* (Gotham, 2003); Kruszelnicki, Karl, "What Are the Odds of Getting a Double Yolk Egg?," www.abc.net.au **p.252–253 Lost for Words** "UNESCO Atlas of the World's Languages in Danger," www.unesco.org; Austin, Peter and Sallabank, Julia. *The Cambridge Handbook of Endangered Languages* (Cambridge University Press, 2011) **Language Lovers** "What Countries Have the Most Languages?," www.ethnologue.com; "Papua New Guinea's Incredible Linguistic Diversity," www.economist.com **Word Power** Morin, Roc, "How to Say (Almost) Everything in a Hundred-Word Language," www.theatlantic.com; "The 10 Most Obscure Languages in the World," www.translatemycert.ie **p.254–255 Ker-ching!** Toscano, Paul, "The Weirdest Currencies in the World," www.cnbc.com; Poole, Robert Michael, "The Tiny Island with Human-Sized Money," www.bbc.com

p.256-257 Odd Jobs Winter, Caroline, "Towing an Iceberg: One Captain's Plan to Bring Drinking Water to 4 Million People," www.bloomberg.com; Rigby, Rhymer, "The Job: Professional Queuer," www.ft.com; **p.258–259 Big Countries** "Largest Countries in the World," www.worldometers.info **Small Countries** "Klein, Christopher, 10 Things You May Not Know About the Vatican," www.history.com; "National Day," www.liechtenstein.li **p.260–261 Unusual Rules** Wade, Alex, "The World's Strangest Laws," www.thetimes.co.uk; "23 Surprising Laws Around the World You Probably Didn't Know," www.telegraph.co.uk **p.262–263 Reaching For the Sky** Ghosh, Iman, "These Are the World's Tallest Structures Throughout History," www.weforum.org; "Burj Khalifa: The Tallest Building in the World," www.guinnnessworldrecords.com **p.264–265 Tunnel Vision** McFadden, Christopher, "The Top 9 Longest Tunnels in the World," www.interestingengineering.com; Holloway, April, "Qanat Firaun, the Most Spectacular Underground Aqueduct of the Ancient World," www.ancient-origins.net **p.266–267 Monumental** Buchholz, Katharina, "The Most Visited Monuments in the World," www.statista.com; Smith, Sophie, "50 Fascinating Things You (Probably) Didn't Know About the Statue of Liberty," www.telegraph.co.uk **p.268–269 The Magnificent Seven** Adhikari, Saugat, "The 7 Wonders of the Ancient World," www.ancienthistorylists.com; Montero Fenollós, J. L., "We Know Where the 7 Wonders of the Ancient World Are—Except for One," www.nationalgeographic.co.uk **p.270–271 Grow Your Own** "World Data Atlas: Crops Production," www.knoema.com; Sterling, Justine, "7 Things You Never Knew About Rice," www.foodandwine.com **Humans' Best Friends** "Domestication Timeline," www.amnh.org; Yong, Ed, "A New Origin Story for Dogs," www.theatlantic.com **Animal Farm** "(Farm) Animal Planet," www.storymaps.arcgis.com; "World Data Atlas: Livestock Production," www.knoema.com **p.272–273 Making Shapes** Fulton, Wil, "Every Important Italian Noodle Illustrated," www.thrillist.com; "Longest Strand of Pasta," www.guinnessworldrecords.com **p.274–275 Hot Stuff** "The Scoville Scale," www.alimentarium.org; "Most Carolina Reaper Chilis Eaten in One Minute," www.guinnessworldrecords.com **Chocolate Eaters** "Lindt & Sprüngli: Annual Report," www.lindt-spruengli.com **Sweet Spot** McCarthy, Niall, "Switzerland Comes First for Chocolate Consumption," www.statista.com; Synan, Mariel, "Hot Chocolate for Strength," www.history.com **p.276–278 Celebrate in Style** Mack, Lauren, "Chinese Birthdays," www.thoughtco.com **p.278–279 All Together Now** "Orchestra Size and Setting," www.theidiomaticorchestra.net; "The Vegetable Orchestra," www.vegetableorchestra.org **p.280–281 Read All About It** "The All-Time Most Popular Books in the World Revealed," www.stylist.co.uk; "500 Million Harry Potter Books Have Now Been Sold Worldwide," www.wizardingworld.com **p.282–283 Brushstrokes** Beale, Charlotte, "The World's 10 Most Valuable Artworks," www.weforum.org; López, Alejandro I., "The Most Intriguing Mysteries Behind Leonardo Da Vinci's Salvator Mundi," www.culturacolectiva.com **p.284–285 Hats Off** McDowell, Colin. Hats: Status, Style and Glamour (Thames & Hudson Ltd, 1997) **p.286–287 Faithful Followers** Lloyd, Christopher (Ed.). *Britannica All New Children's Encyclopedia: What We Know and What We Don't* (Britannica Books, 2020); Taylor, Alan, "The 15 Tallest Statues in the World," www.theatlantic.com **p.288–289 Brief Battles** Rentoul, John,

"Top Ten Shortest Wars," www.independent.co.uk; Luckhurst, Toby, "Honduras v El Salvador: the Football Match That Kicked Off a War," www.bbc.co.uk **Keeping the Peace** "16 Countries That Don't Have an Army," www.telegraph.co.uk; "Swiss in Liechtenstein "Invasion"," www.news.bbc.co.uk **p.290–291 The Long Game** "Longest Marathon in History: the Athlete That Took More Than Half a Century to Cross the Finish Line," www.guinnessworldrecords.com; "They Also Serve," www.theguardian.com **Going for Gold** "5 Unusual Olympic Sports," www.britannica.com; Gibson, Megan, "9 Really Strange Sports That Are No Longer in the Olympics," www.olympics.time.com **p.292–293 Fool's Game** "Fairies, Rabbit Births and an "Ancient" Tiara: What Are the Greatest Historical Hoaxes?," www.historyextra.com; "Saitaphernes' Golden Tiara," www.archive.archaeology.org; "Clever Hans: Story, Effect & Facts," www.britannica.com **p.294–295 Treasure Hunt** Jarus, Owen, "30 of the World's Most Valuable Treasures That Are Still Missing," www.livescience.com; Stevens, Rob, "How Pickles the Dog Found the World Cup Trophy," www.bbc.co.uk

Chapter 7: Inventions

p.298–299 Eureka! "History of Technology Timeline," www.britannica.com; "Technology Timeline," www.explainthatstuff.com **Easy Does It** "Simple Machine," www.britannica.com; "Who Invented Scissors?," www.wonderopolis.org **p.300–301 Child's Play** Breyer, Melissa, "8 Brilliant, Everyday Things Invented by Kids," www.treehugger.com; "10 Great Inventions Dreamt Up by Children," www.greatbusiness.org; Black, Jane, "Saving Food, One Sheet of Paper at a Time," www.washingtonpost.com **p.302–303 Accidental Genius** "9 Things Invented or Discovered by Accident," www.science.howstuffworks.com; Lallensack, Rachael, "The Accidental Invention of the Slinky," www.smithsonianmag.com **p.304–305 Turning Back the Clock** Atherton, Kelsey, "A brief, 20,000-year history of timekeeping," www.popsci.com; Margolis, Helen, "A Brief History of Timekeeping," www.physicsworld.com; Andrewes, William J. H., "A Chronicle of Timekeeping," www.scientificamerican.com **p.306–307 All Around the World** "Federation Aéronautique Internationale: Records," www.fai.org; Andrews, Evan, "Was Magellan the First Person to Circumnavigate the Globe?," www.history.com **Daredevils** Individual records listed here: www.guinnessworldrecords.com **p.308–309 Monster Machines** "The Large Hadron Collider," www.home.cern; "The Crawlers," www.nasa.gov **p.310–311 Micro Machines** "Physicists Create World's Smallest Engine," www.sciencedaily.com; "Smallest Medical Robot for the Guinness World Records," www.sciencedaily.com **p.312–313 Pedal Power** "From Boneshakers to Bicycles," www.britannica.com; Wenz, John, "10 of the Weirdest Pedal-Powered Machines," www.popularmechanics.com **p.314–315 Balancing Act** "The History of the Unicycle," www.barthaynes.com; "Tallest Rideable Unicycle," www.guinnessworldrecords.com **p.316–317 Track Records** Drescher, Cynthia, "The 10 Fastest Trains in the World," www.cntraveler.com; Chandler, Nathan, Bonsor, Kevin, "How Maglev Trains Work," www.science.howstuffworks.com **Fast Track** Dugdale, Magdalena, "World's Oldest Metro Systems," www.railway-technology.com; "9 Oldest Subway Systems in the World," www.oldest.org **Hustle and Bustle** "The World's Top 10 Busiest Metros," www.railway-technology.com **p.318–319 Big Birds** Bennett,

Jay, "14 Monster Planes That Dominate the Skies," www.popularmechanics.com; Ros, Miquel, "Giant Flying Machines: 10 of the World's Largest Aircraft," www.edition.cnn.com; "The Spruce Goose," www.evergreenmuseum.org **p.320-321 In the Driver's Seat** "The World's Most Expensive Car Is Not a Rolls Royce or Aston Martin!," www.theweek.in; "Karl Benz," www.britannica.com **Hot Wheels** Thiel, Wade, "The 25 Best-Selling Cars of All Time," www.motorbiscuit.com; "Top 10 Ways Ford's Model T Changed the World," www.reliableplant.com **Under the Bonnet** "16 Different Fuels that Could Power Your Car," www.autocar.co.uk **p.322-323 Trade Secrets** Matthews, Kayla, "The History of Spy Gadgets and Our Fascination with 007," www.interestingengineering.com; Garber, Megan, "How Monopoly Games Helped Allied POWs Escape During World War II," www.theatlantic.com **Playtime** Bedford, Emma, "Toy Industry—Statistics & Facts," www.statista.com; "Fun Facts," www.jenga.com **p.324-325 At Your Convenience** McFadden, Christopher, "49+ Interesting Vending Machines Around the World," www.interestingengineering.com; Jaffe, Eric, "Old World, High Tech," www.smithsonianmag.com; Hinson, Tamara, "10 of the World's Weirdest Vending Machines," www.roughguides.com **Glorious Technicolor** Blandino, Giovanni, "Four-Colour Printing: How Does It Work?," www.pixartprinting.co.uk; Hadhazy, Adam, "What Are the Limits of Human Vision?," www.bbc.com **p.326-327 Hole Numbers** Rakowski, Leo, "Non-Traditional Methods for Making Small Holes," www.mmsonline.com **p.328-329 Be Prepared** "Swiss Army Knife Tools," www.knife-depot.com **p.330-331 Siege Engines** "Castle Siege Weapons," www.medievalchronicles.com **p.332-333 Mechanical Marvels** Andrews, Evan, "7 Early Robots and Automatons," www.history.com; Gorvett, Zaria, "Leonardo da Vinci's Lessons in Design Genius," www.bbc.com **p.334-335 Human Versus Machine** Peek, Sitala, "Knocker Uppers: Waking Up the Workers in Industrial Britain," www.bbc.co.uk; Radzicki McManus, Melanie, "10 Extinct Job Titles," www.money.howstuffworks.com **p.336-337 Rules for Robots** Salge, Christoph, "Asimov's Laws Won't Stop Robots from Harming Humans, So We've Developed a Better Solution," www.scientificamerican.com **Rise of the Machines** Marr, Bernard, "13 Mind-Blowing Things Artificial Intelligence Can Already Do Today," www.forbes.com; S. Smith, Craig, "Computers Already Learn From Us. But Can They Teach Themselves?," www.nytimes.com **p.338-339 01010000 01000011** "The 10 Most Influential Computers in History," www.techradar.com; Douglas, Ian, Richmond, Shane, "The 20 Most Important Computer of All Time," www.telegraph.co.uk; "Top Ten Most Influential Computers Since 1940," www.sacatech.com **Connected World** Ahlgren, Matt, "100+ Internet Statistics and Facts for 2020," www.websitehostingrating.com; "Global Digital Population as of October 2020," www.statista.com **p.340-341 Second Sight** "German Scientist Discovers X-rays," www.history.com; "The World's Most Powerful Microscope," www.kqed.org **p.342-343 Coming Soon?** "Future Technology: 22 Ideas About to Change Our World," www.sciencefocus.com; Koerth-Baker, Maggie "32 Innovations That Will Change Your Tomorrow," www.archive.nytimes.com; Puiu, Tibi, "The "Next Big Things" in Science Ten Years from Now," www.zmescience.com **Bizarre Inventions** "8 Tech Inventions and Gadgets That Never Took Off," www.brandwatch.com; Pyne, Holly, "The 20 Most Pointless Inventions to Have Ever Been Invented," www.shortlist.com

Chapter 8: Game Changers

p.346-347 Whiz Kids Bowman, Verity, "Moment in Time: 18 July, 1976—Nadia Comaneci's Perfect 10," www.telegraph.co.uk; Gunther, Shea, "5 Teens Who Have Sailed Around the World," www.treehugger.com **p.348-349 Brothers and Sisters** "All in the Family: 8 Famous Sets of Siblings," www.britannica.com; "Famous Sporting Siblings," www.bbc.co.uk **p.350-351 King or Queen for the Day** Kantor, Jonathan H., "10 of the Shortest-Reigning Leaders in History," www.listverse.com; "Daughter of Emperor Xiaoming of Northern Wei," www.community.worldheritage.org **Game of Thrones** Greenberg, Isabel, "These Are the World's Longest-Reigning Royals," www.harpersbazaar.com; Klein, Christopher, "7 Fascinating Facts About King Louis XIV," www.biography.com **p.352-353 The Real Deal?** "Homer: Greek Poet," www.britannica.com; "Mu-lan Shih," www.britannica.com **p.354-355 Role Swap** "Who Was Hatshepsut?," www.nationalgeographic.com; Fletcher, Abner, "How a Freed Slave Disguised Herself as a Man and Fought with the Buffalo Soldiers," www.houstonpublicmedia.org **p.356-357 Incredible Journeys** Odell, Michael, "Sacha Dench: the Woman Who Flies with Swans," www.thetimes.co.uk; Hembrey, Jon, "Jean Béliveau's 11 Years on the Road," www.cbc.ca **p.358-359 Runners-Up** Worrall, Simon, "Buzz Aldrin Hates Being Called the Second Man on the Moon," www.nationalgeographic.com; "Scott of the Antarctic," www.bbc.co.uk **Unlucky Charms** "From Haiti to Chile: Family Survives Two Quakes in Two Months," www.theguardian.com; Hough, Andrew, "Frano Selak: "World's Luckiest Man" Gives Away His Lottery Fortune," www.telegraph.co.uk; Roos, Dave, "10 People with Incredibly Bad Luck," www.people.howstuffworks.com **p.360-361 The Invincibles** "History of the America's Cup," www.americascup.com; "Top 10 Winning Streaks," www.tennishead.net **p.362-363 Faster, Higher, Stronger** Amos, Jonathan, "Skydiver Felix Baumgartner Breaks Sound Barrier," www.bbc.co.uk; Chappell, Bill, "Woman Rides Bicycle to 183.9 mph—a World Record," www.npr.org **p.364-365 Record Breaker** "Ashrita Furman: Guinness World Records' Most Prolific Record-Breaker," www.guinnessworldrecords.com **Great All-Rounders p.366-367** "Babe Didrikson Zaharias," www.biography.com; "Test Cricketers Who Played International Field Hockey," www.theroar.com.au **p.368-369 Keep It Down** Individual records listed here: www.guinnessworldrecords.com; "Boys And Girls, Welcome to Sneezing 101," www.eastbaytimes.com; Crew, Bec, "Scientists Have Confirmed What Really Happens When You Crack Your Knuckles," www.sciencealert.com **p.370-373 Rebel Spirit** "Martin Luther and the 95 Theses," www.history.com; Whipps, Heather, Specktor, Brandon "13 Significant Protests That Changed the Course of History," www.livescience.com **p.374-375 Seeing the Future** Handwerk, Brian, "The Many Futuristic Predictions of HG Wells That Came True," www.smithsonianmag.com; Aguirre, Abby, "Octavia Butler's Prescient Vision of a Zealot Elected to 'Make America Great Again,'" www.newyorker.com **p.376-377 Friends of the Earth** Walsh, Bryan, "Heroes of the Environment," www.content.time.com; Yanes, Javier, "Jane Goodall, the Human Voice of Chimpanzees," www.bbvaopenmind.com **p.378-379 Lifesavers** "Mary Seacole Biography," www.biographyonline.net; Jorgensen, Timothy J., "How Marie Curie Brought X-Ray Machines to the Battlefield," www.smithsonianmag.com **p.380–381 Making It Big** "John Cage Organ Project," www.universes. art; "Largest Painting," www.guinnessworldrecords. com; "Longest Play," www.guinnessworldrecords.com; Fawbert, Dave, "The 10 Longest Novels Ever Written," www.shortlist.com; "Top 10 Interesting Facts About Marcel Proust," www.discoverwalks.com; "Longest Novel," www. guinnessworldrecords.com **Making It Small** Ponsonby, Shaun, "There's a Riot Goin' On—The Rise and Fall of Sly & The Family Stone," www.getintothis.co.uk; Street, Jacqui, "Australian Painter Wayne Malkin Claims Unofficial World Record with Matchstick Portrait," www.abc.net.au; Churchwell, Sarah, "For Sale, Baby Shoes, Never Worn— The Myth of Ernest Hemingway's Short Story'; Ponsford, Matthew, "A Nude Sculpture So Small It's 'Walking on Hair,'" www.edition.cnn.com; "Smallest Sculpture of a Human," www.guinnessworldrecords.com; "The Shortest…," interestingliterature.com **p.382–383 Colorful Characters** Ferrier, Morwenna, "This Colour Might Change Your Life," www.theguardian.com; Wainwright, Oliver, "Meet Minion Yellow by Pantone: the World's First Character-Branded Colour," www.theguardian.com **p.384– 385 Celebrity Creatures** Jinkinson, Bethan, "10 Species Named After Famous People," www.bbc.co.uk; Merolla, Lisa, "Top 18 Species Named After Famous People," www. popularmechanics.com **p.386–387 Deep Thoughts** Giles, Lionel (Trans.). *The Sayings of Lao Tzu* (A&D Books, 2014) **Wise Words** Calaprice, Alice. *The Ultimate Quotable Einstein* (Princeton University Press, 2013) **p.388–389 Still Here** Latson, Jennifer, "5 Times Ernest Hemingway Cheated Death," www.time.com; Memmott, Mark, "Margaret Thatcher Is Not Dead, But Text Message About Cat Starts Rumor," www.npr.org **p.390–391 Just One More Thing** Holodny, Elena, "Famous Last Words of 19 Famous People," www.independent.co.uk; "What Are the Best Last Words Ever?," www.theatlantic.com

Picture Credits

t = top; l = left; r = right; c = center; b = bottom

p.11 Alfred Pasieka/Science Photo Library/Getty Images; **p.13(1)** ESA/Hubble & NASA, Acknowledgement: Flickr user Det58; **p.13(2)** ESA/Hubble & NASA, Acknowledgement: Judy Schmidt; **p.13(3)** ESO/SPECULOOS Team/E. Jehin; **p.13(4)** NASA/JPL-Caltech/Roma Tre Univ.; **p.13(5)** ESA/Hubble, NASA, D. Calzetti (UMass) and the LEGUS Team; **p.14** Mark Garlick/Science Photo Library/Getty Images; **p.17** Michael Miller/Stocktrek Images/Getty Images; **p.18** Stocktrek Images/ Getty Images; **p.28** NASA/JPL-Caltech/SETI Institute; **pp.34– 35** NASA; **p.39** NASA; **p.43** Worldspec/NASA/Alamy; **p.45** NASA/Goddard Space Flight Center/Arizona State University; **p.50** NASA/ David Higginbottom; **p.61** Gary Hincks/Science Photo Library; **p.65** tom pfeiffer/Alamy; **p.67** Sumiko Scott/ Getty Images; **p.69tl** NASA; **p.69tr** RusianKain/iStockphoto; **p.69cl** Totajla/iStockphoto; **p.69cr** Altor/123rf.com; **p.69b** frentusha/iStockphoto; **p.73t** Carmen Hauser/iStockphoto; **p.73cl** Education Images/Getty Images; **p.73cr** SamCastro/

iStockphoto; **p.73bl** Eivaisla/iStockphoto; **p.73br** FlowerStock/ Alamy; **p.76tl** Arsgera/iStockphoto; **p.76tr** dibrova/ iStockphoto; **p.76cl** R.M. Nunes/iStockphoto; **p.76c** jd_field/ iStockphoto; **p.76cr** MARIO VAZQUEZ/Getty Images; **p.76bl** Ella_Ageeva/iStockphoto; **p.76br** Lara_Uhryn/iStockphoto; **p.83** Minden Pictures/Alamy; **p.87** Giordano Cipriani/Getty Images; **p.89** A. T. Willett/Alamy; **p.101** SERGEY ALESHIN/ iStockphoto; **p.111** Minden Pictures/Alamy; **p.125t** De Agostini Picture Library/Getty Images; **p.125b** Julius T Csotonyi/Science Photo Library; **p.126** Ryan M. Bolton/Alamy; **p.135** Mikkel Juul Jensen/Science Photo Library; **p.139** AGEphotography/ iStockphoto; **pp.140–141** Martin Shields/Science Photo Library; **p.144** James L. Amos/Science Photo Library; **p.146** Universal History Archive/Getty Images; **p.155** cinoby/Getty Images; **p.156** Steve Gschmeissner/Science Photo Library; **p.161** Johan Roux/Alamy; **p.164** seakitten/iStockphoto; **p.167** GlobalP/iStockphoto; **p.170** samopinny/iStockphoto; **p.173** Shawshank61/iStockphoto; **p.180** kuritafsheen/Getty Images; **p.182** Thomas Kaestner; **p.186** Geoff Smith/Alamy; **pp.192– 193** indianoceanimagery/iStockphoto; **p.197** Rodrigo Vaz/Getty Images; **p.204** Science Source/Science Photo Library; **p.208(1)** twinsterphoto/iStockphoto; **p.208(2)** Caroline Schiff/ Getty Images; **p.208(3)** ferrantraite/iStockphoto; **p.208(4)** IndiaPicture/Getty Images; **p.208(5)** Surasak Soothikarn/ EyeEm; **p.208(6)** SensorSpot/iStockphoto; **p.208(7)** Yasser Chalid/Getty Images; **p.213** Alfred Pasieka/Science Photo Library/Getty Images; **p.216t** Peter Hermes Furian/Alamy; **p.216c&b** Chris Madden/Alamy; **p.223** Nik Bruining/Alamy; **p.231** Martin81/Dreamstime; **p.247** Prisma Archivo/Alamy; **p.264** qaphotos.com/Alamy; **p.267** Tuul & Bruno Morandi/ Getty Images; **p.277** Amelia Fuentes Marin/iStockphoto; **p.283** Kunstmuseum Basel/Martin P. Bühler; **p.293** Glenn Hill/Getty Images; **p.309** Imaginechina Limited/Alamy; **p.315** Jordi Vidal/Getty Images; **pp.318–319** Bob Sharples/Alamy; **p.329** Victorinox (main image); **p.329** zabo69005/iStockphoto (attachments); **p.333** INTERFOTO/Alamy; **p.336** AHowden - Japan Stock Photography/Alamy; **p.341** Tomatito/Shutterstock; **p.347** Michael Ochs Archives/Getty Images; **p.353** Culture Club/Getty Images; **p.361** Robert Prezioso/Getty Images; **p.371** Don Cravens/Getty Images; **p.373** Everett Collection Inc/ Alamy; **p.377** RvS.Media/Basile Barbey/Getty Images; **p.381tr** Used by permission of Aram Saroyam; **p.388** Michael Ochs Archives/Getty Images; **p.390** Heritage Images/Getty Images

Trademark Notices